VALUE

THE FOUR CORNERSTONES OF CORPORATE FINANCE

VALUE

THE FOUR CORNERSTONES OF CORPORATE FINANCE

McKinsey & Company

Tim Koller
Richard Dobbs
Bill Huyett

WILEY

JOHN WILEY & SONS, INC.

Published by John Wiley & Sons, Inc., Hoboken, New Jersey.
Published simultaneously in Canada.

For general information on our other products and services or for technical support, please contact our Customer Care Department within the United States at (800) 762-2974, outside the United States at (317) 572-3993 or fax (317) 572-4002.

Wiley also publishes its books in a variety of electronic formats. Some content that appears in print may not be available in electronic books. For more information about Wiley products, visit our web site at www.wiley.com.

Library of Congress Cataloging-in-Publication Data:

Value : the four cornerstones of corporate finance / McKinsey and Company ; Tim Koller, Richard Dobbs, Bill Huyett.
    p. cm.
  Includes index.
  ISBN 978-0-470-42460-5 (cloth); ISBN 978-0-470-94906-1 (ebk);
  ISBN 978-0-470-94907-8 (ebk); ISBN 978-0-470-94908-5 (ebk)
    1. Corporations—Valuation.   2. Corporations—Finance.   3. Stockholder wealth.
 I. Koller, Tim.   II. Dobbs, Richard.   III. Huyett, Bill.   IV. McKinsey and Company.
  HG4028.V3V36 2010
  658.15–dc22

                                        2010032747

Printed in the United States of America

10 9 8 7 6 5 4 3 2

Contents

Many companies make decisions that compromise value in the name of creating value. But with courage and independence, executives can apply the four cornerstones of finance to make sound decisions that lead to lasting value creation.

Return on capital and *growth* are the twin drivers of value creation, but they rarely matter equally. Sometimes raising returns matters more, whereas other times accelerating growth matters more.

You can create the illusion of value or you can create real value. Sometimes acquisitions and financial engineering schemes create value, and sometimes they don't. No matter how you slice the financial pie, only improving cash flow creates value.

Good investor communications can ensure that a
company's share price doesn't become misaligned with its
intrinsic value. And communication isn't just one way:
executives should listen selectively to the right investors as
much as they tell investors about the company.

It's not easy to strike the right balance between shorter-term
financial results and longer-term value creation—especially
in large, complex corporations. The trick is to cut through
the clutter by making your management processes more
granular and transparent.

About the Authors

McKinsey & Company is a management-consulting firm that helps leading private, public, and social sector organizations make distinctive, lasting, and substantial performance improvements. Over the past seven decades, the firm's primary objective has remained constant: to serve as an organization's most trusted external advisor on critical issues facing senior management. With consultants deployed from more than 90 offices in over 50 countries, McKinsey advises companies on strategic, operational, organizational, financial, and technological issues. The firm has extensive experience in all major industry sectors and primary functional areas.

McKinsey's corporate finance practice, along with the firm's strategy and risk practices, uniquely integrates industry insights, the firm's global presence, and proprietary knowledge as it advises clients. Together, these practices help clients set corporate portfolio direction, manage risk in investment choices, and build effective value-management capabilities.

Tim Koller is a partner in McKinsey's New York office, the head of the firm's Corporate Performance Center, and a member of the leadership group of the firm's global corporate finance practice. During his 25 years of consulting based in New York and Amsterdam, Tim has served clients globally on corporate strategy and capital markets, mergers and acquisitions, and value-based management. He is the co-author of *Valuation: Measuring and Managing the Value of Companies*, which is now in its fifth edition and used around the world by banks, corporations, and leading business schools as the authoritative text on the subject. Tim leads the firm's research activities in valuation and capital markets. Prior to joining McKinsey, Tim was with Stern Stewart & Company and Mobil Corporation. He received an MBA from the University of Chicago.

Richard Dobbs is a partner in McKinsey's Seoul office and a director of the McKinsey Global Institute, the firm's business and economics research arm. Prior to this, Richard oversaw R&D for McKinsey's corporate finance practice. Since joining McKinsey in London in 1988, Richard has served clients globally on corporate strategy and capital markets, mergers and acquisitions, and value-based management. He is a graduate of Oxford University, an associate fellow of the Saïd Business School at Oxford and, as a Fulbright Scholar, received an MBA from the Stanford Graduate School of Business.

Bill Huyett is a partner in McKinsey's Boston office and a leader of the firm's strategy, corporate finance, and health care practices. During his 23 years in consulting based in Boston, Zurich, and Washington D.C., Bill has served clients globally on product development and commercialization, growth, innovation, corporate strategy, mergers and acquisitions, and corporate leadership. Before joining McKinsey, Bill held a variety of line management positions in the electronics industry. His degrees in electronics engineering and computer science are from the University of Virginia, as is his MBA.

Preface

Most executives have figured out how to create value for shareholders. Through experience, observation, and intuition, they've developed a wealth of personal wisdom that, with some luck, typically takes them in the right direction.

But let's face it: that wisdom doesn't always prevail. Indeed, the run-up to the financial crisis of 2008 is but one example of how easily finance myths, fads, and misconceptions overwhelm wisdom, even in the most sophisticated organizations.

Executives don't have it easy. It's tough to hold steady when shareholders expect absurdly high returns during periods of relative alignment between companies' share prices and underlying economic value. It's even tougher to stick with fundamentals as peers' profits skyrocket in seemingly irrational ways, as they did in 2008, or when share prices reach unprecedented and unsustainable levels, as they did during the Internet-bubble era.

During such periods, seductive new economic theories emerge. These theories catch the attention of journalists, traders, boards, investors, and executives—even though they're blatantly at odds with the tenets of finance that have held true for more than 100 years.

These episodes of wishful thinking have only reinforced the immutable principles of value creation. These four principles, which we call *the cornerstones of corporate finance*, start with the axiom that companies exist to meet customer needs in a way that translates into reliable returns to investors. Together, the cornerstones form a foundation upon which executives can ground decisions about strategy, mergers and acquisitions, budgets, financial policy, technology, and performance measurement—even as markets, economies, and industries change around them.

For executives with functional, business, or corporate responsibilities, ignoring the cornerstones can lead to decisions that erode value or lead to outright corporate disaster. Let's take two examples.

First, leverage: As the market heated up in 2007 and 2008, many savvy financial services executives thought leverage could be used to create (as opposed to merely redistribute) value. That misconception clashes with the cornerstones. Leverage is a quick way to manufacture accounting profits, but it doesn't add real value to the company or the economy, because it merely rearranges claims on cash flow and increases risk.

Second, volatility: Some say companies are better valued when they deliver steady, predictable earnings growth. That, too, is an assumption that doesn't emerge from the cornerstones. The truth is that the most sophisticated investors—the ones who should matter most to executives—expect some earnings volatility, if only as recognition of changing economic dynamics beyond any one company's control. Related is a belief that earnings per share guidance, and the significant executive time consumed by managing guidance, is valued by investors even though empirical evidence clearly shows otherwise.

Compounding the misconceptions are apparent disconnects in how financial performance reflects economic theory and empirical data. These disconnects can cloud top-management judgments about business strategies and investment cases. Basic economics suggest, for example, that above-cost-of-capital returns will be competed away. Data show, though, that some companies earn consistently superior returns using business models that vaccinate themselves against competitors and new entrants.

In our practice we see uneven development of finance capabilities among general managers and functional leaders. All too often, these leaders have picked up their finance knowledge without a grounding in the cornerstones, leading to such overly simplistic refrains as "We need to grow earnings faster than revenue." Or the ungrounded might overemphasize earnings per share at the expense of capital productivity or growth.

When we combine the misconceptions, the contradictions between finance and economics, and the uneven development of finance skills, we understand the roots of decisions that diverge from the perennial principles. The voices of the media don't often shed light, the views expounded by investors about what constitutes value and what doesn't are splintered, and traders cause further confusion by unnaturally bidding up or down stock prices of individual companies and even entire sectors.

Internalizing the four cornerstones of finance, understanding how they relate to the real economy and the public stock markets (or private-owner expectations), and having the courage to apply them across the enterprise have significant upside and little downside. At least, the four cornerstones can prevent executives from making strategic, financial, and business decisions that undermine value creation. At best, the cornerstones can encourage a more constructive, value-oriented dialogue among executives, boards, investors, bankers, and the press—resulting in courageous and even unpopular decisions that build lasting corporate value.

To this end we offer you *Value: The Four Cornerstones of Corporate Finance*.

Our hope is that this book will be a catalyst and concrete guide for improving how executives plan strategy, make decisions, and build the next generation of leaders. Ultimately, we hope the collective impact of more companies embracing these principles creates a more stable and productive economy.

Acknowledgments

In 1990, McKinsey first published *Valuation: Measuring and Managing the Value of Companies*. After having sold more than 500,000 copies in 10 languages, the fifth edition of *Valuation* was released in mid-2010.

We are greatly indebted to *Valuation*'s authors, because their success led to the formulation of this book. Tom Copeland and Jack Murrin were co-authors of *Valuation*'s first three editions, while Marc Goedhart and David Wessels co-authored the fourth and fifth editions. Without their insight and industry, this book (*Value*) would not exist today, so we are eternally grateful for these fine colleagues.

We definitely couldn't have created this work without our clients, who hone our thoughts and insights as they interact with us. They provide the reality against which we constantly test our assumptions and ideas, and their experience is the very matter that we combine with academic theory to ferret out the truth.

The intellectual origins of this book lie in the present value method of capital budgeting and in the valuation approach developed by Professors Merton Miller and Franco Modigliani in their 1961 *Journal of Business* article, "Dividend Policy, Growth and the Valuation of Shares." Others have gone far to popularize their approach. In particular, Professor Alfred Rappaport of Northwestern University and Joel Stern of Stern Stewart & Company were among the first to extend the Miller-Modigliani enterprise valuation formula to real-world applications.

Ennius Bergsma deserves our special thanks for initiating the development of McKinsey's corporate finance practice in the mid-1980s. He inspired the original internal McKinsey valuation handbook and mustered the support to turn that handbook into a published book for an external audience. We also owe a special debt to Dave Furer for help, and late nights, developing the original drafts of *Valuation* more than 20 years ago.

We couldn't have devoted the time and energy to this book without the support and encouragement of McKinsey's corporate finance practice leadership, in particular Christian Caspar, Bernie Ferrari, Massimo Giordano, Ron Hulme, Rob Latoff, Thomas Leudi, Nick Leung, Michael Patsalos-Fox, Jean-Marc Poullet, Pedro Rodeia, Michael Silber, Vincenzo Tortoricci, and Felix Wenger.

Likewise we couldn't have devoted the proper time and energy to this work if it weren't for the vision of McKinsey's former managing director, Ian Davis, and the firm's current managing director, Dominic Barton.

We would also like to thank those who have personally shaped our knowledge of corporate finance, strategy, and economics, often through their challenging questions. We thank Buford Alexander, Ennius Bergsma, Peter Bisson, Tom Copeland, Mike Dodd, Bill Fallon, Bernie Ferrari, Richard Foster, Marc Goedhart, John Goetz, Robert Harris, Tim Jenkinson, Larry Kanarek, Jack McDonald, Michael Mauboussin, Colin Meyer, Michael Mire, Jack Murrin, Jonathan Peacock, Chandan Sengupta, Bennett Stewart, Bill Trent, Robert Uhlaner, James Van Horn, and David Wessels.

The authors are honored to work with McKinsey's Corporate Performance Center (CPC), a group of dedicated finance experts who influence our thinking every day. The CPC's leaders include: Ankur Agrawal, André Annema, Andres Cottin, Bas Deelder, Susan Nolen Foushee, Marc Goedhart, Regis Huc, Mimi James, Mauricio Jaramillo, Bin Jiang, Marc Metakis, Jean-Hugues Monier, Rishi Raj, Werner Rehm, Ram Sekar, and Zane Williams.

We've made extensive use of McKinsey's Corporate Performance Analytical Tool (CPAT), which provides a great database and deep analytical capability. Thank you to Bin Jiang, who developed and oversees CPAT, and to Bing Cao, who analyzed the data for us. Dick Foster, a retired McKinsey partner, inspired the development of CPAT.

Neil DeCarlo, our lead editor, was our sounding board, coach, and occasional arbiter, debating the structure of each chapter and helping us find the best language to convey our ideas. He was also incredibly flexible, accommodating our hectic schedules regardless of when it was in his time zone. He was, in many ways, the fourth author of this book.

Rik Kirkland and Michael Stewart ensured that we received great help from McKinsey's external publishing and external communications teams. Bill Javetski and Dennis Swinford, from McKinsey's editorial team, have been serial collaborators with us on the numerous articles and other work that ultimately found its way into this book. Additionally, Joanne Mason orchestrated our marketing and distribution efforts, and fact-checking and editorial support was circumspectly provided by Drew Holzfeind, Joe Mandel, and Katherine Boas.

Kim Bartko expertly oversaw the production of the exhibits in this book, a herculean task given the variety of formats and technologies employed. We can't say enough about the way Kim wielded her visual-communications talent in improving many of our original exhibits. Kim was supported by the efficient and expert production work of Mark Bergeron, Gail Farrar, and Richard Peal.

The ideas in some chapters can be traced to individuals who've influenced our thinking over the years: Rob McLean and John Stuckey for the best-owner principle in Chapter 5, Werner Rehm and Rob Palter for the investor segmentation in Chapter 6 and investor communications in Chapter 16, Marc Goedhart for the discussion of stock market bubbles in Chapter 8, Lee Dranikoff and Antoon Schneider for the discussion of divestitures in Chapter 12, and Marc Goedhart and Werner Rehm for the discussion of capital structure in Chapter 15.

The five editions of *Valuation* drew upon work, ideas, and analyses from Carlos Abad, Paul Adam, Buford Alexander, Petri Allas, Alexandre Amson, André Annema, the late Pat Anslinger, Vladimir Antikarov, Ali Asghar, Bill Barnett, Dan Bergman, Olivier Berlage, Peter Bisson, the late Joel Bleeke, Nidhi Chadda, Carrie Chen, Steve Coley, Kevin Coyne, Johan Depraetere, Mikel Dodd, Lee Dranikoff, Will Draper, Christian von Drathen, David Ernst, Bill Fallon, George Fenn, Susan Nolen Foushee, Russ Fradin, Gabriel Garcia, Richard Gerards, Alo Ghosh, Irina Grigorenko, Fredrik Gustavsson, Marco de Heer, Keiko Honda, Alice Hu, Régis Huc, Mimi James, Chris Jones, William Jones, Phil Keenan, Phil Kholos, David Krieger, Shyanjaw Kuo, Bill Lewis, Kurt Losert, Harry Markl, Yuri Maslov, Perry Moilinoff, Fabienne Moimaux, Mike Murray, Terence Nahar, Juan Ocampo, Martijn Olthof, Rob Palter, Neha Patel, John Patience, Bill Pursche, S. R. Rajan, Frank Richter, David Rothschild, Michael Rudolf, Yasser

Salem, Antoon Schneider, Meg Smoot, Silvia Stefini, Konrad Stiglbrunner, Ahmed Taha, Bill Trent, David Twiddy, Valerie Udale, Sandeep Vaswani, Kim Vogel, Jon Weiner, Jack Welch, Gustavo Wigman, David Willensky, Marijn deWit, Pieter deWit, Jonathan Witter, David Wright, and Yan Yang.

For help in preparing the manuscript and coordinating the flow of paper, e-mails, and phone calls, we owe our thanks to our assistants, Jennifer Fagundes, Sumi Choi, and Alice Morris.

We also extend heartfelt thanks to the team at John Wiley & Sons, including Tiffany Charbonier, Mary Daniello, Bill Falloon, Meg Freeborn, Mike Freeland, Pamela van Giessen, Emilie Herman, Joan O'Neil, and Cristin Riffle-Lash. We can't say enough about the quality and professionalism of the John Wiley team. We're indebted as well to the team at Cape Cod Compositors for their exacting work in polishing our manuscript into its final form as a published book.

Finally, thank you to Melissa Koller, Cathy Dobbs, and Lauren Huyett, and our children. Our wives and families are our true inspirations. This book would not have been possible without their encouragement, support, and sacrifice.

Part One

The Four Cornerstones

1

Why Value Value?

There's no disputing that value is the defining metric in a market economy. When people invest, they expect the value of their investment to increase by an amount that sufficiently compensates them for the risk they took, as well as for the time value of their money. This is true for all types of investments, including bonds, bank accounts, real estate, or company shares.*

Therefore, knowing how to create and measure value is an essential tool for executives. If we've learned anything from the latest financial crisis, and from periods of economic bubbles and bursts in our history, it's that the laws of value creation and value measurement are timeless. Financial engineering, excessive leverage, the idea during inflated boom times that somehow the old rules of economics no longer apply—these are the misconceptions upon which the value of companies are destroyed and entire economies falter.

In addition to their timelessness, the ideas in this book about creating and measuring value are straightforward. Mathematics professor Michael Starbird is noted for his saying: "The typical 1,200 page calculus text consists of two ideas and 1,198 pages of examples and applications." Corporate finance is similar. In our view, it can be summarized

---

* Throughout this book we use the terms value and value creation. In its purest form, value is the sum of the present values of future expected cash flows—a point-in-time measure. Value creation is the change in value due to company performance. Sometimes we'll refer to value and value creation based on explicit projections of future growth, returns on capital, and cash flows. Other times we'll use the market price of a company's shares as a proxy for value, and total return to shareholders (share price appreciation plus dividends) as a proxy for value creation.

by four principles or cornerstones.* Applying these principles, executives can figure out the value-creating answers to most corporate finance questions, such as which business strategy to pursue, whether to undertake a proposed acquisition, or whether to repurchase shares.

The cornerstones are intuitive as well. For example, most executives understand that it doesn't affect a company's value whether executive stock options are recorded as an expense in a company's income statement or cited separately in the footnotes of the financial statements, because cash flow doesn't change. Executives are rightly confused when it takes more than a decade of bickering over the accounting rules to reflect the economics of these options.

THE FOUR CORNERSTONES

What are the four cornerstones of finance and how do they guide the creation of lasting corporate value?

The first and guiding cornerstone is that *companies create value by investing capital from investors to generate future cash flows at rates of return exceeding the cost of that capital* (that is, the rate investors require to be paid for the use of their capital). The faster companies can grow their revenues and deploy more capital at attractive rates of return, the more value they create. In short, the combination of growth and return on invested capital (ROIC) drives value and value creation.†

Named, in short, *the core of value,* this combination of growth and ROIC explains why some companies typically trade high price to earnings (P/E) multiples despite low growth. In the branded consumer-products industry, for instance, the global confectioner Hershey Company's P/E was 18 times at the end of 2009, which was higher than 70 percent of the 400 largest U.S. nonfinancial companies. Yet, Hershey's revenue growth rate has been in the 3 to 4 percent range.

What's important about this is that where a business stands in terms of growth and ROIC can drive significant changes in its strategy. For businesses with high returns on capital, improvements in growth create

---

* Throughout this book we use the terms cornerstones and principles interchangeably.
† We define growth in terms of revenues and earnings. We define return on capital as operating profits divided by the capital invested in fixed assets, working capital, and other assets.

the most value. But for businesses with low returns, improvements in ROIC provide the most value.

The second cornerstone of finance is a corollary of the first: *Value is created for shareholders when companies generate higher cash flows, not by rearranging investors' claims on those cash flows.* We call this *the conservation of value,* or anything that doesn't increase cash flows via improving revenues or returns on capital doesn't create value (assuming the company's risk profile doesn't change).

When a company substitutes debt for equity or issues debt to repurchase shares, for instance, it changes the ownership of claims to its cash flows. However, this doesn't change the total available cash flows or add value (unless tax savings from debt increase the company's cash flows). Similarly, changing accounting techniques may create the illusion of higher performance without actually changing the cash flows, so it won't change the value of a company.

We sometimes hear that when a high P/E company buys a low P/E company, the earnings of the low P/E company get rerated at the P/E of the higher company. If the growth, ROIC, and cash flows of the combined company don't change, why would the market revalue the target company's earnings? In addition to bad logic, the rerating idea has no empirical support. That said, if the new, combined earnings and cash flows improve as a result of the acquisition, then real value has been created.

The third cornerstone is that a company's performance in the stock market is driven by changes in the stock market's expectations, not just the company's actual performance (growth, ROIC, and resulting cash flow). We call this *the expectations treadmill*—because the higher the stock market's expectations for a company's share price become, the better a company has to perform just to keep up.

The large American retailer Home Depot, for instance, lost half the value of its shares from 1999 through 2009, despite growing revenues by 11 percent per year during the period at an attractive ROIC. The decline in value can mostly be explained by Home Depot's unsustainably high value in 1999 at $132 billion, the justification of which would have required revenue growth of 26 percent per year for 15 years (a very unlikely, if not impossible, feat).

In a reverse example, Continental AG's (the German-based global auto supplier) shareholders benefited from low expectations at the beginning of 2003, when Continental's P/E was about six. Over the next three years, the shareholders earned returns of 74 percent per year, about one-third of which can be attributed to the elimination of the negative expectations and the return of Continental's P/E to a more normal level of 11.

As the old adage says, good companies aren't necessarily good investments. In a world where executive compensation is heavily linked to share-price performance over relatively short time periods, it's often easier for executives to earn more by turning around a weak performer than by taking a high-performing company to an even higher level.

The fourth and final cornerstone of corporate finance is that *the value of a business depends on who is managing it and what strategy they pursue.* Otherwise called *the best owner,* this cornerstone says that different owners will generate different cash flows for a given business based on their unique abilities to add value.

Related to this is the idea that there is no such number as an inherent value for a business; rather, a business has a given value only relative to who owns and operates it. Some, for instance, add value through unique links with other businesses in their portfolios, such as those with strong capabilities for accelerating the commercialization of products formerly owned by upstart technology companies.

The four cornerstones of finance provide a stable frame of reference for making sound managerial decisions that lead to lasting value creation. Conversely, ignoring the cornerstones leads to poor decisions that erode the value of companies and, in some cases, create widespread stock market bubbles and painful financial crises.

CONSEQUENCES OF NOT VALUING VALUE

The first cornerstone of value creation—that ROIC and growth generate value—and its corollary, the conservation of value, have stood the test of time. Alfred Marshall wrote about return on capital relative to its cost in 1890.* When managers, boards of directors, and investors have forgotten these simple truths, the consequences have been disastrous.

The rise and fall of business conglomerates in the 1970s, hostile takeovers in the United States in the 1980s, the collapse of Japan's bubble economy in the 1990s, the Southeast Asian crisis in 1998, the Internet bubble, and the economic crisis starting in 2007—all of these can

---

* A. Marshall, *Principles of Economics,* vol. 1 (New York: MacMillan & Co., 1890), 142.

be traced to a misunderstanding or misapplication of the cornerstones. During the Internet bubble, for instance, managers and investors lost sight of what drives ROIC, and many even forgot its importance entirely.

When Netscape Communications went public in 1995, the company saw its market capitalization soar to $6 billion on an annual revenue base of just $85 million—an astonishing valuation. The financial world was convinced by this phenomenon that the Internet could change the basic rules of business in every sector, setting off a race to create Internet-related companies and take them public. Between 1995 and 2000, more than 4,700 companies went public in the United States and Europe, many with billion-dollar-plus market capitalizations.

Some of the companies born in this era, including Amazon, eBay, and Yahoo!, have created and are likely to continue creating substantial profits and value. But for every solid, innovative new business idea, there were dozens of companies (including Netscape) that couldn't similarly generate revenue or cash flow in either the short or long term. The initial stock market success of these companies represented a triumph of hype over experience.

Many executives and investors either forgot or threw out fundamental rules of economics in the rarified air of the Internet revolution. Consider the concept of *increasing returns to scale,* also known as "network effects" or "demand-side economies of scale." The idea enjoyed great popularity during the 1990s after University of California–Berkeley professors Carl Shapiro and Hal Varian described it in their book, *Information Rules: A Strategic Guide to the Network Economy.**

The basic idea is this: in certain situations, as companies get bigger, they can earn higher margins and return on capital because their product becomes more valuable with each new customer. In most industries, competition forces returns back to reasonable levels; but in increasing-return industries, competition is kept at bay by the low and decreasing unit costs of the market leader (hence the tag "winner takes all" in this kind of industry).

The concept of increasing returns to scale is sound economics. What was unsound during the Internet-bubble era was its misapplication to almost every product and service related to the Internet and, in some cases, to all industries. The history of innovation shows how difficult

* C. Shapiro and H. Varian, *Information Rules: A Strategic Guide to the Network Economy* (Boston: Harvard Business School Press, 1999).

it is to earn monopoly-sized returns on capital except in very special circumstances.

Many market commentators ignored history in their indiscriminate recommendation of Internet stocks. They took intellectual shortcuts to justify absurd prices for shares of technology companies, which inflated the Internet bubble. At the time, those who questioned the new economics were branded as people who simply didn't get it—the new-economy equivalents of those who would defend Ptolemaic astronomy.

When the laws of economics prevailed, as they always do, it was clear that Internet businesses (such as online pet food or grocery delivery) didn't have the unassailable competitive advantages required to earn even modest returns on capital. The Internet has revolutionized the economy, as have other innovations, but it didn't and can't change the rules of economics, competition, and value creation.

Ignoring the cornerstones also underlies financial crises, such as the one that began in 2007. When banks and investors forgot the conservation-of-value principle, they took on a level of risk that was unsustainable.

First, homeowners and speculators bought homes—essentially illiquid assets. They took out mortgages with interest set at artificially low teaser rates for the first few years, but then those rates rose substantially. Both the lenders and buyers knew that buyers couldn't afford the mortgage payments after the teaser period. But both assumed that either the buyer's income would grow by enough to make the new payments, or the house value would increase enough to induce a new lender to refinance the mortgage at similarly low teaser rates.

Banks packaged these high-risk debts into long-term securities and sold them to investors. The securities, too, were not very liquid, but the investors who bought them, typically hedge funds and other banks, used short-term debt to finance the purchase, thus creating a long-term risk for those who lent the money.

When the interest on the homebuyers' adjustable rate increased, many could no longer afford the payments. Reflecting their distress, the real estate market crashed, pushing the value of many homes below the value of loans taken out to buy them. At that point, homeowners could neither make the required payments nor sell their houses. Seeing this, the banks that had issued short-term loans to investors in securities backed by mortgages became unwilling to roll those loans over, prompting all the investors to sell their securities at once.

The value of the securities plummeted. Finally, many of the large banks themselves had these securities on their books, which they, of course, had also financed with short-term debt that they could no longer roll over.

This story reveals two fundamental flaws in the decisions taken by participants in the securitized mortgage market. First, they all assumed that securitizing risky home loans made them more valuable because it reduced the risk of the assets—but this violates the conservation-of-value rule. The aggregated cash flows of the home loans were not increased by securitization, so no value was created and the initial risks remained.

Securitizing the assets simply enabled risks to be passed on to other owners; some investors, somewhere, had to be holding them. Yet the complexity of the securities chain made it impossible to know who was holding precisely which risks. After the housing market turned, financial service companies feared that any of their counterparties could be holding massive risks and almost ceased to do business with one another. This was the start of the credit crunch that triggered a protracted recession in the real economy.

The second flaw in thinking made by decision makers during the past economic crisis was believing that using leverage to make an investment in itself creates value. It doesn't because, according to the conservation-of-value principle, leverage doesn't increase the cash flows from an investment. Many banks, for example, used large amounts of short-term debt to fund their illiquid long-term assets. This debt didn't create long-term value for shareholders in those banks. On the contrary, it increased the risks of holding their equity.

Market bubbles and crashes are painfully disruptive, but we don't need to rewrite the rules of competition and finance to understand and avoid them. Certainly the Internet changed the way we shop and communicate—but it didn't create a materially different economic mechanism, the so-called *new economy*. On the contrary, the Internet made information, especially about prices, transparent in a way that intensifies market competition in many real markets.

Similarly, the financial crisis triggered in 2007 will wring out some of the economy's recent excesses, such as enabling people to buy houses they can't afford, and uncontrolled credit card borrowing by consumers. But the key to avoiding the next crisis is to reassert the fundamental economic rules, not to revise them.

ADVANTAGES OF VALUING VALUE

There has long been vigorous debate on the importance of shareholder value relative to a company's record on employment and social responsibility—also measures of success. In their ideology and legal frameworks, the United States and the United Kingdom have given most weight to the idea that the main function of a corporation is to maximize shareholder value.

An explicitly broader view of a corporation's purpose, governance structures, and forms of organization has long been influential in continental Europe. In the Netherlands and Germany, for example, the board of a large corporation has a duty to support the continuity of the business in the interests of all the corporation's stakeholders, including employees and the local community, not just shareholders.

Our analysis and experience suggests that for most companies anywhere in the world, pursuing the creation of long-term shareholder value doesn't mean that other stakeholders suffer. We would go further and argue that companies dedicated to value creation are more robust and build stronger economies, higher living standards, and more opportunities for individuals.

Consider employee stakeholders. A company that tries to boost profits by providing a shabby work environment, underpaying employees, and skimping on benefits will have trouble attracting and retaining high-quality employees. With today's more mobile and more educated workforce, such a company would struggle in the long term against competitors offering more attractive environments. While it may feel good to treat people well, it's also good business.

Value-creating companies also generate more jobs. When examining employment, we found the United States and European companies that created the most shareholder value in the past 15 years have shown stronger employment growth. In Exhibit 1.1, companies with the highest total returns to shareholders (TRS) also had the largest increases in employment. We tested this link for individual sectors of the economy and found similar results.

An often expressed concern is that companies must focus on near-term accounting earnings to create shareholder value. We disagree. In fact, we've found a strong positive correlation between long-term shareholder returns and investments in R&D evidence of a commitment to creating value in the longer term. As shown in Exhibit 1.2,

EXHIBIT 1.1 **Correlation between Total Returns to Shareholders (TRS) and Employment Growth**

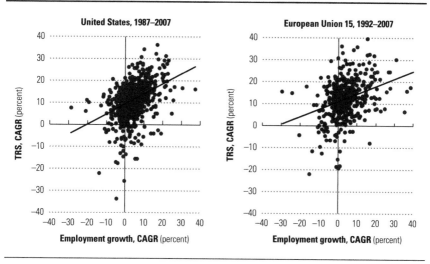

companies that earned the highest shareholder returns also invested the most in R&D. These results also hold within individual sectors in the economy.

Another myth is that value-creating companies tend to ignore their social responsibilities—but it's the opposite that appears to be true: our

EXHIBIT 1.2 **Correlation between TRS and R&D Expenditures**

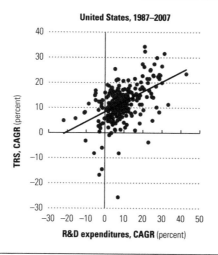

research shows many corporate social responsibility initiatives help create shareholder value.*

IBM, for instance, provides free Web-based management resources to small and midsize enterprises in developing economies. Helping to build such businesses not only improves IBM's reputation in new markets, but it also fosters relationships with companies that could become future customers. Best Buy has a targeted program to reduce employee turnover among women, helping them create their own support networks and build leadership skills. Turnover among women decreased by more than five percent as a result of the program.

In all, the evidence shows that managers who make the effort to create longer-term value for shareholders see that effort rewarded in their companies' stock market performance. In turn, companies that create more lasting value for their shareholders have more financial and human capital to foster behaviors that beneficially impact other stakeholders too.

CHALLENGES FOR EXECUTIVES

There's no doubt that focusing on ROIC and revenue growth over the long term is a tough job for executives—and they won't take it on unless they're sure it wins them more investors and a stronger share price. But as later chapters will show, the evidence is overwhelming that investors do indeed value long-term cash flow, growth, and ROIC, and companies that perform well on these measures perform well in the stock market.

Still, despite the evidence that shareholders value value, companies continue to listen to misguided advice about what the market wants. They fall for the promise of creating value in various unproven ways, such as questionable accounting treatments, elaborate financial structures, or a myopic focus on earnings per share (EPS). But this won't happen.

When analyzing a prospective acquisition, the question often posed is whether the transaction will accrete or dilute EPS over the first year or two. It doesn't matter. No empirical link exists showing that predicted EPS accretion or dilution is an important indicator of whether

---

* Sheila Bonini, Timothy Koller, and Philip H. Mirvis, "Valuing Social Responsibility Programs," *McKinsey on Finance*, no. 32 (Summer 2009): 11–18.

an acquisition will create or destroy value. Deals that strengthen EPS and deals that dilute EPS are equally likely to create or destroy value.

Our intuition tells us value creation from an acquisition can't be as simple as short-term EPS accretion/dilution. After all, EPS accretion/dilution is affected by many factors, some of which are clearly important to value creation, such as the growth rate of the target company and the timing of synergy realization; other factors aren't important, such as the way the transaction is structured or how the accountants apply the accounting rules.

But if such concepts like EPS dilution/accretion and the like are fallacies, why do they prevail? Why, despite the simple and intuitive nature of finance, do executives frequently make decisions that defy axiomatic principles and their own instincts?

In our recent discussion with a company and its bankers, the EPS dilution question came up. To paraphrase one of the bankers: "We know that any impact on EPS is irrelevant to value, but we use it as a simple way to communicate with boards of directors."

Yet company executives say they too don't believe the impact on EPS is so important. They tell us they're just using the measures that Wall Street uses. As well, investors tell us that the short-term impact of a deal on EPS is not that important for them. In sum, we hear from almost everyone that a transaction's short-term impact on EPS doesn't matter, yet they all pay homage to it.

This type of groupthink and lack of valuing value often leads to decisions that either erode value or pass up opportunities to create value. In fact, trying to correlate earnings growth with value creation is a fool's game, because creating longer-term value often necessitates some decisions that reduce earnings in the short term. Moreover, when executives use EPS as a basis for decision making, they can confuse more junior people responsible for analyzing the decisions in question.

From 1997 to 2003, a leading company consistently generated annual EPS growth of between 11 percent and 16 percent. Seems impressive, until you look at other measures important to value creation, like revenue growth. During the same period, the company increased revenues by only 2 percent a year.

The company achieved its profit growth by cutting costs, but as these opportunities became depleted, the company reduced its marketing and product development expenses to maintain earnings growth. After the company's stock price crashed in 2003, managers admitted that they had underinvested in longer-term growth drivers and needed to go through a painful rebuilding period.

The pressure to show strong short-term results often mounts when businesses mature and their growth moderates. Investors go on baying for high growth. Managers are tempted to find ways to keep profits rising in the short term while they try to stimulate growth in the longer term. To be sure, there are situations where raising shorter-term profits should be a priority, and it's very easy for managers to use the long-term value argument as an excuse for neglecting what can and should be done in the short term. But short-term efforts to massage earnings (that undercut productive investment) make achieving long-term growth even more difficult, spawning a vicious downward spiral.

Some analysts and investors will always clamor for short-term results. However, even though a company bent on growing long-term value will not always meet their demands, this continuous pressure has the virtue of keeping managers on their toes. Sorting out the trade-offs between short-term earnings and long-term value creation is part of a manager's job, just as having the courage to make the right call is a critical personal quality.

In other words, *applying the principles of value creation requires independence and courage.*

Just as important, it's up to corporate boards to investigate and understand the economics of the businesses in their portfolio well enough to judge when managers are making the right trade-offs and, above all, to protect managers when they choose to build long-term value at the expense of short-term profits.

Applying the cornerstones of value creation sometimes means going against the crowd. It means accepting that there are no free lunches. It means relying on data, thoughtful analysis, and a deep understanding of the competitive dynamics of one's industry. We hope the rest of this book helps you in this regard so you can make and defend decisions that will create value for investors and society at large.

2

The Core of Value

Companies create value for their owners by investing cash now to generate more cash in the future. The amount of value created is the difference between investments made and cash inflows—adjusted for the fact that tomorrow's cash flows are worth less than today's, due to the time value of money and riskiness of future flows. As we demonstrate later, a company's return on invested capital (ROIC),* and its revenue growth, determine how revenues get converted into cash flows. Therefore, value creation is ultimately driven by ROIC, revenue growth and, of course, the ability to sustain both over time. This first cornerstone, *the core of value*, is illustrated by Exhibit 2.1.

One might expect universal agreement on how to measure and manage value, but this isn't the case—as many executives, boards, and journalists still focus almost obsessively on earnings and earnings growth. Although earnings and cash flow are usually correlated, they don't tell the whole story of value creation, and focusing too much on earnings often leads companies astray.

Earnings growth alone can't explain why investors in two successful, but different, companies like Walgreens and Wm. Wrigley Jr. earned similar shareholder returns between 1968 and 2007, despite much different growth rates. During the period, the drugstore chain (Walgreens) had a growth rate of 12 percent per year, increasing revenues from

---

* A simple definition of return on capital is after-tax operating profit divided by invested capital (working capital plus fixed assets).

EXHIBIT 2.1 **Growth and ROIC Drive Value**

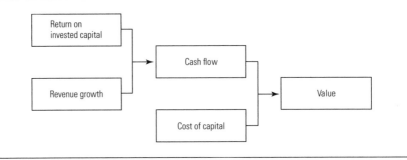

$623 million to $54 billion; at the same time, the chewing-gum maker (Wrigley) grew revenues at 9 percent, from about $160 million to $5.4 billion.

Even though Walgreens was one of the fastest-growing companies in the United States during this time, its average annual shareholder returns were 16 percent compared with 17 percent for the significantly slower growing Wrigley. The reason Wrigley could create slightly more value than Walgreens, despite 25 percent slower growth, was because it earned a 28 percent return on capital—while Walgreens earned a 14 percent return (good for a retailer).

This is what many executives, analysts, bankers, and journalists miss: overwhelming evidence that earnings growth is just one element (and an imperfect one) driving company performance. Earnings or earnings growth alone doesn't reflect the importance of capital utilization.

To be fair, if all companies in an industry earned the same returns on capital, then earnings growth would be the differentiating metric. For reasons of simplicity, analysts and academics have sometimes made this assumption, but, as we show in Chapter 10, returns can vary considerably, even within the same industry.

Deere and Co. knew this in 2001 when it changed its executive compensation scheme to focus more on ROIC, bucking the trend to compensate executives only on the basis of earnings and earnings growth—in essence dulling incentive to drive capital productivity. The results were impressive, as Deere's ROIC increased from less than 10 percent to more than 40 percent in recent years, and its share price tripled between 2001 and 2007.*

---

* "The Future of Corporate Performance Management: A CFO Panel Discussion," *McKinsey on Finance*, no. 29 (Autumn 2008): 14–17.

RELATING GROWTH, ROIC, AND CASH FLOW

Disaggregating cash flow into revenue growth and ROIC clarifies the underlying drivers of a company's performance. Say a company's cash flow was $100 last year and will be $150 next year. This doesn't tell us much about its economic performance since the $50 increase in cash flow could come from many sources, including revenue growth or a reduction in capital spending, or a reduction in marketing expenditures. But if we told you that a company was growing revenues at 7 percent per year, and would earn an ROIC of 15 percent, you could evaluate its performance. You could, for instance, compare the company's growth to the growth of its industry or the economy, and you could analyze its returns on capital relative to peers and its own historical performance.

Growth, ROIC, and cash flow are tightly linked. Consider two companies, Value Inc. and Volume Inc., whose projected revenues, earnings, and cash flows are displayed in Exhibit 2.2.

Both companies earn $100 in year one and grow their revenues and earnings at 5 percent per year. Value generates higher cash flows with the same earnings because it invests less than Volume to achieve the same profit growth. While Value invests 25 percent of its profits, Volume invests 50 percent of its profits to generate the same growth (called its investment rate). Value's lower investment rate leads to 50 percent higher cash flows than Volume with the same level of profits. This simple example illustrates how wrong it can be to focus only on earnings. You might ask whether companies really have such extreme differences in investment rates. The answer is yes, as we show in Chapter 10, Return on Capital.

We can value the two companies by discounting their cash flows at a discount rate that reflects what investors expect to earn from investing in the company (called their cost of capital). Most large companies have a cost of capital between 8 and 10 percent. Exhibit 2.3 shows

EXHIBIT 2.2 **Tale of Two Companies: Same Earnings, Different Cash Flows**

$ million

	Value Inc.					Volume Inc.				
	Year 1	Year 2	Year 3	Year 4	Year 5	Year 1	Year 2	Year 3	Year 4	Year 5
Revenue	1,000	1,050	1,102	1,158	1,216	1,000	1,050	1,102	1,158	1,216
Earnings	100	105	110	116	122	100	105	110	116	122
Investment	(25)	(26)	(28)	(29)	(31)	(50)	(53)	(55)	(58)	(61)
Cash flow	75	79	82	87	91	50	52	55	58	61

EXHIBIT 2.3 **Value Inc.: Discounted Cash Flow Valuation**

$ million

	Value Inc.						
	Year 1	Year 2	Year 3	Year 4	Year 5	Year X	Sum
Earnings	100	105	110	116	122	. . .	–
Investment	(25)	(26)	(28)	(29)	(31)	. . .	–
Cash flow	75	79	82	87	91	. . .	–
Value today	68	65	62	59	56	. . .	1,500

Present value of 75
discounted at 10% for
one year

Present value of 87
discounted at 10% for
four years

how Value is valued. We discounted each year's cash flow to the present at a 10 percent cost of capital, then summed the results to derive a total present value of all future cash flows of 1,500. Using the same technique, Volume's value is 1,000.

We can also express the companies' values as P/E ratios by dividing their values by their first-year earnings of $100. Value's P/E is 15, while Volume's is only 10. Despite identical earnings and growth rates, the companies have different earnings multiples because of different cash flows.

Value generates higher cash flows because it doesn't have to invest as much as Volume. Value's lower investment needs are driven by its higher return on capital. In this case, Value invested $25 (out of $100 earned) in year one to grow its revenue and profits by $5 in year two. Its return on new capital is 20 percent ($5 of additional profits divided by $25 of investment).* Volume's return on capital is 10 percent, $5 in additional profits in year two divided by $50 of investment.

Growth, ROIC, and cash flow (as represented by the investment rate) are tied together mathematically in the following relationship:

$$\text{Investment Rate} = \text{Growth} \div \text{ROIC}$$

For Value,

$$25\% = 5\% \div 20\%$$

For Volume,

$$50\% = 5\% \div 10\%$$

* We assumed that all of the increase in profits is due to the new investment, with the return on Value Inc.'s existing capital remaining unchanged.

EXHIBIT 2.4 **Payout Ratio Varies with Growth and ROIC**

Cash flow/earnings

Growth					
	3%	53%	67%	77%	88%
	6%	14%	33%	54%	76%
	9%	−29%	0%	31%	64%
		7%	9%	13%	25%

ROIC

Because the three variables are tied together, you only need two to know the third, so you can describe a company's performance with any two of the variables. From an economic perspective, describing a company in terms of growth and ROIC is most insightful. Value's growth rate is 5 percent and its ROIC is 20 percent, while Volume's growth rate is also 5 percent, but its ROIC is only 10 percent.

Exhibit 2.4 portrays how much cash flow a company can pay to its investors depending on its returns on capital and growth in a single year. You can see from the exhibit that both factors are important in driving cash flow. As a percentage of profits, cash flow is highest when growth is slow and ROIC is high. When growth is high, cash flow can be negative, but this doesn't mean that slow growth is better. Exhibit 2.4 is only a one-year snapshot, and higher growth today means lower cash flow today, but presumably higher cash flow later.

Now in Exhibit 2.5, we show how different combinations of growth and ROIC translate into value, discounting cash flows to the present at the company's cost of capital. In this case, we're assuming a 9 percent cost of capital and a company that earns $100 in the first year.*

These calculations are consistent with what we find in the real world. Take the typical large company, which grows at about 5 to 6 percent per year (nominal), earns about a 13 percent return on equity

---

* We've assumed that after 15 years, growth slows to 4.5 percent. If a company grew faster than the economy forever, it would eventually overtake the entire world economy.

EXHIBIT 2.5 **Translating Growth and ROIC into Value**

Value,[1] dollars

Growth		7%	9%	13%	25%
	3%	900	1,100	1,400	1,600
	6%	700	1,100	1,600	2,100
	9%	400	1,100	1,900	2,700

ROIC

[1] Present value of future cash flows, assuming year 1 earnings of $100 and a 9% cost of capital. After 15 years all scenarios grow at 4.5%.

and has a 9 percent cost of capital. Finding the intersection of the typical company's return and growth leads you to a value of about 1,500–1,600, which, when divided by earnings of 100, gives a P/E ratio of 15–16 times. Fifteen times is the median P/E ratio for large companies in nonrecessionary periods.

Observe that for any level of growth, value always increases with improvements in ROIC. In other words, when all else is equal, higher ROIC is always good.

The same can't be said of growth. When ROIC is high, faster growth increases value, but when ROIC is low, faster growth decreases value. The dividing line between whether growth creates or destroys value is when the return on capital equals the cost of capital. When returns are above the cost of capital, faster growth increases value. At the line where returns equal the cost of capital, value is neither created nor destroyed regardless of how fast the company grows.

We sometimes hear the assertion and objection that if a company grows, its return on capital will naturally increase; therefore, even low-ROIC companies should strive for growth. But we find this to be true only for young start-up businesses and businesses with extremely low capacity utilization. Most often, a low ROIC indicates a flawed business model or unattractive industry structure.

If you're curious and mathematically inclined, Appendix A shows the core-of-value cornerstone as a simple formula along with its derivation.

REAL-WORLD EVIDENCE

The logic we've laid out earlier is reflected in the way companies perform in the stock market. We mentioned earlier why Walgreens and Wrigley's shareholder returns were the same even though Walgreens grew much faster.

Another example is GE, the share price of which increased from about $5 in 1991 to about $40 in 2001, earning investors $519 billion of share-value increase and distributions during the last 10 years of Jack Welch's tenure as CEO. A similar amount invested in the S&P 500 index would have returned only $212 billion.

How did GE do it? In different ways, GE's industrial and finance businesses both contributed significantly to its overall value creation. Over the 10-year period, the industrial businesses increased revenues by only 4 percent per year (less than the growth of the economy), but their ROIC increased from about 13 to 31 percent. The finance businesses performed in a more balanced way, demonstrating growth of 18 percent per year and increasing returns on capital from 14 to 21 percent. In the industrial businesses, ROIC was the key driver of value creation, while in the financial businesses, both growth and ROIC contributed significantly to value creation.

So we see that the core-of-value cornerstone applies at the company level, but what about the sector level? To answer, consider companies as a whole in the consumer packaged-goods sector. Even though certain companies in this sector (like Procter & Gamble and Colgate Palmolive) aren't high-growth companies, the market values them at high earnings multiples.

The typical large packaged-goods company grew its revenues only 6 percent from 1998 to 2007, slower than the average of about 8 percent for all large companies. Yet at the end of 2007 (before the market crash), the median price-earnings ratio of consumer packaged-goods companies was about 20, compared with 17 for the median large company. The high valuation of companies in this sector is explained by their high returns on capital—typically above 20 percent compared with returns on capital of 13 percent for the median large company (for 1998–2007).

Comparing Campbell Soup Company ($8 billion in 2008 revenue) with fast-growing discount retailer Kohl's ($16 billion revenue in 2008) is also instructive. In the mid-2000s, Kohl's revenue grew 15 percent annually, while Campbell's achieved only 4 percent organic growth. Yet the two had similar P/E ratios. Despite its slow growth, Campbell's higher ROIC of 50 percent made up for its slower growth, while Kohl's ROIC averaged only 15 percent.

Now let's see how well the core-of-value cornerstone applies at the country and global levels by asking why large U.S.-based companies typically trade at higher multiples than their counterparts in Japan and the Asian-tiger countries (Hong Kong, South Korea, Taiwan, and Singapore).* Some executives assume the reason is because investors are simply willing to pay higher prices for U.S. companies. In some cases, non-U.S. companies even considered moving their share listing to the New York Stock Exchange to increase their value.

The real reason U.S. companies trade at higher multiples is because they typically earn higher returns on capital. The median large U.S. company earned a 16 percent ROIC in 2007, while the median large Asian company earned 10 percent. Historically, Asian companies have focused more on growth than profitability or ROIC, which explains the large valuation differences.

Of course these broad comparisons hide differences across companies and industries, where some Asian companies outperform their U.S. counterparts (Toyota in automobiles, for example).

We've also used the core-of-value cornerstone to understand how P/E ratios behave over time. Exhibit 2.6 plots the median P/E ratio for the S&P 500 index from 1962 to 2009, as well as an estimate of what the P/E ratio should have been given underlying fundamentals, using a formula based on the core-of-value cornerstone (growth, returns on capital, and cost of capital). As you can see, the predicted P/E ratios closely track the actual P/E ratios (look to Chapter 7, The Stock Market and the Real Economy, for details of this relationship).

Let's look at how the core principle works for a sample of companies in the consumer-staples industry. Exhibit 2.7 shows the median P/E ratios for companies with different combinations of revenue growth and ROIC. As you can see in the first two rows, higher returns

---

* The median large company in the United States had a market-to-book ratio of 2.4 in 2007, while the median large company in the Asian tiger countries had a median market-to-book of about 1.8.

EXHIBIT 2.6 **Estimating Fundamental Market Valuation Levels**

Price/earnings

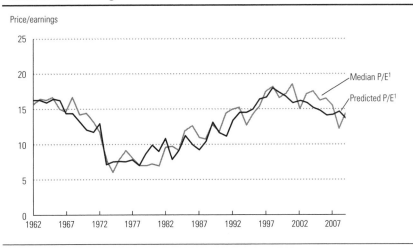

[1] P/E is 12-month forward-looking price-to-earnings ratio.

Source: McKinsey Corporate Performance Center analysis.

EXHIBIT 2.7 **Consumer Staples Sector: Growth and ROIC Drive P/E Multiples**

Median forward P/E, December 2007

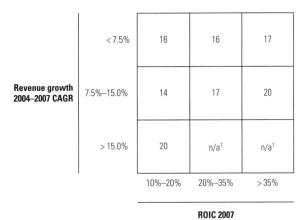

Revenue growth 2004–2007 CAGR			
< 7.5%	16	16	17
7.5%–15.0%	14	17	20
> 15.0%	20	n/a[1]	n/a[1]
	10%–20%	20%–35%	> 35%
		ROIC 2007	

[1] Fewer than two companies in these cells.

Source: McKinsey Corporate Performance Center analysis.

lead to a higher P/E ratio for a given level of growth. Note that for the two higher ROIC columns, higher revenue growth also leads to higher P/E ratios, but the first column is worth explaining. The very high growth companies (greater than 15 percent per year) have high P/E ratios despite lower ROIC. When we dig deeper, we find that all these companies are quite young—their modest returns on capital are partly because they're growing so fast and investing a lot of capital several years ahead of those returns. Note that the medium-growth companies with low returns have the lowest P/E, reflecting the fact that their growth is not expected to create much, if any, value.

To demonstrate the relevance of growth and ROIC, we've been using earnings multiples, particularly the P/E ratio, as a shorthand for summarizing a company's value. In practice, analyzing and interpreting earnings multiples can be messy. Appendix B tackles some of the subtleties of analyzing multiples properly.

MANAGERIAL IMPLICATIONS

We dive more deeply into the managerial dimensions of return on capital and growth in Chapters 10 and 11, respectively. For now, we refer back to Exhibit 2.5 because it contains important strategic insights for managers. Namely, we can use the matrix to examine the relative impact of changes in ROIC and growth on a company's value.

In general, high-return companies generate more value from growth (assuming ROIC remains constant), while low-return companies generate more value from increasing ROIC. Exhibit 2.8 shows that a typical high-return company, such as a branded consumer-products company, can increase its value by 10 percent by increasing its growth

EXHIBIT 2.8 **Increasing Value: Impact of Higher Growth and ROIC**

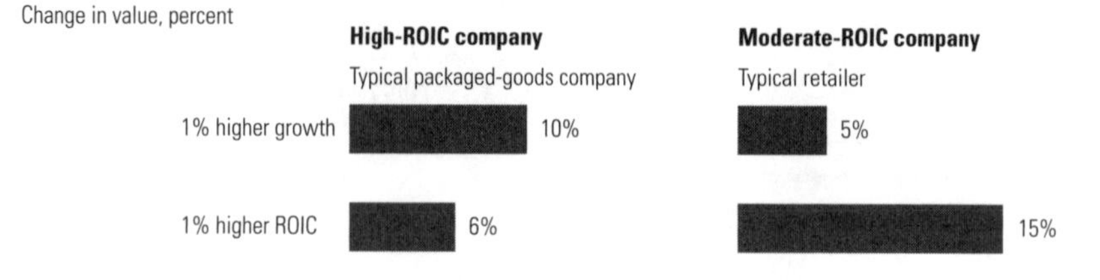

Change in value, percent	High-ROIC company Typical packaged-goods company	Moderate-ROIC company Typical retailer
1% higher growth	10%	5%
1% higher ROIC	6%	15%

Source: McKinsey Corporate Performance Center analysis.

EXHIBIT 2.9 **Value Creation by Type of Growth: Consumer Products Company**

Shareholder value created for incremental $1.00 of revenue

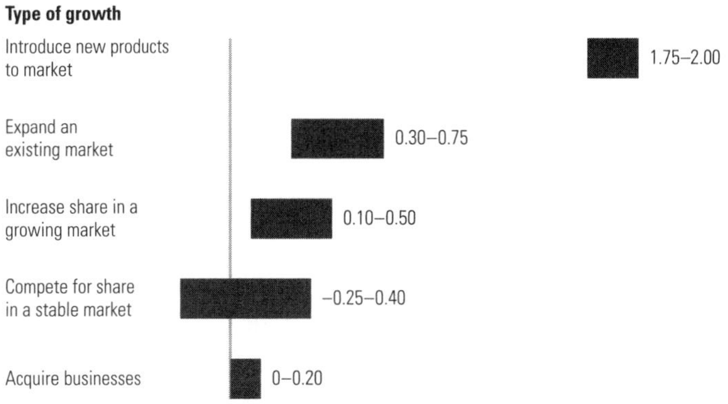

Type of growth

Introduce new products to market	1.75–2.00
Expand an existing market	0.30–0.75
Increase share in a growing market	0.10–0.50
Compete for share in a stable market	−0.25–0.40
Acquire businesses	0–0.20

Source: McKinsey Corporate Performance Center analysis.

rate by 1 percent. A typical moderate-return company, such as the average retailer, will increase its value by only 5 percent for the same increase in growth.

On the other hand, the moderate-return company gets a 15 percent bump from increasing its ROIC by 1 percent, while the high-return company gets only a 6 percent bump from the same increase in ROIC.

The general lesson is that high-return companies should focus on growth, while low-return companies should focus on improving returns before growing. Of course this analysis assumes that it's equally difficult to achieve a 1 percent increase in growth as a 1 percent increase in ROIC, everything else constant. In reality, degrees of difficulty will be different for different companies in different industries, as will the relative impact of growth and returns on invested capital, but the analysis is essential for a company to set its strategic priorities.

Until now we've assumed that all growth earns the same return on capital and, therefore, generates the same value—but this isn't true. Different types of growth create different amounts of return and value, depending on the industry and company.

Exhibit 2.9 shows the value created from different types of growth for a typical consumer-products company. These results are based on specific cases with which we are familiar, not on a comprehensive analysis, but we believe they are reflective of broader reality.* (See Chapter 11 for more discussion about the different amounts of value created from different types of growth.)

The results in Exhibit 2.9 are expressed in terms of value created for one dollar of incremental revenue. For example, one dollar of additional revenue from a new product creates $1.75 to $2.00 of value in this industry. The most important implication of this chart is the rank order. New products typically create more value for shareholders, while acquisitions typically create the least. The key at these extremes is, you guessed it, returns on capital.

Growth strategies based on organic new-product development frequently have the highest returns because they don't require much new capital; companies can add new products to their existing factory lines and distribution systems. Furthermore, investments required for new products are doled out over time; if preliminary results aren't promising, funding can be scaled back or canceled.

Acquisitions, on the other hand, require all the investment be made up front. The up-front payment reflects the expected cash flows from the target plus a premium to stave off other bidders. So even if the buyer can improve the target company enough to generate an attractive return on capital, the return is typically only a small amount over its cost of capital.

To be fair, this analysis doesn't reflect the risk of failure. Most product ideas fail before reaching the market, and the cost of failed ideas aren't in the numbers. By contrast, acquisitions typically bring existing revenues and cash flows that limit the downside risk to the acquirer.

The second-lowest source of value creation for consumer goods companies is achieving additional share in a stable market. This is because competitors are unlikely to give up share without a fight, which often leads to a price war in which all the companies in the industry lose (but it's great for the consumer).

The next rung up on the ladder, growing share in a growing market, typically creates more value than growing share in a stable market, because when a market is growing faster, competitors can grow quickly even if they are losing some market share. They are, therefore, less likely to retaliate with price wars.

---

* We identified examples for each type of growth and estimated their impact on value creation. For instance, we obtained several examples of the margins and capital requirements for new products.

Last, expanding an existing market creates high value because it typically means finding new customers in markets the company already serves. Therefore, the incremental costs and capital required to serve those customers is low.

The interaction of growth and ROIC is also important. For example, we've seen some very successful, high-return companies in the United States that are reluctant to invest in growth if it reduces ROIC (or profit margin). One technology company we know had 30 percent operating margins and a 50+ percent ROIC, so it didn't want to invest in projects that might earn only 25 percent returns, fearing this would dilute its average returns. But as you might expect, even a 25 percent return opportunity would still create value, even though the company's average return would decline.

But the evidence is clear that this indeed creates value. We examined the performance of 78 high-return-on-capital companies (greater than 30 percent returns on capital) from 1996 to 2005.* Not surprisingly, the companies that created the most value (measured by total returns to shareholders) were those that grew fastest and maintained their high returns on capital. But the second-highest value creation came from those that grew fastest even though they experienced moderate declines in return on capital. They created more value than companies that increased their return on capital but grew slowly.

We've also seen companies with low returns pursue growth on the assumption that this will also improve their profit margins and returns, reasoning that growth will increase returns by spreading fixed costs across more revenues. Except for small start-up companies, or companies with low capacity utilization, we find that faster growth rarely fixes a company's return-on-capital problem. Low returns usually indicate a poor industry structure (e.g., airlines), a flawed business model (think Webvan), or weak execution. Until you fix the return-on-capital problem, you shouldn't grow.

Having examined the performance of 64 low return-on-capital companies from 1996 to 2005, the evidence backs this up. The companies that had low growth but increased their returns on capital outperformed the faster-growing companies that did not improve their return on capital.

---

* Bin Jiang and Timothy Koller, "How to Choose between Growth and ROIC," *McKinsey on Finance*, no. 25 (Autumn 2007): 19–22.

3

The Conservation
of Value

Recall that the first cornerstone is that value is created when a company generates higher cash flows through high revenue growth or high return on capital, or some combination thereof. The second cornerstone, *the conservation of value*, is a corollary of the first principle: anything that doesn't increase cash flows doesn't create value.

Value is conserved, or unchanged, when a company shifts the ownership of claims to its cash flows, but doesn't change the total available cash flows (such as when substituting debt for equity or issuing debt to repurchase shares). Similarly, changing the appearance of the cash flows without actually changing the cash flows, say by changing accounting techniques, doesn't change the value of a company.*

Although this principle may seem obvious, we make it explicit because executives, investors, and pundits often fall for the allure of the elusive free lunch, hoping, for example, that one accounting treatment will lead to a higher value than another or that some fancy financial structure will turn a mediocre deal into a winner.

The battle over how companies should account for executive stock options illustrates the extent to which executives continue to believe that the stock market is uninformed. Companies issue executive stock

---

* In some cases, a company can increase its value by reducing its cost of capital by using more debt in its capital structure. However, even in this case the underlying change is to reduce taxes, but the overall pretax cost of capital doesn't change. See Chapter 15, Capital Structure, for a further discussion.

options in lieu of cash compensation, creating incentives for employees to act in the interests of the companies and to conserve cash (especially important for young start-up companies).

Even though there is no cash effect when executive stock options are issued, they reduce the cash flow available to existing shareholders by diluting their ownership when the options are exercised. But under accounting rules dating back to the 1970s, companies were allowed to ignore the effect of issuing options in their income statements.

As options became more material, in the early 1990s the Financial Accounting Standards Board (FASB) recognized the error of this treatment and proposed to change it, requiring companies to record an expense for the value of options when they're issued.

Warren Buffett and others saw clearly that if options were valuable to employees, they must be costly to shareholders. But a large group of executives and venture capitalists thought that investors would be spooked if options were brought onto the income statement. Some claimed that the entire venture capital industry would be decimated because young start-up companies that pay much of their compensation with options would show low or negative profits. They even convinced Senator Joe Lieberman to introduce legislation to stop the FASB from proceeding.

The FASB finally issued its new rules in 2004,* more than a decade after they took up the issue, and only after the dot-com bubble burst and the accounting scandals of the early 2000s weakened the opposition. Despite dire predictions, the stock prices of companies didn't change when the new accounting rules were implemented—because the market already reflected the cost of the options in their valuations of companies.

One respected analyst said to us, "I don't care whether they are recorded as an expense or simply disclosed in the footnotes. I know what to do with the information."

As we'll see, the conservation-of-value cornerstone is important for far more than just stock option accounting; it also answers such questions as whether an acquisition creates value simply because reported earnings increase, whether a company should return cash to shareholders through share repurchases instead of dividends, and whether financial engineering creates value.

---

* Financial Accounting Standard 123R, released in December 2004, effective for periods beginning after June 15, 2005.

Executives should focus on increasing cash flows rather than finding gimmicks that merely redistribute value among investors or improve the appearance of reported results. Executives should also be wary of proposals that claim to create value unless they're clear about how their actions will materially increase the size of the pie. If you can't pinpoint the tangible source of value creation, you're probably looking at an illusion.

FOUNDATIONS OF VALUE CONSERVATION

The value-conservation cornerstone or principle rests on the pioneering work of Nobel prize winners Franco Modigliani and Merton Miller, financial economists who in the late 1950s and early 1960s questioned whether managers could change capital structure to increase share prices. In 1958, they showed that the value of a company shouldn't be affected by changing the structure of the debt and equity ownership unless the overall cash flows generated by the company also change.[*]

Consider a company that has no debt and generates $100 of cash flow each year before paying shareholders. Suppose the company is valued at $1,000. Now suppose the company borrows $200 and pays it out to the shareholders. Our knowledge of the core value cornerstone, and the value conservation cornerstone, tells us that the company would still be worth $1,000, with $200 for the creditors and $800 for the shareholders, because its cash flow available to pay the shareholders and creditors is still $100 per year.

In most countries, however, borrowing money does change cash flows because interest payments are tax deductible. The total taxes paid by the company are lower, thereby increasing the cash flow available to pay both shareholders and creditors. In addition, having debt may induce managers to be more diligent and, therefore, increase the company's cash flow.

On the other hand, having debt could make it more difficult for managers to raise capital for attractive investment opportunities, thereby reducing cash flow. The point is that it isn't the substitution of debt for equity in and of itself that matters; it only matters if the

---

[*] F. Modigliani and M. H. Miller, "The Cost of Capital, Corporate Finance and the Theory of Investment," *American Economic Review* 48 (1958): 261–297.

substitution changes the company's cash flows through tax reductions, or if associated changes in management decisions change value.

In a related vein, finance academics in the 1960s developed the idea of efficient markets. Although the meaning and validity of efficient markets is a continuing debate, especially after the bursting of the dot-com and real estate bubbles of the 2000 decade, one implication of efficient market theory remains: the stock market isn't easily fooled when companies undertake actions to increase reported accounting profit without increasing cash flows.

We mentioned the example of accounting for employee stock options in the introduction to this chapter. Similarly, when the FASB eliminated goodwill amortization effective in 2002, and then when the International Accounting Standards Board (IASB) did the same in 2005, many companies reported increased profits—but their underlying value didn't change because the accounting change didn't affect cash flow. The evidence is overwhelming that the market isn't fooled by actions that don't affect cash flow.*

MANAGERIAL IMPLICATIONS

The conservation-of-value cornerstone is useful because it tells us what to look for when analyzing whether some action will create value: look for the cash flow impact. It also applies across a wide range of important business decisions, such as accounting policy (see Chapter 9), acquisitions (Chapter 13), corporate portfolio decisions (Chapter 12), dividend payout policy (Chapter 15) and capital structure (also Chapter 15).

Following is a discussion of how the conservation-of-value cornerstone applies to share repurchases, acquisitions, and financial engineering.

Share Repurchases

Covered more deeply in Chapter 15, "Capital Structure," share repurchases have become a popular way for companies to return cash to investors. Until the early 1980s, more than 90 percent of the total

---

* See Chapters 15 and 16 of *Valuation: Measuring and Managing the Value of Companies*, 5th edition, by Tim Koller, Marc Goedhart, and David Wessels (Hoboken, NJ: John Wiley & Sons, 2010).

distributions made by large U.S. companies to shareholders were dividends and less than 10 percent were share repurchases. However, since 1998, about 50 to 60 percent of total distributions have been share repurchases.*

To determine if share repurchases create value or not, we must consider the source of the cash used to repurchase the shares. For example, let's assume that a company borrows $100 to repurchase 10 percent of its shares. For every $100 of shares repurchased, the company will pay, say, 6 percent interest on its new debt. After taxes of, say, 35 percent, its total earnings would decline by $3.90 (100 × .06 × 1 − Tax rate). However, the number of shares has declined by 10 percent, so its earnings per share would increase by about 5 percent.

A 5 percent increase in EPS without working very hard sounds like a great deal. Assuming the company's P/E ratio doesn't change, then its market value per share will also increase by 5 percent. In other words, the assumption is that you can get something for nothing; you can increase EPS while keeping your P/E ratio constant.

Unfortunately, this doesn't square with the conservation-of-value principle because the total cash flow of the business hasn't increased. While EPS has increased by 5 percent, the company's debt has increased as well. With higher leverage, the company's equity cash flows will be more volatile and investors will demand a higher return. This will bring down its P/E ratio, offsetting the increase in EPS.

However, even if cash flow isn't increased with a buyback, some have rightly argued that repurchasing shares can reduce the likelihood that management will invest the cash at low returns. If this is true, and it is likely that management would invest the money unwisely, then you have a legitimate source of value creation because the operating cash flows of the company would increase. Said another way, when the likelihood of investing cash at low returns is high, share repurchases make sense as a tactic for avoiding value destruction.

Some argue that management should repurchase shares when its shares are undervalued. Let's suppose management believes that the current share price of the company doesn't reflect its underlying potential, so it buys back shares today. One year later, the market price adjusts to reflect management's expectations. Has value been created? Once again the answer is no, value has not been created; it's only been

* Michael J. Mauboussin, "Clear Thinking about Share Repurchases," in *Mauboussin on Strategy* (Legg Mason Capital Management, 2006).

shifted from one set of shareholders (those that sold) to the shareholders that did not sell. So the holding shareholders may have benefited, but the shareholders as a whole were not affected.

Buying shares when they're undervalued may be good for the shareholders who don't sell, but studies of share repurchases have shown that companies aren't very good at timing share repurchases, often buying when their share prices are high, not low.

As a rule, executives need to exercise caution when presented with transactions that appear to create value by boosting EPS. Always ask, where is the source of the value creation?

Companies in R&D-intensive industries, for example, have searched for ways to capitalize R&D spending with complex joint ventures, hoping to lower R&D expenses that reduce EPS. But does the joint venture create value by increasing short-term EPS? No, and in fact it may erode value because the company now transfers upside potential (and risk, of course) to its partners.

Acquisitions

Covered more extensively in Chapter 13, acquisitions create value only when the combined cash flows of the two companies increase due to accelerated revenue growth, cost reductions, or better use of fixed and working capital.

When Johnson & Johnson purchased Pfizer's consumer health business for $16 billion in late 2006, it immediately announced that the combination would reduce costs by $600 million per year. These savings increased the combined operating profits of J&J/Pfizer's consumer businesses by 30 percent—equal to about $5 billion to $6 billion in present value. Taking these numbers, the acquisition's cost savings alone would recoup one-third of the purchase price, making it a clear value creator.

Another value-creating example, based on revenue acceleration, also comes from Johnson & Johnson, which acquired Neutrogena (skin care products) in 1994 for $924 million. With new product development and by increasing the brand's presence outside the United States, J&J was able to increase Neutrogena's sales from $281 million to $778 million by 2002. Exhibit 3.1 shows the extent of the new products J&J introduced under the Neutrogena brand.

The common element of both these acquisitions was radical performance improvement, not marginal changes. But sometimes we've seen acquisitions justified by what could only be called magic.

EXHIBIT 3.1 **How Johnson & Johnson Turbocharged Neutrogena's Growth**

Product launches	Launch year		
	1994–1996	**1997–1999**	**2000–2002**
Men			• Complete men's product line
Cosmetics			• "Dermatologist Developed" line with 85+ SKUs
Hair products		• New line under "Clean" sub-brand	
Sun protection	• No-stick sunscreen • SPF hand treatment	• Transparent sunscreen	• Healthy Defense brand
Body care	• Rainbath brand (relaunch) • Norwegian Formula foot cream brand	• Body Clear brand	
Facial care			
Acne	• On-the-Spot brand acne treatment	• Multivitamin acne treatment • Oil-free acne treatment	
Moisturizers	• Healthy Skin Care brand	• Light night moisturizer products	• Visibly Firm brand
Cleansers	• Clear Pore treatment • Deep Clean, Deep Pore brands	• Extra Gentle brand • Pore Refining brand	• Skin Clearing brand

Source: McKinsey Corporate Performance Center analysis.

Assume for example that Company A is worth $100, and Company B is worth $50 based on their respective expected cash flows. Company A buys Company B for $50, issuing its own shares. For simplicity, let's assume that the combined cash flows are not expected to increase. What's the new Company AB worth?

Immediately after the acquisition, the two companies are the same as they were before with the same expected cash flows, and the original shareholders of the two companies still own the shares of the combined company. So AB should be worth $150, and the original A shareholders' shares of AB should be worth $100, while the original B shareholders' shares of AB should be worth $50.

As simple as this seems, some executives and financial professionals add some extra value to the transaction. Let's assume that Company A is expected to earn $5 next year, so its P/E ratio is 20 times. Company B is expected to earn $3 next year, so its P/E is 16.7 times. What then will be the P/E ratio of AB? A straightforward approach suggests that the value of AB should remain $150. Its earnings will be $8, so its P/E ratio will be about 18.8, between A's and B's respective P/E ratios.

But here's where the magic happens. Some would believe that once A buys B, the stock market will apply A's P/E ratio of 20 to B's earnings. In other words, B's earnings are worth more once they are owned by A. So by this thinking, the value of AB would be $160, an increase in the combined value of $10.

There's even a term for this: *multiple expansion* in the United States, or *rerating* in the UK. The multiple of B's earnings expands to the level of A's because the market doesn't recognize that perhaps the new earnings added to A are not as valuable. This must be so, because B's earnings will now be all mixed up with A's, and the market won't be able to tell the difference.

Of course, an illusion like this doesn't have to be logical or symmetrical. Another version of the multiple-expansion idea works the other way around, supposing company B purchases A. We've heard the argument that since a lower-P/E company is buying a higher-P/E company, it must be getting into higher-growth businesses. Higher growth is generally good, so another theory postulates that because B is accelerating its growth, its P/E ratio will increase.

If multiple expansion and similar fallacies were true, all acquisitions would create value, because the P/E ratio of the lower P/E company would rise to the level of the higher P/E company, regardless of which is the buyer or seller. Although a concept like multiple expansion may seem attractive, value isn't created just because a lower P/E company merges with a higher P/E company.

You must be saying to yourself, why are we discussing such obvious fantasies? Doesn't every corporate leader know this? The answer is that companies often justify acquisitions with this very logic, believe it or not, even though there is no data to support such ideas. Our approach on the other hand is simple: if you can't point to specific sources of increased cash flow, the stock market won't be fooled.

Financial Engineering

Covered more broadly in Chapter 15, financial engineering is another area where the conservation-of-value cornerstone is important. For our purposes, we define financial engineering as *the use of financial instruments or structures, other than straight debt and equity, to manage a company's capital structure and risk profile.*

Financial engineering can include the use of derivatives, structured debt, securitization, and off-balance-sheet financing. While some of these activities can create real value, most don't—yet the motivation to engage in non-value-added financial engineering remains strong because of its short-term, illusory impact.

Consider that many hotel companies don't own most of the hotels they operate. Instead, the hotels themselves are owned by other companies, often structured as partnerships or real estate investment trusts (REITs). Unlike corporations, partnerships and REITs don't pay U.S. income taxes; taxes are only paid by their owners.

Therefore, an entire layer of taxation is eliminated by placing hotels in partnerships and REITs in the United States. With ownership and operations separated in this manner, total income taxes paid to the government are lower, so investors in the ownership and operating companies are better off as a group because their aggregate cash flows are higher. This is an example of financial engineering that adds real value by increasing cash flows.

On the other hand, consider the collateralized debt obligations (CDO) that contributed to the 2007–2009 financial crisis as an example of questionable financial engineering. Here's how a CDO works. The sponsor of a CDO (typically a bank) creates a new legal entity called a special purpose vehicle (SPV) that buys up a lot of loans. These loans can be corporate loans, mortgage loans, or even other CDOs. The new legal entity then issues debt securities that will be paid off by the cash flows from the loans in the SPV's portfolio.

Exhibit 3.2 illustrates the cash flows related to a CDO. Individual homeowners pay interest and principal to their mortgage servicer, who forwards it to an SPV that has issued collateralized mortgage obligations. That entity pays interest and principal to its investors, which could include a CDO entity that, in turn, pays principal and interest to the various CDO investors.

But the total cash flows received by the investors can't be more than they would receive if they directly owned the loans and securities; in fact, due to fees and transaction costs, the total cash flow to the CDO holders must be lower than the cash flows from the underlying loans.

The benefit of a CDO is that it allows banks to remove assets from their balance sheets by selling them to investors (through the CDO), thereby freeing up some of the bank's equity capital to make new loans. Making more loans in turn, with their associated transaction fees, increases the banks' cash flows.

EXHIBIT 3.2 **Cash Flows Related to Collateralized Debt Obligations**

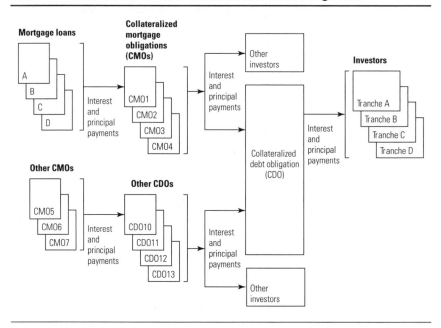

CDOs worked well for over 20 years, doing exactly what they were intended to do. The early CDOs were pools of home mortgages that allowed banks to originate loans and then take them off their books so they could originate more loans. But the CDOs issued in 2005 and 2006 were different and fundamentally flawed.

Unlike the early CDOs, these new CDOs were so complex and intransparent that even the most sophisticated investors and banks couldn't assess their risks, so they relied on the ratings agencies to do this. The problem was that the ratings agencies earned large fees from the banks for their ratings, and they didn't want the banks to take their business elsewhere.

With no money of their own at stake, the ratings agencies pronounced many of these securities AAA or AA, the safest securities. In the process, pools of risky subprime loans were turned into AAA-rated securities, but that violated the conservation-of-value principle. The total risks and cash flows hadn't changed, so the total risk of the CDOs couldn't have been reduced.

When homeowners with subprime mortgages started to miss payments in 2006, or default, housing prices fell. Investors then realized that the CDOs and CMOs were riskier than they thought, so they rushed to sell their stakes. The CDOs and CMOs became unsellable, but investors and banks who owned these securities had often financed them with short-term debt that had to be renewed every month or quarter (or sometimes daily).

Seeing that the value of their collateral (the CDOs and CMOs) had dropped, creditors would not refinance the short-term debt as it came due. The banks and the investors holding the CDOs couldn't do anything but sell assets at fire-sale prices, go out of business, or get a government bailout.

You might ask why the banks were so exposed. Wasn't the idea that they were just creating these CDOs, and not actually investing in them? The banks were caught with three types of risky inventory. One, they held loans that they hadn't yet been able to package and securitize. Two, they often owned the riskiest tranches of CDOs because they weren't able to sell them when they created them. Three, they were frequent purchasers of long-term CDOs because they believed they could profit by buying them and financing them with cheap short-term debt.

Another indirect benefit proposed was that CDOs created additional investment opportunities for investors, but this argument doesn't hold up to scrutiny. The claim was that investors liked CDOs because they yielded higher returns than other similarly rated securities. In other words, the yield on an AA-rated CDO was higher than an AA-rated corporate bond. But if these CDOs were rated the same as corporate bonds, why did they have higher yields? The answer, which we know from hindsight, is that they were riskier, and the market knew they were riskier even if the ratings agencies didn't. The market saw through the illusion.

So a good idea taken too far almost destroyed the financial markets.

4

The Expectations
Treadmill

The first two cornerstones of finance defined what drives real value creation in a corporation. The third cornerstone, *the expectations treadmill*, explains how that value is reflected in the returns that equity investors earn.

The return on invested capital (ROIC) that a company earns is not the same as what its shareholders earn. Suppose a company can invest $1,000 in a factory and earn $200 every year. The first investors in the company pay $1,000 for their shares, and if they hold the shares they will earn 20 percent per year ($200 divided by $1,000).

Suppose then, after one year, the investors decide to sell their shares and find buyers who pay $2,000 for the shares. Because of the higher price, and assuming it doesn't rise further, these new buyers will earn only 10 percent per year on their investment ($200 divided by $2,000), compared to the original owners who earned a 120 percent return (ROIC of 20 percent and share-price appreciation of 100 percent).

Although all the investors collectively will earn the same return as the company (on a time-weighted average), individual groups of investors will earn very different returns because they pay different prices for the shares based on their expectations of future performance.

A useful analogy, the speed of a treadmill represents the expectations built into a company's share price. If the company beats expectations, and if the market believes the improvement is sustainable, its stock price goes up, in essence capitalizing the future value of this incremental improvement. But this then accelerates the treadmill, so as performance improves, the treadmill quickens, and the company has to run ever faster just to keep up and maintain its new stock price. Conversely, a company with low expectations at the beginning of a period may have an easier time outperforming in the stock market simply because the low expectations are easier to beat.

The expectations treadmill describes the difficulty of continuing to outperform the stock market. At some point it becomes impossible for management to deliver on accelerating expectations without faltering, just as anyone will eventually stumble on a treadmill that moves ever faster.

Consider the case of Tina Turnaround, a fictional character based on the experience of many CEOs we know. Tina has just been hired as the CEO of Widgets R Us, a company with below-average returns on capital and growth relative to competitors. Because of this, the market doesn't expect much, so the value of Widgets R Us is low relative to competitors.

Tina hires a top-notch team and gets to work. After two years, Widgets is catching up to its peers in margins and ROIC, and its market share is rising. Widgets' stock price rises twice as fast as its peers' because the market wasn't expecting the company's turnaround.

Tina and her team continue their hard work. After two more years, Widgets has become the industry leader in operating performance, with the highest ROIC. Because of its low starting point, the company's share price has risen at four times the rate of the industry. Given Widgets' new trajectory and consistent performance, the market expects continued above-average returns and revenue growth.

As time goes by, Widgets maintains its high ROIC and leading market share. But two years later, Tina is frustrated that her company's shares are now doing no better than her peers' shares, even though Widgets has outperformed rivals.

Tina's been caught by the expectations treadmill: she and her team have done such a good job that the expectation of continued high performance is already incorporated into the company's share price. As long as she delivers results in line with the market's expectations, her company's share-price performance will be no better or worse than average.*

---

* Theoretically, if a company's performance exactly matches expectations, its total return to shareholders will equal the cost of equity. In practice, however, with continual changes in interest rates, inflation, and economic activity, comparison to the broader market is sometimes preferable.

This explains why extraordinary managers may deliver only ordinary total return to shareholders (TRS),* or why managers of companies with low performance expectations might find it easy to earn a high TRS, at least for a short time. Even for the extraordinary manager, it can be extremely difficult to keep beating the high share-price expectations. For the company with low expectations, managers can create a higher TRS by raising expectations up to the level of its peers.

The danger for companies with already high expectations is that, in their quest to achieve above-peer TRS, they may resort to misguided actions, like pushing for unrealistic earnings growth or pursuing risky, major acquisitions. This was seen in the late 1990s and early 2000s when the U.S. electric power industry boomed. During this time, deregulation led to high hopes for power generation companies, which spun out energy producers from their regulated parents at extremely high valuations.

Mirant, for instance, was spun out from Southern Co. in October 2000 with a combined equity and debt capitalization of almost $18 billion, a multiple of about 30 times EBITA (for a power generation company!). To justify its value, Mirant expanded aggressively, as did other similar companies, investing in power plants in the Bahamas, Brazil, Chile, the UK, Germany, China, and the Philippines, as well as 14 different states in the United States. The debt burden from these investments quickly became too much to handle, and Mirant filed for bankruptcy in July 2003.

The expectations treadmill is the dynamic behind the adage that a good company and a good investment may not be the same. In the short term, good companies may not be good investments because future great performance might already be built into the share price. On the other hand, smart investors often prefer weaker-performing companies because they have more upside potential, as the expectations are easier to beat.

SHAREHOLDER RETURNS AND UNDERLYING VALUE

The differing fortunes of Wal-Mart and Target, two of the largest retailers in the world with $403 billion and $65 billion in respective 2008 sales, illustrate the expectations treadmill and its complications. From 1995 through 2005, Wal-Mart outperformed Target on the key value

---

* Total return to shareholders is stock price appreciation plus dividends.

drivers, growth, and ROIC, but Target's shareholders earned higher returns. The expectations treadmill effect explains this contradiction.

Exhibit 4.1 shows the revenue growth and returns on capital for Wal-Mart and Target, as well as TRS (stock price appreciation plus dividends). Wal-Mart's sales grew 13 percent per year compared with Target's 9 percent, and Wal-Mart also earned a higher ROIC throughout the period. Yet Wal-Mart investors earned an annualized return to shareholders of only 15 percent per year compared with Target's much higher return of 24 percent per year.

The expectations treadmill explains the contradiction between TRS and the underlying value created by the two companies. Using P/E ratios as a proxy for market expectations, Wal-Mart's ratio at the beginning of 1995 was 15 times, compared with only 11 for Target. By the beginning of 2006, Wal-Mart's P/E ratio had increased slightly to 16 times, whereas Target's caught up with and surpassed Wal-Mart's reaching 18 times (Exhibit 4.2).

Target's low P/E ratio in 1995 reflected serious concerns about its Mervyn's brand, which was struggling to perform. Target eventually sold its Mervyn's and Marshall Field's brands, after which it then beat expectations, thereby raising expectations for future performance. Meanwhile, Wal-Mart delivered roughly in line with some very high expectations.

Which one did a better job? You can make arguments both ways: Target did a great job of turning its business around, and Wal-Mart did a great job delivering against very high expectations.

Exhibit 4.3 quantifies the components of TRS, an aggregate measure that can mask big differences in how TRS results are achieved. Two of the components in the exhibit are related to expectations: *zero-growth return* (TRS assuming no future growth) and *change in P/E* (change in investor expectations). Together, these components account for seven percent of the total nine percent difference in TRS between the two companies.

In 1995, Target's P/E was only 11 while Wal-Mart's was 15. This converts to a lower TRS for Wal-Mart, even if neither company grew at all and their multiples remained the same. Because investors paid less for a dollar of Target's earnings in 1995, Target's existing (no-growth) earnings generated a higher yield than Wal-Mart's existing earnings. When Target's P/E increased from 11 to 18 times, this alone generated a 5 percent annual TRS, while Wal-Mart's P/E increased only slightly, generating less than a 1 percent TRS (rounded to zero).

EXHIBIT 4.1 **Wal-Mart vs. Target: Wal-Mart Ahead on Growth, ROIC, Not TRS**

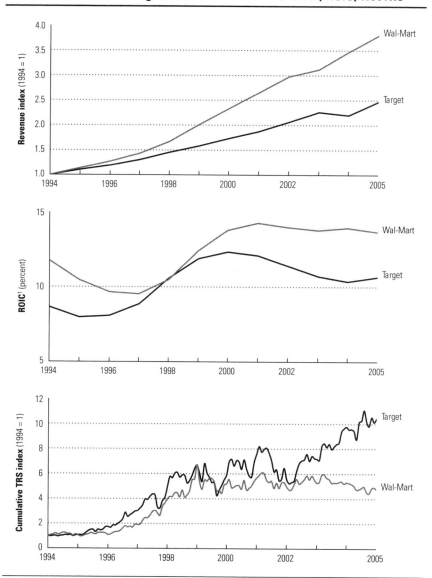

[1] 3-year rolling ROIC without goodwill, adjusted for leases.

Source: McKinsey Corporate Performance Center analysis.

EXHIBIT 4.2 **Wal-Mart vs. Target: P/E Increase Helps Target's TRS**

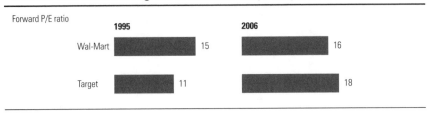

Source: McKinsey Corporate Performance Center analysis.

We also see that 3 percent of Target's higher TRS was due to higher financial leverage. Target used much more debt than Wal-Mart in 1995, with a debt-to-capital ratio of 48 percent, compared with 21 percent for Wal-Mart. But Target's higher leverage in 1995 was probably not sustainable and, in fact, Target eventually reduced its debt.

Leverage has a multiplier effect on TRS relative to underlying economic performance. In other words, a 1 percent increase in revenues and profits has a greater impact on Target's share price than the same increase on Wal-Mart's share price. As we discuss in Chapter 15, greater leverage doesn't necessarily create value, because the amplification works both ways: greater leverage equals greater risk, and greater risk can amplify both stronger and weaker performance.

From an operating perspective, the two companies were about even. Wal-Mart's growth rate of 13 percent was higher than Target's rate of 9 percent, while Target's increasing margin was higher than

EXHIBIT 4.3 **Wal-Mart vs. Target: TRS Decomposition**

1995–2005, percent annualized

	Target	Wal-Mart	Difference
Revenue growth	9	13	(4)
Investment for growth	(5)	(3)	(2)
Change in margin	4	–	4
TRS from performance	8	10	(2)
Zero-growth return	6	4	2
Change in P/E	5	–	5
Impact of financial leverage	5	2	3
Other	–	(1)	1
Sum	24	15	9

Wal-Mart's relatively constant margin. Better performance in the one domain by the one company was offset by better performance in the other domain by the other company.

The decomposition of shareholder returns can also show what a company must do to achieve various levels of future TRS. For example, at the time of this writing, both Wal-Mart and Target had similar expectations built into their share prices (based on similar multiples), and those expectations were near the long-term averages for companies sharing their performance characteristics.

Therefore, Target could no longer expect to earn a higher TRS than Wal-Mart simply by improving its earnings multiple. Nor could it benefit from reducing its debt level since it was already on par with Wal-Mart's debt level. The TRS differentiator for the two companies over the next several years would have to be underlying growth and returns on capital.

UNDERSTANDING EXPECTATIONS

In addition to understanding TRS, companies also gain insight by examining the performance they need to justify their current share price. What are your performance plans and are they aligned with the market's expectations? What performance is required to justify or beat the expectations built into your current share price?

You can estimate the required performance by reverse engineering your share price in terms of expected revenue growth and ROIC. Take Home Depot, which, at the beginning of 1999, had a market value of $132 billion, with an earnings multiple of 47. Using a discount cash flow model, assuming constant margins and ROIC, Home Depot would have had to grow revenues 26 percent per year over the next 15 years to maintain its 1999 share price.

Home Depot's actual revenue growth through 2007 was 11 percent, an impressive number for such a large company, but far below the growth required to justify its share price in 1999. It's no surprise that Home Depot's shares underperformed the S&P 500 by 7 percent per year over the period.

What should Home Depot's board of directors have done given its high market value in 1999? Celebrate is definitely not the answer. Some companies would try to justify their high share price by considering all sorts of risky strategies. But given Home Depot's size, the chances of finding enough high-ROIC growth opportunities to justify its 1999 share price were virtually nil.

There wasn't much Home Depot could have realistically done except prepare for an inevitable sharp share-price decline (Home Depot's market value dropped from $132 billion in January 1999 to $80 billion in January 2004). Yes, some companies can take advantage of their high share prices to make acquisitions, but that probably wasn't a good idea for Home Depot because its organic growth was 11 percent—a large management challenge to maintain in and of itself.

In our experience, at least 80 percent of the companies we evaluate have performance expectations built into their share prices that are in line with industry growth expectations and returns on capital. Future TRS for these companies will approximate the cost of equity capital, adjusted for the effects of any macro changes like interest rates or aggregate economic growth. But if you're not in that 80 percent, brace yourself for a significantly faster or slower ride on the treadmill.

MANAGERIAL IMPLICATIONS

The expectations treadmill makes it unwise to use TRS as a performance-measurement tool. As we saw in the Wal-Mart/Target case, the sizeable differences in TRS for the two companies from 1994 to 2005 masked the big difference in expectations at the beginning of the measurement period. In Home Depot's case, living up to the expectations was virtually impossible, because no company can run that fast for very long.*

The expectations treadmill means that many executive compensation systems tied to TRS don't reward managers for their performance as managers, because the majority of a company's short-term TRS is driven by movements in its industry and the broader market. Many executives became wealthy from stock options in the 1980s and 1990s when share prices increased primarily because of falling interest rates rather than anything managers did. Conversely, many stock-option

---

* As we see in Chapter 8, Stock Market Bubbles and Financial Crises, most significant overvaluations are industry-wide rather than specific companies, so there isn't much executives can do to manage the situation. They and their boards should, however, be aware of the consequences.

gains were wiped out during the recent financial crisis. These gains and losses were largely disconnected from anything managers did or didn't do.

In addition to focusing on growth and return on capital, compensation systems should be linked to TRS performance relative to peers rather than absolute TRS. That would eliminate much of the TRS that is not driven by company-specific performance.

So why hasn't this simple structure been adopted by companies? It goes back to the influence of accounting rules. Until 2004, stock options weren't reported as an expense on the income statement as long as they met certain criteria, one of which was that the exercise price had to be fixed. Any approach based on relative performance would show up in a company's income statement, so naturally companies adopted fixed-price options that led to higher accounting income.

A few companies have moved to share-based compensation systems that are tied to relative performance. GE for one granted its CEO a performance award based on the company's TRS relative to the TRS of the S&P 500 index. More companies should follow this direction.

In addition to fixing compensation systems, executives need to become much more sophisticated in their interpretation of TRS, especially short-term TRS. If executives and boards understand what expectations are built into their share price, and their peers' share prices, then they can anticipate how their share price might perform as their actions become known to the market.

For example, if you're executing a great strategy that will create significant value, but the market already expects you to succeed, you can't expect to outperform on TRS. The management team and board need to know this so the board can support management's priorities, even if its share price isn't outperforming.

Executives also need to move away from the practice of incessantly monitoring their stock prices, because TRS is largely meaningless over short periods. In a typical three-month time frame, more than 40 percent of companies experience a share-price increase or decrease by more than 10 percent*—movements that are nothing more than random. Therefore, executives shouldn't even try to understand share-price changes unless they move more than

---

* Share-price movement relative to the S&P 500 index for a sample of nonfinancial companies with greater than $1 billion market capitalization, measured during 2004–2007.

2 percent in a single day or 10 percent in a quarter (versus a relevant benchmark).

Finally, be careful what you wish for. We all like to see our company's share price increase, but once your share price rises, it's hard to keep it rising faster than the market. The expectations treadmill is virtually impossible to escape, and we don't know any easy way to manage expectations down.

5

The Best Owner

The fourth and final cornerstone states that the value of a business depends on who owns or manages it, because different owners will generate different cash flows from the same business.* We call this cornerstone *the best owner* because value is maximized when it's owned by whomever can generate the highest cash flows from it. A corollary is that there is no such thing as an inherent value for a business; it always depends on who's operating it.

Acquisitions are a good example of the best-owner principle. Shortly after buying Pillsbury from Diageo in 2001 for $10.4 billion, General Mills increased Pillsbury's pretax cash flows by at least $400 million per year, roughly increasing Pillsbury's operating profits by 70 percent.

Diageo's core business is alcoholic beverages, while Pillsbury and General Mills sell packaged foods. Under Diageo, Pillsbury's operations were run entirely apart from Diageo's core business because there were few overlaps in manufacturing, distribution, and marketing. On the other hand, General Mills was able to substantially reduce costs in purchasing, manufacturing, and distribution—and it boosted revenues after introducing Pillsbury's products to schools in the United States where General Mills already had a strong presence. Also, General Mills used Pillsbury's refrigerated trucks to distribute its newly branded, refrigerated meals.

---

* By *owner*, we mean the organization that governs and operates the business, not the shareholders per se.

General Mills was a better owner of Pillsbury than Diageo. In truth, we never know who the very best owner is; we only know who the better owner is among competing alternatives. It could be that some company other than General Mills could generate even higher cash flows as the owner of Pillsbury.

The $10.4 billion that General Mills paid for Pillsbury was not its value—it was the *price*. Pillsbury had at least two values: its value to General Mills and its value to Diageo. For General Mills to consider the deal attractive, the value of Pillsbury (to General Mills) had to be greater than the price paid; for Diageo to consider the deal attractive, the price it received had to be greater than the value of Pillsbury as Diageo was operating it.

The General Mills/Pillsbury example shows just how large the impact of the best owner can be (70 percent in this case). Best ownership also helps the economy by redirecting resources to their highest-value use.

WHO'S THE BEST OWNER?

So how do we identify the best owner of a business at any time under any industry circumstances? We have to examine the sources of how value is added by the potential new owners.

Some owners add value through linkages with other activities in their portfolio, such as using established sales channels to reach new customers, or sharing an existing production infrastructure. Some owners add value by replicating such distinctive skills as operational or marketing excellence. Some add value by providing better governance and incentives for the management team. Finally, some add value through distinctive relationships they hold with governments, regulators, or customers.

Of course, in some cases, the best owner has multiple sources for adding value, but let's examine each of these categories one at a time.

Unique Links with Other Businesses

The most straightforward way that owners add value is through links to other businesses within the portfolio, especially when such links are unique to the parent company.

Suppose, for instance, that a mining company has the rights to develop a coal field in a remote location far from any rail lines or other infrastructure. Another mining company already operates a coal mine just 10 miles away and has built the necessary rail line and other infrastructure. The second mining company would be a better owner of the new mine because its incremental costs to develop the mine are much lower than anyone else's. It can afford to purchase the undeveloped mine at a higher price than anyone else and still earn an attractive return on capital.

These unique links can occur across the value chain, from R&D to manufacturing to distribution to sales. For instance, a large pharmaceutical company with a sales force dedicated to oncology might be the best owner of a small pharmaceuticals company with a promising new oncology drug but no sales force.

In many cases, the link isn't entirely unique to a single company but might apply to several companies. IBM for one has successfully acquired a large number of small software companies to exploit its global sales force. IBM was a better owner than the standalone owners of the acquired companies, because IBM could quickly sell the products globally.

Distinctive Skills

Better owners may have distinctive and replicable functional or managerial skills in any number of areas across the business system, but to make a difference the skill has to be a key success driver in the industry. For example, a company with great manufacturing skills probably wouldn't be a better owner of a consumer-packaged-goods business, because manufacturing costs are rarely large enough to affect a company's competitive position.

In consumer packaged goods, distinctive skills at developing and marketing brands could make a company a better owner. Take Procter & Gamble (P&G), which as of 2009, had 23 billion-dollar (net sales) brands and 20 half-billion-dollar brands spread across a range of product categories, including laundry, beauty products, pet food, and diapers. Almost all of P&G's billion-dollar brands rank first or second in their respective markets.

What's special about P&G is that it developed these brands in different ways. Some have been P&G brands for decades, such as Tide and Crest. Others were acquired in the last 10 years, including Gillette and Oral-B. Finally, Febreze and Swiffer were developed from scratch in the past 10 years. As a group, these brands grew sales at an average of 11 percent per year for the decade (2001–2009).

Better Insight/Foresight

Owners who have insight into how a market and industry will evolve, and can then capitalize on that insight, can sometimes expand existing businesses or develop new ones as innovators. One example is Intuit, which noticed in the late 1990s that many small businesses were using its Quicken software, originally designed to help individual consumers manage their personal finances.

The observation led to an important insight: most business-accounting software was too complex for the small business owner. So Intuit designed a new product for small business accounting, and within two years it had claimed 80 percent of this burgeoning market.

While many companies in the mid-1980s saw that fiber-optic networks would be the future of communications, Williams Companies, an oil and natural gas company, had an additional insight: fiber-optic cable could be installed into its decommissioned oil and gas pipelines at a fraction of the cost that most of its competitors would have to pay. Combining its own network with those acquired from others, Williams eventually controlled 11,000 miles of cable, transmitting digital signals from one end of the United States to the other.

Williams's insight combined with its pipeline infrastructure made it a good or best owner of this network in the emerging digital communications industry. Williams also reduced its stake in fiber-optic cable at the right time when prices were inflated, selling most of its telecommunications businesses in 1994 for $25 billion.

Better Governance

Better owners can also add value through better governance of a company without necessarily having its hands on the day-to-day operations of the business. Better governance refers to the way the company's owners (or their representatives) interact with the management team to drive maximum long-term value creation. For example, the best private equity firms don't just recapitalize companies with debt; they improve the performance of the company through improved governance.

Two of our colleagues analyzed 60 successful investments by 11 leading private equity firms. They found that in almost two-thirds of the transactions, the primary source of value creation was improving the operating performance of the company relative to peers.* The use of financial leverage or good timing of investments was not, contrary to some claims, the major source of their success.

Private equity firms don't have the time or skills to run their portfolio companies on a day-to-day basis, but they do govern these companies very differently than many listed companies, and this is a big source of outperformance. Typically, firms introduce a stronger performance culture and make quick management changes when necessary. They encourage managers to abandon sacred cows and give them leeway to focus on a five-year horizon rather than the typical one year for a listed company.

Also, the boards of private equity companies spend three times as many days in their roles than those at public companies, and most of their time is spent on strategy and performance management rather than compliance and risk avoidance as at public companies.[†]

Distinctive Access to Talent, Capital, Government, Suppliers, and Customers

This category applies more often to companies in emerging markets where running a business is complicated by an inherently truncated pool of managerial talent, undeveloped capital markets, and high levels of government involvement in business as customers, suppliers, and regulators. In these markets, diversified conglomerates such as Tata and Reliance in India, and Samsung in Korea, can be better owners of many businesses because they're more attractive employers, have more capital, and know how to work with the government.

Missing from our categories are some often cited but, in our experience, weak sources of best ownership—such as size, scale, and diversification. We discuss why these don't confer best-owner status in Chapter 12.

BEST-OWNER LIFE CYCLE

The best owner of a business isn't static but changes over time. The best owner could be a larger company, a private equity firm, a sovereign

---

* Conor Kehoe and Joachim Heel, "Why Some Private Equity Firms Do Better," *The McKinsey Quarterly*, no. 1 (2005): 24–26.
† Viral Acharya, Conor Kehoe, and Michael Reyner, "The Voice of Experience: Public versus Private Equity," *McKinsey on Finance* (Spring 2009): 16–21.

wealth fund, a family, or the business's customers or employees. Or the best-ownership situation could be one in which a business becomes an independent public company listed on a stock exchange.

Furthermore, ownerships are continually evolving in different regions. In the United States, most large companies are either listed or owned by private equity funds. In Europe, government ownership also plays an important role. In Asia and South America, large companies are often controlled by the founding families, and there are ownership links between businesses.

Here's an example of how a company's best owner might evolve. Naturally, a business's founders are typically its first best owner. The founders' entrepreneurial drive, passion, and tangible commitment to the business is necessary to get the company off the ground.

Then, as the company grows, it often needs more capital, so it sells a stake to a venture capital (VC) fund that specializes in helping new companies grow. At this point it's not unusual for the fund to bring in new managers to supplant or supplement the founders; these new managers are better suited to handle the complexities and risks of a larger organization.

To provide even more capital, the VC firm may take the company public, selling shares to a range of investors, and in the process enable itself, the founders, and the managers to realize the value of the company they've created. As a public company, control shifts to an independent board of directors (though the founders may still have great influence if they still own substantial stakes).

As the industry evolves, the company might find that it can't compete with larger companies because, for instance, it needs global distribution capability far beyond what it can build in reasonable time. So it may sell itself to a larger company that has such capability, thereby becoming a product line within a division of the larger company. Now the original company has become merged into the manufacturing, sales, distribution, and administrative functions of the larger company's division. (Other external factors, such as regulatory or technological changes, can also drive the need to change owners.)

As the division's market matures, the larger company decides to focus on other faster growing businesses, so it sells its division to a private equity firm. Now that the division stands alone, the private equity firm attacks excess corporate overhead that is inconsistent with its slower growth. So the private equity firm restructures the division with a leaner cost structure. Once the restructuring is done, the private equity firm sells the division to another large company that specializes in running slow-growth brands.

At each stage of the company's life, the next best owner took actions to increase its cash flows, thereby adding value. The founder came up with the idea for the business. The VC firm provided capital and professional management. Going public provided the early investors a way to realize the value of their work and raised more cash. The large company accelerated the company's growth with a global distribution capability. The private equity firm restructured the company when growth slowed. The last best-owner company applied its skills in managing low-growth brands.

MANAGERIAL IMPLICATIONS

The best-owner life cycle means that executives need to continually look for acquisitions of which they could be the best owner; they also need to continually examine opportunities for divesting businesses of which they might no longer be the best owner. Unfortunately, in our experience too few executives are able to articulate how they are the best owner, and too few make portfolio decisions on this basis.

Because the best owner for a given business is fluid, a company needs to have a structured corporate strategy process that regularly reviews and renews an active list of acquisition targets, and also regularly tests its existing businesses to see if they've reached their sell-by date.

For acquirers, applying the best-owner cornerstone often leads to very different targets than traditional screening approaches might produce. Specifically, traditional approaches often focus on finding potential targets that perform well financially and are somehow related to the parent's business lines. But through the best-owner lens, such characteristics might be irrelevant or of low importance.

It might be better to seek a financially-weak company that has great potential, especially if you have proven performance improvement expertise. It might also be better to focus attention on tangible opportunities for cost reduction, or on the existence of common customers, rather than on such vague notions as how the target may be related to your company.

Keeping the best-owner principle front and center can also help with acquisition negotiations, because this keeps managers focused on what the target is specifically worth to their company, as well as to any other bidders, and to the seller. Many managers err in M&As by estimating only the value to their own company. Because they're unaware of the value to potential better owners or how high those other owners might be willing to bid, they get lulled into negotiations right up to the break-even point. But, of course, the closer they get to that point, the less value the deal would create for their own shareholders.

Instead of asking how much they can pay, bidders should be asking what's the least they need to pay to win the deal and create the most value.

Consider the example of an Asian company that was bidding against a private equity firm to purchase a European contract pharmaceuticals manufacturer. The Asian company estimated the value of the target to itself and also to the private equity firm, which could add value by reducing overhead costs and attracting customers who wouldn't use the target because it was owned by their competitor. They estimated the contract company was worth $96 million to the private equity firm.

But the Asian company could also make the same overhead cost reductions and customer additions, and on top of this it could move some of the manufacturing to its lower-cost plants. Therefore, the value to the Asian company was $120 million, making it the best owner and enabling it to pay a higher price than the private equity firm while still capturing a significant amount of value. As a side note, the value to the European parent of the target was only $80 million.

Knowing the relative values, the Asian company could afford to bid, say, $100 million, pushing out the private equity firm and capturing $20 million in potential value creation for itself.

The Asian company could even push its share further in this case by announcing that it's entering the business even without making the acquisition. If the seller and the private equity firm were convinced of this competitive threat, they would have to reduce their estimates of the target's value, and the Asian company could reduce its bid, capturing more of the value.

We mentioned that the best-owner idea also encourages divestitures, including both sales and spin-offs. If we go back more than 50 years we find that many pharmaceutical and chemical companies were combined because they required similar manufacturing processes and skills. But as the two industries matured, their research, manufacturing, and other skills considerably diverged such that they became distant cousins rather than sisters.

Today the key to running a commodity chemicals company is scale, operating efficiency, and managing costs and capital expenditures— while the key to running a pharmaceutical company is managing an R&D pipeline, a sophisticated sales force, the regulatory approval process, and government relations in state-run health systems that buy prescription drugs. Although it may have made sense to share a common owner once, it no longer does, which is why nearly all formerly combined chemical/pharmaceutical companies have split up. Most recently, Zeneca was split from Imperial Chemical Industries in 1993 (and later merged into AstraZeneca), and Aventis was split from Hoechst in 1999 (and later merged into Sanofi Aventis).

Executives are often concerned that divestitures are an admission of failure and they'll make a company smaller. Yet the research shows that the stock market consistently reacts positively to divestitures, both sales and spin-offs.* Research has also shown that spun-off businesses tend to increase their profit margins by one-third during the three years after the transactions are complete.†

Simply stated, if a board and management team is to maximize the value of the businesses in their portfolio, they must be clear about how their corporation adds value to each (and to businesses outside its portfolio that could be added to the portfolio). As companies reexamine their portfolio of businesses, they must, at a minimum, specifically understand their sources of best ownership. They should also consider whether others could be better owners. And since the sources of best ownership are not static, they should examine what conscious decisions they might make on a continuous basis to evolve their own source(s) of best ownership.

---

* J. Mulherin and A. Boone, "Comparing Acquisitions and Divestitures," *Journal of Corporate Finance* 6 (2000): 117–139.
† P. Cusatis, J. Miles, and J. Woolridge, "Some New Evidence That Spinoffs Create Value," *Journal of Applied Corporate Finance* 7 (1994): 100–107.

Part Two

The Stock Market

6

Who Is the
Stock Market?

A prerequisite for managing a listed company is understanding how the stock market works. By understanding the market better, executives can have more confidence that their decisions will both create value and be reflected in the price of their shares.* When executives don't understand how the stock market works, and how it values companies, they can make such poor strategic decisions as passing up value-creating acquisitions or making value compromising acquisitions.

In this chapter we examine how the market works, in particular the interaction of investors who have different strategies and different beliefs about the future. The market isn't a monolith, and the interaction of investors creates volatility that isn't necessarily driven by new information. We also show that stock price levels are largely influenced by the most sophisticated investors.

A MODEL OF THE MARKET

Executives and journalists often talk about the market as if it were a monolithic entity with a single point of view, but if that were the case it wouldn't be a market. What makes a market is different investor strategies and points of view that interact to set prices and also drive

* Most of our analysis is based on listed companies from developed economies where the stock markets are liquid and open to investors from outside the country.

volatility. So understanding investors and their strategies is the best way to understand the market.

We begin with a simple illustration of how different strategies by different investors can drive market behavior. Assume that the stock market has two types of investors (A and B) trading one company's stock. The A investors research the performance of the company and develop a point of view about the value of its shares. Some A investors believe the shares are worth $40, others $50, and others $60.

B investors, on the other hand, haven't done any research about the company and are more concerned about short-term movements. Their strategy is to follow trends. When shares are going up, they buy, assuming they will continue to increase. When shares go down, they sell. B investors make money by speed: once the share price turns direction, they reverse their position quickly so their losses are small relative to their gains.

Let's assume that the company's share price is $30 when trading starts. The A investors start purchasing shares because they believe the shares should be worth $40 to $60, and their purchases begin to drive up the share price. The B investors notice the rising share price and begin to purchase shares as well, further accelerating the share-price increase.

More and more B investors jump on the bandwagon creating upward momentum. As the share price increases, the A investors gradually slow their purchases. At $40, some A investors stop buying, but the B investors continue to buy. Once the share price nears $60, some of the A investors believe the shares are overvalued and begin to sell. Once the share price passes $60, all A investors stop buying and many are selling. This slows the momentum, which some of the B investors sense, so they begin to sell.

Eventually the selling pressure is greater than the buying pressure, and the stock price begins to fall. The momentum investors accelerate the fall until the price reaches a low enough level that the A investors begin to buy shares again, thus reversing the fall.

The pattern continues, with the share price oscillating within a band set by the A investors, as shown by the left side of Exhibit 6.1. There is a natural volatility to the market even without new information.

Let's now suppose that the company announces a new product that no investors anticipated. The A investors revise their estimates of the company's value to the range of $60 to $80. They begin buying, causing the share price to begin a new oscillating cycle, but around a higher level, as shown by the right side of Exhibit 6.1.

EXHIBIT 6.1 **Model of the Stock Market**

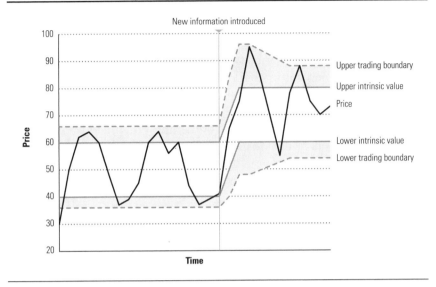

This model demonstrates two important aspects of the market. First, the share price moves up and down, even when there is no new information about the company. Second, the A investors ultimately drive the level of the share price.

CONVENTIONAL WISDOM

Although there were only two types of investors in the model we described earlier, the real market is of course more complex, with many different types of investors and investment strategies. Retail investors hold about 40 percent of the total market in the United States, but they rarely matter when it comes to influencing a company's share price because they don't trade very much. Professional investors—whether they manage hedge funds, mutual funds, or pension funds—are the real drivers of share prices, accounting for virtually all large trades (over 10,000 shares).

Common approaches to understanding institutional investors, such as classifying them as growth or value investors, aren't helpful in figuring out which ones really matter. While the growth and value concepts are deeply embedded in the language of investing, the terms are misleading.

From the name *growth*, you might logically conclude that growth stocks grow revenues faster than value stocks. We examined the companies in the S&P 500 that were included in the growth or value subindexes.* We found that the median revenue growth rate for the growth companies was only slightly higher than for the value companies, and 46 percent of the value companies grew faster than the median growth company. Statistically, there was no difference in the distribution of growth rates.

In fact, the primary factor distinguishing growth companies from value companies is return on capital. For the value companies, the median ROIC was 15 percent, versus 35 percent for the growth companies. So the companies classified as growth didn't grow faster, but they did have higher returns on capital.

How did these misleading labels arise? If you go back to the core-of-value principle, you'll remember that for any given level of growth, higher return on capital leads to a higher value (also true when expressed as a price-earnings ratio or a market-book value ratio). For simplicity, academics traditionally assumed that returns on capital were the same across time and companies and, therefore, differences in multiples reflected different growth expectations. But we know this isn't true.

The fallacy is perpetuated in the investing world by the way growth and value stock indexes are constructed. Most growth/value indexes, like that of Standard & Poors, use market-book ratios to divide between value and growth companies. High market-book is considered a growth company, and low market-book is a value company, even though growth is only one factor driving market-book ratios.

So we really just have a naming problem, and perhaps it would have been better to call growth stocks high market-book stocks and value stocks low market-book stocks. But the names do have real consequences. At the least, it's misleading for retail investors choosing among mutual funds. It also has a pernicious effect on decision making, encouraging executives to focus more on growth than ROIC.

The growth/value classification also influences executives to believe that if they can just convince growth investors to buy their stock, the share price will go up—but they would be disappointed by our findings. Our analysis of companies whose stocks have recently

---

* Bin Jiang and Timothy Koller, "The Truth About Growth and Value Stocks," *McKinsey on Finance* (Winter 2007): 12–15.

been moved from the value to the growth index (because of an increase in share price) clearly shows that growth investors don't precipitate the change in share price. Rather, they respond to it, moving into a stock only after the share price has already moved to a higher market-book ratio.

The same result happens when a company moves from the growth index to the value index. Growth investors sell their shares after the decline in share price, not before.

BETTER WAY TO UNDERSTAND INVESTORS

A more useful way to categorize and understand investors is to categorize them by their investment strategies. Do they develop a view on the value of a company, or do they look for short-term price movements? Do they conduct extensive research and make a few big bets, or do they make a lot of small bets (with less information)? Do they build their portfolios from the bottom up, or do they mirror an index?

Using this approach we classify institutional investors into four types: intrinsic investors, traders, mechanical investors, and closet indexers.* These groups differ in their investment objectives and how they build their portfolios. As a result, their portfolios vary along a number of important dimensions, including turnover rate, number of shares held, and the number of positions held per investment professional (Exhibit 6.2).[†]

Intrinsic Investors

Intrinsic investors take positions in companies only after rigorous due diligence (typically taking longer than a month) of their inherent ability to create long-term value. Their due diligence covers not only the financial performance of the company and its strategic position, but also the strength of the management team as leaders and strategists.

---

* Some companies have one or two strategic investors. Because these investors rarely trade their shares, we've excluded them from this analysis.
[†] The investor segmentation and statistics are from Robert N. Palter, Werner Rehm, and Jonathan Shih, "Communicating with the Right Investors," *McKinsey on Finance* (Spring 2008): 1–5. A similar classification comes from Brian Bushee, "Identifying and Attracting the 'Right' Investors: Evidence on the Behavior of Institutional Investors," *Journal of Applied Corporate Finance* 16, no. 4 (Fall 2004): 28–35.

EXHIBIT 6.2 **Investors Segmented by Investment Strategies**

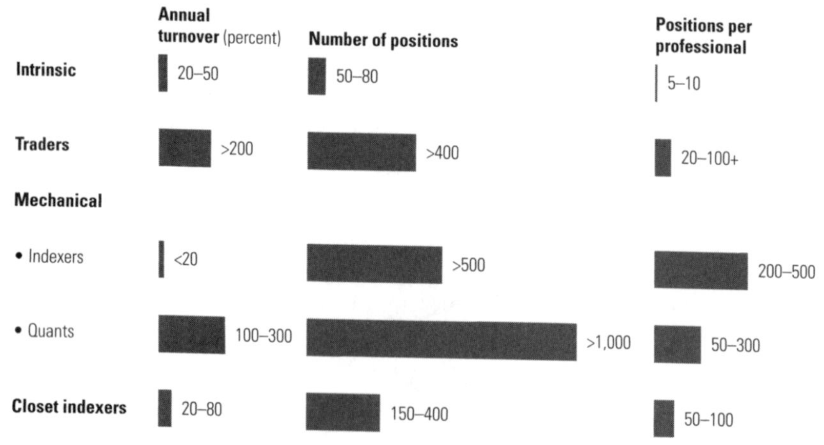

	Annual turnover (percent)	Number of positions	Positions per professional
Intrinsic	20–50	50–80	5–10
Traders	>200	>400	20–100+
Mechanical			
• Indexers	<20	>500	200–500
• Quants	100–300	>1,000	50–300
Closet indexers	20–80	150–400	50–100

Source: McKinsey Corporate Performance Center analysis.

We estimate that these investors hold 20 percent of U.S. assets and contribute 10 percent of the trading volume in the U.S. market.

Portfolio turnover is low for intrinsic investors, who typically accept that any price-to-value discrepancies could persist for up to three or four years before equalizing. Intrinsic investors are willing to wait, knowing that the probability of reward over time is greatly in their favor as a critical mass of investors eventually recognize the undervaluation and demand the stock.

The depth of intrinsic investors' research can be seen because they typically hold fewer than 75 stocks at any time and they have few positions per professional. They often view short-term price declines, not based on fundamental changes in a company's long-term outlook, but as buying opportunities.

Mutual funds that are intrinsic investors include Legg Mason Value Fund, which holds less than 50 stocks in its portfolio at any time and has a turnover rate of less than 10 percent. From the hedge fund world, Maverick Capital (managed by Lee Ainslie) is a good example of an intrinsic investor. Mr. Ainslie is proud that Maverick holds only five positions per investment professional, and many of his staff have followed a single industry for 10, 20, or more years.*

---

* Richard Dobbs and Timothy Koller, "Inside a Hedge Fund: An Interview with the Managing Partner of Maverick Capital," *McKinsey on Finance* (Spring 2006): 6–11.

Traders

Traders seek profits by betting on short-term movements in share prices (less then a month and often less than a week), typically based on news announcement about the company, or on technical factors like the momentum of the company's share price. For example, traders may develop a view that a pharmaceutical company is about to announce good news about a drug trial that will boost the company's share price. Traders would buy the shares, wait for the announcement and the share price to go up, then immediately sell their positions. Some traders are in and out of the same stock many times during the year.

Controlling about 35 percent of U.S. equity holdings, traders don't need to develop a point of view about whether a company's shares are over- or undervalued relative to their intrinsic value; they just need to develop a view about whether the shares will go up or down in the very short term. It's not that traders don't understand the companies or industries in which they invest. On the contrary, these investors follow the news about them closely and often approach companies directly, seeking nuances or insights that could matter greatly in the short term. But traders don't focus on strategy, competitive position, and other long-term factors.

The typical investment professional in this segment has 20 or more positions to follow and trades in and out of them quickly to capture small gains over short periods—as short as a few days or even hours. For example, SAC Capital, which manages $16 billion, was reported by *BusinessWeek* to "routinely" account for up to 3 percent of all the daily trading volume on the New York Stock Exchange.* To put that volume in perspective, it's more than all but five of the top brokers trading on behalf of their clients.

Mechanical Investors

Mechanical investors make decisions based on strict criteria or rules. *Indexers*, or index fund managers, are the prototypical mechanical investor; they merely build their portfolio by matching the composition of an index such as the S&P 500. Other mechanical investors are *quants*, who use computer models with no qualitative judgment in building their portfolios.

* Marcia Vickers, "The Most Powerful Trader on Wall Street You've Never Heard Of," *BusinessWeek* online cover story (July 21, 2003).

Closet Indexers

Closet indexers are interesting because they're promoted as active man-agers, but their portfolios look like an index. In addition, they hold a wide range of stocks, so they can't understand a single company too deeply.* In the case of closet index funds, each investment professional handles an average of 100 to 150 positions, making it impossible to do in-depth research that could be influenced by meetings with an investment target's management.

In part, the high number of positions per professional in this group-ing reflects that most closet index funds are part of larger investment houses that separate the roles of fund manager and researcher. A fund manager that largely tracks a given index obviously minimizes the re-search function and resulting requirement for careful, individual stock selection. By contrast, intrinsic investors know every company in their portfolios in depth.

Intrinsic investors and closet indexers build their portfolios in very different ways. Intrinsic investors start from zero. Closet indexers start with the index and make adjustments from there.

For example, Johnson & Johnson's weight in the S&P 500 was 1.4 percent in early 2008. Some of their largest holders, including Put-nam Fund for Growth and T. Rowe Price Value Fund, held almost exactly the same percentage of J&J in their portfolios as the index. By holding J&J's shares in line with the index, they are not taking a point of view on J&J's valuation either positive or negative. So even though these funds are marketed as active managers, they can be considered closet indexers (at least with respect to their holdings of J&J).

INTRINSIC INVESTORS DRIVE VALUATION LEVELS

Our research supports the idea that intrinsic investors are the ultimate drivers of share price for periods longer than the next month or so. Exhibit 6.3 helps make the case. The first two columns show that traders trade more than intrinsic investors. Large traders as a whole bought and sold $11 trillion of shares in 2006, compared with $3 trillion for intrinsic investors. As well, the typical large trader bought and sold

---

* For more on closet index funds, see Martijn Cremers and Antti Petajist, "How Active Is Your Fund Manager? A New Measure That Predicts Performance" (FA Chicago Meetings Paper, January 15, 2007).

EXHIBIT 6.3 **Intrinsic Investors Have Greatest Impact on Share Price**

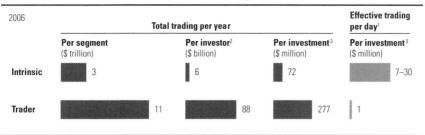

2006	Total trading per year			Effective trading per day[1]
	Per segment ($ trillion)	Per investor[2] ($ billion)	Per investment[3] ($ million)	Per investment[3] ($ million)
Intrinsic	3	6	72	7–30
Trader	11	88	277	1

[1] Trading activity in segment per day that trade is made.
[2] Per investor in segment.
[3] Per investor in segment per investment.

Source: R. Palter, W. Rehm, and J. Shih, "Communicating with the Right Investors," *McKinsey on Finance*, no. 27 (Spring 2008): 1–5.

over $80 billion worth of shares in 2006, much more than the typical intrinsic investor.

Similarly, in the third column, the typical trader also invests much more per investment than the intrinsic investors. But if you look to the last column, you see that when intrinsic investors trade, they buy or sell in much larger quantities. Intrinsic investors also hold larger percentages of the companies they hold.

Indexers, quants, and closet indexers are largely irrelevant from a company's point of view because they follow rather than lead the market. The only investors that matter are traders and intrinsic investors.

Even though traders trade much more in overall transaction volume (albeit much is trading the same investment more than once in shorter time periods), and even though traders control 35 percent versus 20 percent of U.S. equities, intrinsic investors are more important to the manager or executive. Intrinsic investors ultimately drive share price, because when they buy, they buy in much larger quantities. The moves of the best intrinsic investors are also often copied by other investors, so each dollar they invest could be followed by several more dollars from other investors.

Traders can surely make the market move, but their impact is measured in days or weeks, not years. Traders like volatility and they need news, real or manufactured, to make money. Their need for news and events leads them to frequently call companies' investor relations departments and senior executives, looking for little tidbits of information they can exploit before everyone in the market knows.

Traders also focus on near-term events, product announcements, quarterly earnings, and so forth. They may encourage news that affects short-term share prices, like a share repurchase or an extra penny of quarterly EPS. As a result, traders' high visibility to senior executives is way out of proportion with their actual importance in driving share prices.

Meanwhile, intrinsic investors typically go about their business quietly—studying, analyzing, and digging deeply into their portfolio companies. They look at long-term economics; they examine fundamentals; they apply the core-of-value principle to determine what the price of given stocks should be. Perhaps most importantly, intrinsic investors are resources for executives, providing an objective, circumspect view of their companies, industries, and competitors by virtue of their buying and selling decisions.

7

The Stock Market and the Real Economy

So far we've established that at the company level, growth and ROIC are key drivers of market valuation (Chapter 2), and that the investors who matter in driving stock prices are the most sophisticated (Chapter 6). In this chapter, we examine the movements of the aggregate market to show how they can be explained by the performance of the real economy (production, consumption, inflation, interest rates, and profits).

By understanding what's driving the market, executives are better able to interpret their own company's share price performance and how their actions may or may not affect it. Of course investors can also benefit from knowing what underlies stock market performance and the extent to which it is aligned or misaligned with the real economy.

A cursory look at the stock market during the past 50 years would tempt you to conclude that its performance has been too wild to be explained by the performance of the real economy. Here are the annualized inflation-adjusted returns on the S&P 500 by decade compared with GDP growth:

Decade	Real TRS	Real GDP Growth
1960–1970	5%	4%
1970–1980	0%	3%
1980–1990	9%	3%
1990–2000	14%	3%
2000–2009	−5%	2%

While the growth of the economy is very stable across the decades, the stock market returns range from negative 5 percent to positive 14 percent. As you will see later, once we factor in the effect of inflation and interest rates, this performance will make sense.

Ignorance of the linkages between the market and real economy can lead to questionable decisions by executives. For example, in the 1980s and 1990s, many senior executives got very wealthy from the stock options they received from their companies as share prices increased across the board. Between 1983 and 1996, the S&P 500 generated inflation-adjusted returns to shareholders averaging 12 percent per year, nearly twice the long-term average of 7 percent.

Without understanding the source of these returns, many boards of directors and executives believed they could and should continue to generate a similarly high level of returns. Yet the performance of the stock market during this period had little to do with the skill of managers, individually or collectively.

Much of the stock market's stellar performance between 1983 and 1996 was driven by the decline in interest rates and inflation, and the resultant increase in P/E ratios engineered by Federal Reserve Chairman Paul Volcker. Inflation of 14 percent in 1981 led to interest rates on long-term U.S. government bonds of 16 percent, which, in turn, led to P/E ratios of around 8. By 1996, inflation and interest rates were 3 percent and 6.5 percent, respectively, and the median P/E ratio was 16.

By 1996, with low interest rates, P/E ratios couldn't continue to increase, thereby robbing the market of a key source of its returns for the prior 15 years. (Of course, the market went right into the technology bubble until 2000, when P/E ratios went to unsustainable levels. After the technology bubble burst, the P/E ratios returned in 2004 to 1996 levels.) If executives understood what was driving shareholder returns, they would have known returns *had to* revert to normal levels.

Surprisingly little has been written by academics to explain the performance of the stock market in terms of the real economy, and a cursory review of the leading finance textbooks shows no discussion of this topic. The title of a very well-known book, *A Random Walk Down Wall Street*, by Burton Malkiel, neatly summarizes the academic view of markets. The title reflects the interest of most academics in trying to explain stock price patterns merely as a statistical phenomenon, a purely internal system, without regard to any external reference points.

One reason for this cursory approach to understanding the market is that, for most of the past 45 years, the databases most readily available to academics contained only stock price and dividend information.*

SHAREHOLDER RETURNS FOR 100 YEARS

You've probably heard the often quoted statistic that stocks have earned about 10 percent per year over the past 100+ years (dividends and capital appreciation). With volatile inflation, however, that 10 percent number can be misleading. Adjusted for inflation, large U.S. equities have earned returns to shareholders of about 6.5 to 7 percent annually.

That 6.5 to 7 percent long-term real return on common stocks is no random number. It derives from the long-term performance of companies in the aggregate, and the relationship between valuation and performance as described by the core-of-value principle.

Here's how it works. Let's describe the aggregate of all large companies as if they were one company in terms of growth, ROIC, and investment rate. Over the past 75 years, real corporate profits have grown about 3 to 3.5 percent per year. Add about 2 percent for normalized inflation and you get nominal growth of about 5 to 5.5 percent per year. The median ROIC has been about 13 percent. Finally, large corporations typically pay out about 50 percent of their profits to shareholders every year in dividends and share repurchases.

Assuming a 7 percent real cost of capital, and inflation of about 2 percent for a nominal cost of capital of 9 percent, you can derive what the long-term P/E ratio for large companies should be using a formula based on the core-of-value principle. That P/E ratio turns out to be about 15 times. Not coincidentally, that's the average P/E ratio for the past 50 years (excluding the high inflation years and high-tech bubble years).

Over the long-term, P/E ratios keep returning to 15, so we can expect that the value of companies will increase at the same rate as profits (3 to 3.5 percent per year) because the P/E ratio will be constant. In addition, the 50 percent payout of profits to shareholders results in a cash flow (dividends plus share repurchases) yield of 3 to 3.5 percent. Adding the increase in value plus the dividend yields results in a total

* Burton G. Malkiel, *A Random Walk Down Wall Street* (New York: W. W. Norton, 2007).

real return to shareholders of about 6.5 to 7 percent, the historical average.

The consistency of this number, and that it can be explained by fundamental economic forces, has important implications for investors and companies. It tells us that over the longer term, shareholder returns are unlikely to deviate much from this number unless there are radical changes in investor risk preferences or radical changes in the performance of the economy. For example, long-term GDP growth would have to increase or decrease significantly, or the ratio of corporate profits to GDP would need to change (it has been constant for at least 75 years).

STOCK MARKET ERAS 1960–2009

So the market is explainable for 100+ years, but what about shorter horizons? Exhibit 7.1 shows the level of the S&P 500 from the very end of 1959 to the end of 2009. Some researchers would describe the pattern as random, suggesting it could go in any direction over the next time period.

It would be hard to argue that the market's movements over one hour, one day, one week, or one month can be explained by anything

EXHIBIT 7.1 **Inflation-Adjusted S&P 500 Price Index**

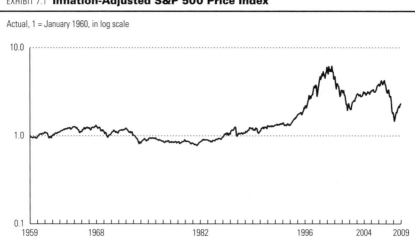

Actual, 1 = January 1960, in log scale

Source: Bloomberg, McKinsey Corporate Performance Center analysis.

other than a random process. There are simply too many moving parts, and, as we saw in Chapter 4, short-term market movements are as much about changes in expectations as they are about actual performance. Short-term prices are also influenced by purely technical factors, such as large investors selling shares to rebalance their portfolios.

So if we can't explain the market over one month, but we can explain it over 100 years, over what time frame can we reasonably expect to explain the market?

One approach is to look at periods of time that correspond to various economic or market events. Common practice is to examine the stock market from peak to trough or vice versa, because that makes for better headlines, even though it may distort our understanding of the underlying economic events. For example, the market in the United States increased consistently from 1983 until 2000, then declined sharply through 2004. However, underlying economic drivers changed in about 1996.

We show that the period 1983 to 1996 represents a long recovery from the high inflation/high interest rates in the late 1970s and the recession induced by the Federal Reserve in 1980–1982 to stop the inflation. Then a new force became dominant in 1997—the technology bubble—so we treat the bubble and its burst from 1997 through 2004 as one era (we examine more about bubbles in the next chapter).

We've identified five eras over the past 50 years that merit distinction with different fundamental forces driving the U.S. economy and stock market:

- The **Carefree 1960s** from 1960 to 1968. During this period, the economy grew at a steady rate, corporate profits grew at a steady rate, and interest rates and inflation were low and stable. It should be no surprise, then, that the real return to shareholders was 9 percent, just above the long-term average.

- The **Great Inflation** from 1969 to 1982. High inflation led investors to reduce P/E ratios from 16 in 1969 to 8 in 1982, leading to negative real returns for investors over this miserable 14-year period.

- The **Return to Normalcy** from 1983 to 1996. P/E ratios and economic growth recovered as inflation was brought under control, leading to real returns of 12 percent for investors.

- The **Technology Bubble** from 1997 to 2004. From beginning to end, real returns and economic growth were near normal levels, with real returns averaging 5 percent. But the real story was the bubble in the middle.

- The **Leveraging and Credit Crisis** from 2005 to 2009. The recklessness of the financial sector wiped out corporate profits, leading to real returns of –5 percent per year (through the end of 2009).

Exhibit 7.2 shows how we smoothed out most of the short-term volatility in the stock market to highlight the underlying movement.

Exhibit 7.3 then compares the stylized movement of the market with similar stylized trends in earnings, P/E ratios, interest, and inflation rates. The top panel compares the inflation-adjusted S&P 500 price index with an index of inflation-adjusted earnings. As you can see, the stock price trend drops below the earnings trend in the early 1980s, then accelerates above the earnings trend in the late 1990s. By the end of 2009, the price index and earnings index are once again aligned.

The divergence between the price trend and earnings trend is illustrated by the P/E ratio, displayed in the second panel of Exhibit 7.3. As you can see, the P/E ratio varies by a large amount. The third panel

EXHIBIT 7.2 **U.S. Equity Market: Five Eras**

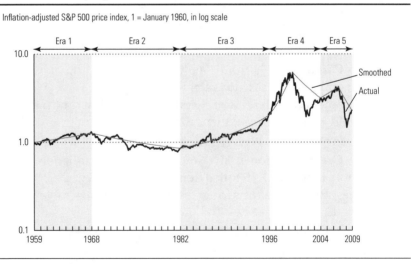

Inflation-adjusted S&P 500 price index, 1 = January 1960, in log scale

Source: Bloomberg, McKinsey Corporate Performance Center analysis.

EXHIBIT 7.3 **Fundamentals Drive Stock Performance over Five Eras**

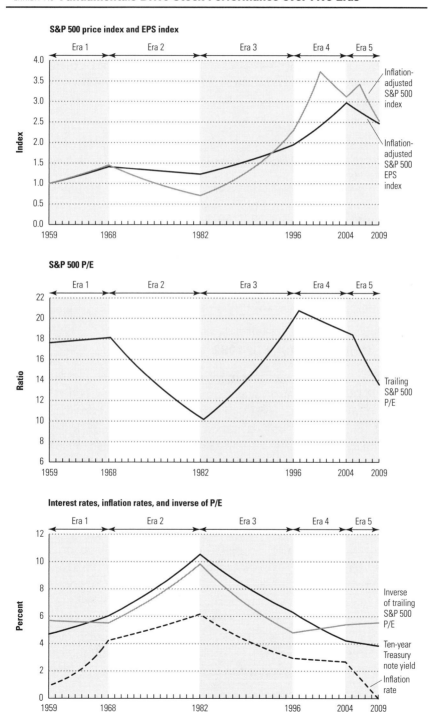

S&P 500 price index and EPS index

Inflation-adjusted S&P 500 index

Inflation-adjusted S&P 500 EPS index

S&P 500 P/E

Trailing S&P 500 P/E

Interest rates, inflation rates, and inverse of P/E

Inverse of trailing S&P 500 P/E

Ten-year Treasury note yield

Inflation rate

Source: Bloomberg, McKinsey Corporate Performance Center analysis, Institutional Brokers' Estimate System, Bureau of Economic Analysis.

shows that most of the variation in the P/E ratio can be attributed to changes in interest rates and inflation. In the third panel, we've shown the inverse of the P/E ratio so that it can be more easily compared to interest rates and inflation.

With these charts in mind, let's now examine each of the five economic eras more closely, pointing out how the behavior of the stock market during each era has reflected events in the underlying real economy.

The Carefree 1960s: 1960 to 1968

During the carefree 1960s, the economy was healthy and stable. Real GDP grew at 2.7 percent per year, and inflation was between 1 and 1.5 percent per year until 1966 when it began to creep up to 4.2 percent by 1968. Corporate profits grew a bit faster than the economy at 3.9 percent, and the P/E ratio stayed within a narrow band of 15 to 18 times. As a result, the S&P 500 index increased about 5 percent per year. Adding dividends, shareholders earned an average real return of about 9 percent per year, slightly above the long-term average.

The Great Inflation: 1969 to 1982

Inflation was the driving force in the economy and the markets during the next 14 years. Inflation was 4.2 percent in 1968 just before this era and gradually increased to 11.0 percent in 1974. It came down a bit over the next several years but remained at historically high levels before increasing again to 13.5 percent in 1980. This era was also one of volatile economic growth with four official recessions (1969–1970, 1973–1975, 1980, 1981–1982), largely driven by inflation and the government's numerous unsuccessful attempts to fix it, until Paul Volcker slammed on the economic brakes by raising interest rates and halting the growth of the money supply in the early 1980s.

Note that we do not blame oil prices. Although oil prices were certainly a problem, government policy had led to higher levels of inflation even before the oil embargo of 1973–1974. Corporate profits were hit hard by the double impact of inflation and recession. Over the 14 years, real corporate profits were flat.

High inflation rates led investors to demand higher interest rates. High interest rates increase the nominal cost of capital, while high inflation increases the proportion of earnings that must be invested for growth. This explains the decline in the P/E ratio from about 18 at the beginning of 1969 to about 10 at the end of 1982. The combination of no-profit growth and a decline in the P/E ratio led to a real TRS of negative 1 percent per year for this period.

The Return to Normalcy: 1983 to 1996

The long period of strong performance from 1983 to 1996 has created much confusion. The S&P 500 index rose from a level of 141 at the start of 1983 to 741 at the end of 1996. Including dividends, the nominal annual return to shareholders was 16 percent, or 12 percent after adjusting for inflation, nearly double the 6.5 to 7 percent average annual real return stocks have delivered over the past 100+ years.

From 1983 to 1996, real earnings for the S&P 500 increased about 3 percent per year, close to the long-term average growth in real profits. Simultaneously, U.S. interest rates and inflation fell dramatically. Ten-year U.S. government bond yields peaked at nearly 15 percent just before this era in 1981 and then fell, more or less steadily, to 6 percent in 1996. The decline in inflation and interest rates drove P/E ratios back up to more typical levels in the mid to high teens by 1996.

Just to give you a sense of how important inflation and interest rates were as drivers of returns during this period, we estimate that without the decline in interest rates and inflation, the real return to shareholders would have been about 7 percent per year, right in line with the long-term average.

The Technology Bubble: 1997 to 2004

The years 1997 to 2004 appear very different depending on whether you look just at the starting and ending points, or whether you look at what happened in the middle. From beginning to end, real returns to shareholders were about 5 percent (3.5 percent increase in the index plus 1.5 percent from dividends), slightly below the long-term average.

What everyone remembers, though, is what happened in the middle. The S&P 500 went from 741 at the beginning of 1997 to 1,527 in mid-2000, before falling back to 1,212 at the end of 2004. As we explain in Chapter 8, this movement was caused by a bubble in the technology and megacap stocks. For example, from 1997 to 2000, the technology and megacap stocks increased by a median of 62 percent (total, not annual), while the rest of the companies in the S&P 500 increased a median of 21 percent.

The ensuing stock market decline was also centered on the technology and megacap stocks, which declined more than 60 percent as the remaining companies declined by a median of only 8 percent. Interestingly, fully 40 percent of the companies in the S&P 500 actually increased in value during the bear market from 2000 to 2004. The bubble of 2000 was not a marketwide bubble but a very large sector bubble, as we demonstrate in the next chapter.

The Leveraging and Credit Crisis: 2005 to 2009

The S&P 500 briefly hit another peak of 1,565 in mid-2007 before dropping to 1,115 at the end of 2009, with a dip along the way to 677 in March 2009. Unlike the 2000 peak that was driven by extraordinary P/E ratios, the 2007 peak was driven by unusually high corporate profits. The subsequent decline was driven by the financial crisis as it spread from the financial sector to the entire real economy.

The market P/E in 2007 was about 40 percent lower than it was in 1999—in line with what we would have expected given the level of interest rates and inflation. The 2007 P/E also resembled the P/Es of the 1960s, when inflation and interest rates were similarly low as they were in 2007.

It was the exceptionally strong corporate earnings that were responsible for the index reaching 1,500. Indeed, the ratio of total profits for the S&P 500 companies to gross domestic product (GDP) soared in 2006 to an unprecedented 5.7 percent—much higher than the historical average of about 2.3 percent.*

The record level of earnings wasn't sustainable because it wasn't broad based but, rather, was concentrated in two sectors: financial companies and energy companies. The profits of the energy companies were driven by high oil prices that peaked in 2008 at $145 per barrel but later fell to $30 before recovering to $71 in June 2009. In the financial sector, higher volumes and fees stoked returns on equity that were around 60 to 80 percent above the historical trend. Much of these higher

---

* In addition, we have examined similar ratios of the profits of top European companies (FTSE 300) to the total GDP of all Western European economies. The pattern is similar, with a more pronounced upward trend. For the U.S. economy, we've also used the corporate profit measures published by the U.S. Bureau of Economic Analysis (BEA) and found a pattern similar to that of the S&P 500.

returns came from subprime and related products that were wiped out in 2008 and 2009.

In December 2009, the S&P 500 traded at 1,115. Based on consensus estimates, that translates to a P/E multiple of 15 for 2010 earnings. Although there was great uncertainty about earnings at that time, the market appeared to be returning to typical valuation levels. Later, we discuss whether the market overreacted to the crisis and whether its reaction was unique relative to other recessions.

MODELING THE MARKET OVER ONE-YEAR PERIODS

Can the value of the stock market be explained over shorter periods of time than the eras we've just discussed? We built a simple annual model based on the core-of-value cornerstone to test the linkage between the stock market and the real economy. We found that the theoretical model does a pretty good job explaining the market, which means that the market is closely linked to the real economy.

Exhibit 7.4 illustrates how the model works. The value of the stock market (in this case the S&P 500) equals a base level of corporate earnings times an expected P/E ratio that is driven off the expected

EXHIBIT 7.4 **Modeling the Stock Market**

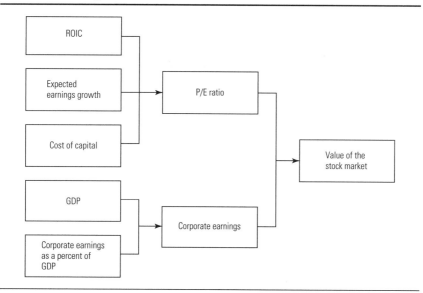

long-term ROIC, the expected growth in corporate earnings, and the expected cost of capital.*

The level of corporate earnings is estimated in two ways. The *trend* model assumes that earnings will follow the long-term trend whether they are currently above or below trend. This is consistent with the empirical observation that, while highly volatile, the long-term growth rate in corporate earnings is the same as the long-term growth rate in GDP. In other words, corporate profits tend to revert to a constant percent of GDP, and GDP growth itself also tends to be stable over long periods of time.

The *anchored* model assumes that investors take current earnings as an anchor for projecting future earnings. In the anchored model, investor expectations overshoot long-term future earnings during earnings peaks and vice versa, when earnings are below trend. This assumption is consistent with what we know of securities analysts' earnings forecasts, which also tend to be too high when markets peak and too low in troughs. Exhibit 7.5 illustrates the differences between the two earnings models.

Before showing the overall results, we compare the predicted P/E ratio to the actual P/E ratio. Exhibit 7.6 compares the median P/E of the companies in the S&P 500 index from 1962 to year-end 2009 with the predicted values from the model. Our simple model does a remarkably good job at mimicking the actual P/E ratios, year by year. For most years the model is within 15 percent of the actual, and the overs/unders are well balanced.†

Is 15 percent accuracy good? Given the complexity of the system and the difficulty of even measuring some of the variables (current earnings, inflation, interest rates, growth expectations), the result provides us with assurance that the fundamental factors do drive share prices within reasonable bounds.

Some may be uncomfortable with the lack of precision in this analysis, but one can't be more precise with markets in which many investors are interacting with different strategies and different amounts of information. Aristotle said, "... it is the mark of an educated man

---

* We estimated the value of these variables based on historical rates that are quite stable. The cost of capital was estimated based on our research showing a constant real cost of equity, which we then adjusted for inflation to derive a nominal cost of equity.

† As we explain in the next chapter, we've used the median of the S&P 500 companies, not the weighted average P/E (which is typically reported in the press). The weighted average is periodically distorted by the valuations of very large capitalization stocks.

EXHIBIT 7.5 **Projections Tend to Anchor on Recent History**

Annual and expected corporate earnings, $ billion

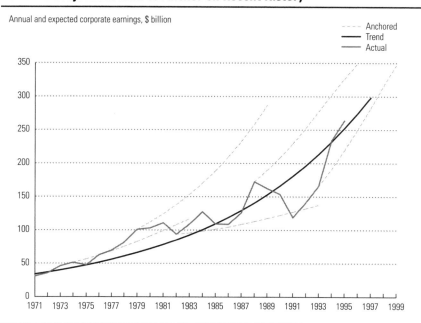

Source: Institutional Brokers' Estimate System, Bloomberg, Bureau of Economic Analysis, McKinsey Corporate Performance Center analysis.

EXHIBIT 7.6 **Modeled P/E Closely Tracks Actual Market**

Price/earnings

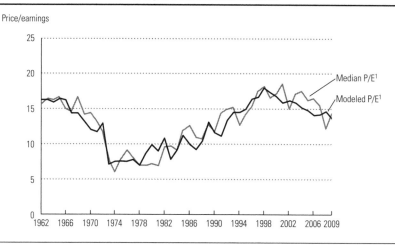

[1] Between 1962 and 1977, 12-month trailing P/E was used (due to lack of data), while all following years use a 12-month forward-looking P/E ratio.

Source: McKinsey Corporate Performance Center analysis.

EXHIBIT 7.7 **Anchored Model Performs Better Than the Trend Model**

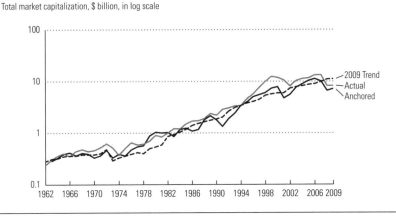

Total market capitalization, $ billion, in log scale

Source: Institutional Brokers' Estimate System, Bloomberg, Bureau of Economic Analysis, McKinsey Corporate Performance Center analysis.

to look for precision in each class of things just so far as the nature of the subject admits."* We have to accept the nature and limitations of what we're analyzing.

Our next step is to combine the predicted P/E ratio with the earnings models to predict the level of the stock market itself. Exhibit 7.7 shows the results of the models compared with the S&P 500 index. Although both models track the long-term trajectory of share prices, the anchored model is better at describing the market's actual price level at any point in time, and the trend model better describes where stock prices should be, given fundamentals.

If the market had perfect foresight, then share prices would be much less volatile than they are because market prices would smooth out all the volatility of future profits and cash flows. Interestingly, smoothing out prices would make P/E ratios much more volatile than they are. That's because prices would remain stable when earnings are low, leading to a high P/E, and vice versa when earnings are high.

You can see this clearly with cyclical companies like chemical companies and paper companies. P/E ratios tend to be very high when profits are low because the market expects profits to rebound; conversely, P/E ratios tend to be very low when profits are high since the market expects profits to decline.

_____
* The Nichomachean Ethics.

So the trend model may better reflect what the market should be, but the anchored model fits actual data better. But this doesn't mean that the anchored model is superior; it simply predicts stock price levels in the short term better than the trend model, reflecting the influence of current earnings and inflation on the investor psyche. In contrast, the trend model comes in more handy when the intent is to predict stock price levels better in the longer run.

What holds for the stock market as a whole is likely to hold for sectors and companies as well. Investors tend to anchor their expectations for growth and profitability too much in the recent past and need time to revise these expectations to reflect long-term fundamentals. In the short term, therefore, the stock market could overvalue (or undervalue) sectors or companies that have experienced strong upturns (or downturns), as investors' expectations tend to overshoot (or undershoot) the actual trends.

MAKING SENSE OF THE MARKET

During the technology bubble, many investors and commentators simply extrapolated from the recent past, predicting ongoing high returns because they could perceive nothing that would stop them. Others developed reasoned arguments to back up the same view.

In 1999, two economists, James Glassman and Kevin Hassett, published a book titled *Dow 36,000: The New Strategy for Profiting from the Coming Rise in the Stock Market*.* Glassman and Hassett predicted that the Dow Jones Industrial index would reach 36,000 sometime in the 2002 to 2004 period, after rising from 700 in 1980 to 11,000 in 1999. Here was their argument: investors were realizing that stocks were low risk and thus were bidding up stock prices. Others argued that stocks were gaining broader acceptance, and that higher demand for stocks would push up prices.

Then the market abruptly fell, tumbling more than 30 percent over the next three years. Such a large run-up, followed by such a sharp decline, led many to question whether the stock market was anything more than a giant roulette table, essentially disconnected from the real world.

---

* James K. Glassman and Kevin A. Hassett, *Dow 36,000: The New Strategy for Profiting from the Coming Rise in the Stock Market* (New York: Three Rivers Press, 2000).

In 1999, investors should have realized that share prices couldn't continue increasing at 17 percent per year. Whereas they might count on corporate profits continuing to increase as the economy grew, interest rates and inflation had reached very low levels and weren't likely to boost P/E ratios by declining further. No matter whether you believed that the valuations of the megacap stocks were valid, it would have been unreasonable to expect that they could continue to boost the overall market's P/E in the way they previously had.

We can make sense of the market, even if it tends to overshoot or undershoot for short periods of time. Executives and investors can be confident that there is a linkage between the stock market and the real economy, and that the market can't randomly soar to 10,000 or drop to 200 (as of December 2009, the S&P was trading at 1,115).

This means that the market as a whole has a more narrow band of longer-term performance than many realize, and that exceptional bull markets will usually be followed by a down market and vice versa—unless corporate profits (and returns on capital) suddenly become a much greater or lesser portion of GDP, or the real cost of equity changes as a result of significant changes in risk preferences.

Market volatility complicates life for managers. But if managers understand what's happening when short-term share prices are off base, they'll be more likely to stick with their longer-term strategic plans.

8

Stock Market Bubbles

If the most sophisticated investors drive share prices, are there stock market bubbles and, if so, why do they occur? The short answer is that yes there are bubbles, but they're generally confined to industry sectors, not the entire market. And they occur because sophisticated investors are sometimes unable to offset the behavior of less rational investors.

It's important to first distinguish between stock market bubbles, bubbles in other assets, and financial crises. The stock market is unique because its underlying assets generate a stream of profit and cash flow; therefore, these assets have intrinsic value. On the other hand, most traded nonfinancial assets—like art, classic cars, and stamps—have no intrinsic value; their value is purely driven by the interaction of buyers and sellers.

The Dutch tulip bubble in 1636–1637 is one of the most talked about and controversial bubbles. Even though tulip bulbs have minimal intrinsic value, bulb prices for some rare varieties in 1636–1637 reached the equivalent of €25,000 for a single bulb. Traders bought and sold bulbs and futures contracts on bulbs based solely on their expectation that prices would continue to increase, expecting they could quickly resell the bulb or the contract to someone else for a handsome profit. Once traders realized that there weren't enough new buyers to keep increasing prices, the prices collapsed within just a few months.

It's difficult to analyze such bubbles because there is no inherent value against which to compare the market value. A reasonable value, for instance, might be bounded by the cash flow an asset generates or the cost to reproduce. These are not relevant to non-stock-market bubbles. For example, one can reasonably assert that a shoe-making company shouldn't be worth $200 billion because the market for shoes simply isn't large enough. One can't say, though, that a painting by van Gogh shouldn't be worth $100 million.

Similarly, a decline in stock prices during a financial crisis doesn't mean that stock prices were at bubble levels. If the stock prices were reasonably valued in light of the economic conditions before the crisis, then you can't characterize the subsequent decline as the bursting of a bubble. An external shock that drives down share prices doesn't mean there was a bubble. For example, the decline in share prices during the 1970s wasn't due to a bubble; it was due to the unexpected rise of inflation and interest rates that eroded the value of companies.

Sharply dropping share prices in the face of uncertainty and new information are not bubbles. For example, when a pharmaceutical company announces that a promising new drug has failed in clinical trials, the share price of the company will usually drop considerably. The steep decline in this case doesn't indicate that the price was originally at a bubble level. The price prior to the announcement may have reflected a reasonable estimate of the company's value given a reasonable estimate of probability for the drug's success.

Suppose that the value of the company would be worth $100 per share if the drug were successful and $20 per share if not successful. Further, suppose that the probability of success was 40 percent. A rational estimate of the value per share prior to the announcement would be between $20 and $100, weighted by the probabilities. In this case the rationale estimate would be $52 ($100 × 40% + $20 × 60%). After the announcement, the share price should drop from $52 to $20. That 61 percent drop in the share price doesn't mean that the earlier price was a bubble.

We define a bubble as a time when the stock price of a company is far above the level that rational, well-informed investors would value the company.

A good example of a stock bubble occurred when 3Com spun off its Palm subsidiary in March 2000. 3Com sold 5 percent of Palm's shares to the public. Immediately after the share sale, the market capitalization of Palm was $45 billion. At the same time, 3Com's market cap was only $28 billion, even though it owned 95 percent of Palm (presumably worth $41 billion). The only way that 3Com could be worth 60 percent of Palm would be if the rest of 3Com's businesses were worth negative $13 billion!

So why didn't rational investors exploit the mispricing by going short in Palm shares and long in 3Com shares? Because they couldn't. The free float of Palm shares was too small after the carve-out because 95 percent of all Palm's shares were still held by 3Com. Establishing a short position in Palm would have required borrowing the shares from a Palm shareholder, but there weren't many. The supply of shares available to borrow increased steadily over the months following the carve-out, and the mispricing gradually decreased.

WHY DO BUBBLES ARISE?

Mainstream academic finance has been criticized for years because some of its underlying assumptions are clearly not true. For example, most finance theories assume that all investors are rational. It's clearly not true that *all* behave rationally, and a growing body of literature has been developed (loosely collected under the title *behavioral finance* or *behavioral economics*) that describes the irrational decisions that investors make.

One study showed that 74 percent of investment professionals believed their performance was better than average, a hindsight bias that leads to overconfidence.* Investors think they can explain historical events and, therefore, are overconfident about their ability to predict the future.

Other biases relate to how investors confirm or refute an investment thesis. Availability bias is the tendency for investors to put undo weight on recent or easily available data. Confirmation bias is the tendency for investors to look for evidence that supports an investment idea while downplaying evidence that might disprove their thesis. These are just a couple examples among many others about how investors can be irrational.

But the fact that investors behave irrationally doesn't necessarily lead to a market with a lot of mispriced shares and bubbles. Individual investor irrationality must be combined with herding behavior and structural constraints for bubbles to occur.

---

* James Montier, "Behaving Badly," *Dresdner Kleinwort Wasserstein—Global Equity Strategy,* February 2, 2006.

As long as irrational investors behave randomly, they should cancel each other out. But there are times when large groups of investors exhibit the same irrational behavior and push a company's share price above or below rational levels, which should in turn create opportunities for more sophisticated investors to take an opposite position, pushing the share price back toward a rational level.

However, as demonstrated in the 3Com/Palm example, there may be structural impediments preventing the smart investors from countering the irrational investors. So bubbles tend to occur when large groups of investors behave irrationally and structural features of the stock market prevent smart investors from moving the share price back to a reasonable level.

Assume that a company's share price has dramatically increased over the past few months because the company surprised the market with better than expected results. Based solely on this strong recent performance, some investors might believe the company will continue to exceed market expectations and thus start bidding for shares. Behavioral finance has shown that many investors demonstrate this type of behavior, creating upward pressure on the share price.

As long as a sufficient number of investors can identify and take short positions against overpricing on the part of these myopic investors, the share price will return to its fundamental level. In practice, however, this may not be the case: the costs, complexity, and risks involved in setting up a short position may be too high.

It's worth exploring the difficulty of short selling in more detail. As the preceding example shows, to correct overpricing, rational investors need to sell shares short (sell shares they don't own). However, the stock exchanges impose a number of obstacles to short selling. For example, from 1938 to 2007, short sales could be made only when the last trade was at a price higher than the second-to-last trade (the uptick rule). In other words, short sellers could not pile on when a company's share price began to decline.

Since the SEC rescinded the uptick rule in 2007, there have been calls for its reinstatement from politicians, regulators, and some stock market participants, despite the lack of any evidence of harm without the uptick rule. In fact, many academics argue that the uptick rule itself was harmful to the functioning of the stock market.

The biggest impediment to short selling, however, is that it creates risks for the short seller that are more difficult to manage than those for a long investor. Suppose I'm a long investor who believes that company A is undervalued. The shares are selling for $100 per share, but I believe they're worth $150. I purchase 10,000 shares at $100 for $1 million. Two years later, the shares hit $150 and I sell my shares for $1.5 million, a nice $500,000 profit.

Let's compare that with the experience of the short seller. Suppose I believe the shares of A are worth only $50. I sell short 10,000 shares for $1 million. Two years later, the share price drops to $50, so I repurchase the shares at $50 for $500,000. I initially received $1 million and paid out $500,000 three years later, for a profit of $500,000—in theory.

The complication is that I need to come up with 10,000 shares to sell. So I go to my broker and borrow the shares. But the brokerage firm won't just give me the shares on my promise to repay them. I need to put up some security. So I deposit $1 million of government bonds with the broker. At the end of the two years, I purchase the shares and return them to the broker. The broker then returns the government bonds to me.

That works fine as long as the share price steadily declines. But what if the share price first goes up before coming down? Assume that the share price rises first to $200 before declining to $50. Does the pattern matter? It may not matter to me, but it does matter to the broker. When the share price hits $200, the shares I have borrowed are worth $2 million, but the government bonds that I have on deposit with the broker are worth only $1 million. The broker asks for another $1 million in collateral. But if I don't have another $1 million to put up, I'm out of business and the broker takes my collateral. So even though my assessment about the ultimate value of the shares was correct, I lose $1 million instead of gaining $500,000.

Shorting is risky without sufficient liquidity to weather adverse movements in the company's share price. The long investor on the other hand can just sit tight and wait until he is proven right. The long investor can't lose more than he has invested, but the short investor can.

A good example of shorting risk is the collapse of Long-Term Capital Management (LTCM) in 1998. Most of LTCM's strategies were based on identifying investments that were not priced at equilibrium values relative to each other. For example, Royal Dutch Shell had a complex dual-share structure with separate legal entities that were economically equivalent, yet the Royal Dutch shares traded at an 8 percent premium to the Shell shares.

LTCM bet that the premium would eventually disappear, so they bought shares of Shell and sold short shares of Royal Dutch. LTCM also used massive leverage, financing its investments with $25 of debt for every dollar of equity. When Russia defaulted on its debts in 1998, the financial markets behaved erratically, and a number of LTCM's positions (like Royal Dutch Shell) generated paper losses. With such high leverage, LTCM's lenders and counterparties reduced their willingness to lend to LTCM in this environment, so the company was forced to liquidate some of its positions.

LTCM liquidated its Royal Dutch Shell position when the Royal Dutch premium had actually increased to 22 percent, generating a cash loss of about $150 million. Eventually, the uncertainty created by LTCM's losses on this position and many others almost created a meltdown of the financial system, so the Federal Reserve got the heads of the banks together to provide enough liquidity to prevent a collapse. The share prices of Royal Dutch Shell did eventually converge when the dual structure was eliminated, but LTCM had closed its position at a substantial loss years earlier.

MARKETWIDE BUBBLES

Bubbles that affect the broad market in developed economies are rare. We identified two periods (1967–1972 and 1997–2001) that might be considered bubbles in the past 50 years in the United States. As you dig deeper, however, even these bubbles weren't broad based but were concentrated on only segments of companies in the market.

We define a marketwide bubble as a time when the market's P/E ratio differs substantially from the P/E you would expect to see given the performance of the economy. Exhibit 8.1 compares the actual P/E ratios of the S&P 500 index to the predicted P/E ratios derived from our economic model based on the core-of-value cornerstone (value is driven by growth, return on capital, and the cost of capital).*

We use two different actual P/E ratios for the S&P 500. The aggregate P/E ratio is a weighted average based on the market capitalization of the companies in the index; this is the number that's headlined in the press. The other P/E ratio is the median of all the companies in the index without regard to size. You can see that the predicted P/E and the median P/E track closely. The aggregate P/E substantially deviates from the predicted P/E in the 1969–1972 and 1997–2001 time frames. These are the periods we've characterized as bubbles.

* This is the same model we displayed in Chapter 7.

EXHIBIT 8.1 **Estimating Fundamental Market Valuation Levels**

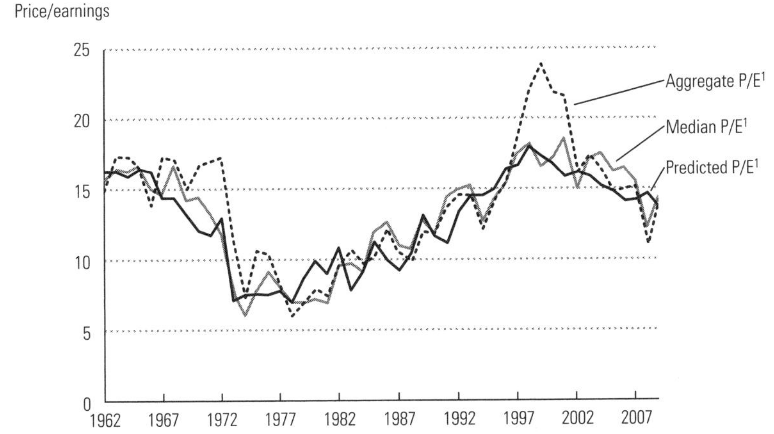

Price/earnings

[1] Between 1962 and 1977, 12-month trailing P/E was used (due to lack of data), while all following years use a 12-month forward-looking P/E ratio.

Source: McKinsey Corporate Performance Center analysis.

During the technology bubble of the late 1990s, the aggregate S&P 500 P/E ratio was greater than 30 times for several years versus a predicted level of about 16 times. Looking deeper, however, the bubble was concentrated in technology stocks and certain very large companies (we'll call them megacaps).

Let's look at the effect of the megacap stocks. Here's where arcane details matter, namely, how the S&P 500 index is constructed. The S&P 500 is a value-weighted index, which means that the largest companies influence the behavior of the index more than the smaller companies. Most often this doesn't matter because the P/E ratios of the largest companies are roughly the same as the rest of the companies. But in the late 1990s, the P/E ratios of the largest 30 companies grew to be far higher than the rest of the market.

Exhibit 8.2 shows what happened. Before and after the bubble, the P/E ratios of the 30 largest companies were the same as the other 470 companies, on average. However, in 1999, the average top-30 company had a P/E ratio of 46 times, compared with an average of 23 times for the other 470 companies. As a result, the overall weighted average P/E ratio reached 30 times.

Most of these large-cap companies with high P/E ratios were clustered in three sectors: technology, media, and telecommunications

EXHIBIT 8.2 **Impact of Largest Stocks on Overall Market Valuation**

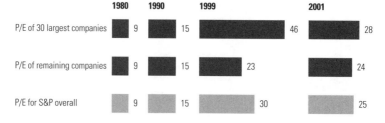

	1980	1990	1999	2001
P/E of 30 largest companies	9	15	46	28
P/E of remaining companies	9	15	23	24
P/E for S&P overall	9	15	30	25

Note: 12-month trailing P/E ratios.

Source: Compustat, McKinsey Corporate Performance Center analysis.

(TMT). P/E ratios were significantly lower in most other U.S. sectors. To illustrate how aggressively investors were valuing the share prices of certain TMT stocks, we analyzed the value of the 10 highest market capitalization U.S. technology companies. At the end of 1999, these 10 companies had a combined market capitalization of $2.4 trillion, annual revenues of $240 billion, and net income of $37 billion, resulting in an aggregate P/E ratio of 64 times.

We built a simple discounted cash flow (DCF) model to estimate what performance would be required to justify this market value. For investors to earn an 11 percent return, these companies would have needed to grow their revenues to approximately $2.7 trillion by 2014 and their net income to about $450 billion. To put this in perspective, assuming that GDP would grow at a healthy rate from 1999 through 2014, and that corporate profits would remain a stable share of GDP (as they have for at least the past 80 years), the total corporate profits of all U.S. companies would be about $1.3 to $1.5 trillion by 2014. So these 10 companies would have needed to earn about one-third of all the profits earned by all U.S. companies.

One would expect rational investors to try and exploit these cases of likely mispricing. Many smart investors questioned the valuations. Julian Robertson, one of the leading investors of the 1980s and 1990s, said:

> Well, we've had a movement away from value investing to momentum investing, where price is not a factor. I can't tell you how many good investors really believe that price no longer matters, and that's not my style. . . . Right now, everybody is chasing

short-term performance. Even the leveraged-buyout people are buying telephone companies instead of industrial companies, in part because they can spin off Internet-type subsidiaries. So everybody—day traders, hedge fund operators, LBO people, right down the line—is piling into the same stocks, which is, in effect, an inadvertent Ponzi scheme. And it will eventually blow up.*

On the other hand, the media found commentators who could explain the high prices with new theories of economics and finance. One idea was the "new economy," although definitions of it were vague. A key aspect of the new economy was *winner take all*—the idea that the largest company in an industry would dominate it and extract all the profits (and even increase the industry's profits once it became a monopoly). Despite what was probably one of the most competitive times in history, the theory essentially suggested that competition would end as the largest companies dominated the economy.

Those who questioned the new economy were said to "not get it." But as we explained, setting up a short position in overpriced stocks is costly and risky. We know of one experienced investor who set up a short position on an overvalued high-tech stock, only to abandon that position at a considerable loss when the share price continued to increase. Just three months after this investor exited his short position, the share price plummeted.

By the way, there were some new business models, like eBay and Google, that did have different economics, but these were rare. eBay's model generates high returns on capital because it needs very little capital, just some computers. It has no inventories or manufacturing facilities. As more buyers use eBay, this attracts more sellers, which in turn attracts more buyers, and so forth in a virtuous spiral. On the other hand, companies that simply made high-tech hardware like PCs or telecommunications equipment, or companies that simply used the Internet to sell products like a brick-and-mortar retailer, were subject to the same old economic laws of competition.

The apparent bubble in the 1970s was also largely driven by a small number of high-capitalization companies. Several established companies traded at extremely high multiples. For example, in 1972, Kodak traded at a P/E multiple of 37 times, Xerox traded at 39 times, and McDonald's traded at 58 times. These companies were part of the

---

* Andy Serwer and Julian Robertson, "Eye of the Tiger," *Fortune* 141, no. 9 (2000): 309–312.

EXHIBIT 8.3 **Stock Market Bubbles: China and Saudi Arabia**

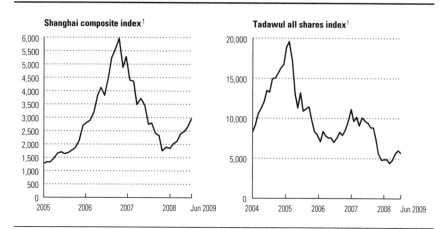

Shanghai composite index[1]

Tadawul all shares index[1]

[1] Estimated index price.

Source: Bloomberg, McKinsey Corporate Performance Center analysis.

so-called *nifty fifty*, 50 large-cap stocks that you supposedly could buy and hold forever. The simplicity of the nifty fifty obviously influenced many investors to follow the herd, leading to inflated share prices.

While bubbles in developed markets are rare, they're more frequent in emerging markets. Exhibit 8.3 shows the performance of the Chinese Shanghai Composite index and the Saudi Arabian Tadawul index.

The Shanghai index increased by more than 150 percent from May 2006 to May 2007. Then, just over one year later, more than two-thirds of the gain was gone. The Saudi Tadawul index more than doubled from February 2005 to February 2006 but then lost all those gains within one year. Emerging markets are susceptible to bubbles because of the same structural constraints we discussed previously, only more extreme.

First, most of the large companies in China have only a small number of shares available for trading, as most are owned by various government entities. For example, the largest company traded on the Shanghai exchange is PetroChina, with only 2 percent of its shares trading on the Shanghai market. Second, Chinese investors have accumulated massive amounts of savings, but most can't easily purchase shares of companies outside China (not even Hong Kong), so their investment opportunities are very limited. Finally, short selling isn't permitted in China, so sophisticated investors can't keep prices at reasonable levels.

The situation is even more complex because many Chinese companies have issued shares on both the Chinese mainland markets and the Hong Kong market. The A shares (traded in China) and the H shares (traded in Hong Kong) have identical rights but can sometimes trade at very different prices because most A shareholders cannot own H shares and vice versa. There are only very limited arbitrage opportunities to keep prices in line. The market capitalization of PetroChina (if the market price on the Shanghai exchange were applied to all shares, both traded and untraded) reached over $700 billion in 2007, while ExxonMobil, a company with twice the profits, traded at only $500 billion.

SECTOR AND COMPANY BUBBLES

Sector and company bubbles are more frequent than marketwide bubbles, but they're still rare. We mentioned the technology bubble of the late 1990s. Another example is the value of biotechnology companies in 2005–2006, when the sum of the market capitalizations of all the listed biotech companies was about $450 billion (excluding the traditional large pharmaceutical companies that were investing in biotech). Making some assumptions about future margins, one can estimate that these companies would need to earn $600 billion in revenues in 2025 (in 2006 dollars). That excludes the existing large pharmaceutical companies not classified as biotech (most of which were aggressively investing in biotech) and any companies that didn't yet exist (except in the minds of scientists). To put that into perspective, all the listed pharmaceutical companies combined earned about $600 billion of revenues in 2006.

Company-specific bubbles are difficult to find. We examined 3,560 U.S.-based companies that traded at a minimum market capitalization of $1 billion any year between 1982 and 2007. Of those, only 123 could be considered to have experienced a bubble in their stock price anytime during those 25 years.* Of those 123, fully 92 were technology/media/telecom companies that experienced their bubbles during the

---

* We considered a company to have experienced a bubble in its share price when the following conditions were met: (1) Its P/E reached twice the P/E of the S&P 500 or at least 40 when the S&P 500's P/E was greater than 20; (2) the drop in the company's share price after the peak year was not due to a substantial decline in earnings; and (3) the share price dropped by 30 percent or more after of its peak P/E.

tech bubble of 1999–2001. That leaves 31 other companies that experienced bubbles in their share prices. Of those, only seven ever reached a market cap greater than $5 billion.

An example of one of these bubbles is Brinker International, a $3 billion company with 1,700 restaurants (including the Chili's chain) in 27 countries. In the early 1990s, Brinker was increasing its revenues by more than 20 percent per year, with improving margins. In 1993, its market capitalization reached $2.1 billion with a P/E ratio of greater than 40 times. Brinker continued its strong revenue growth in 1994 and 1995, but same-store sales began to actually decline. The market realized that without strong same-store sales growth, the company's economics were vulnerable. In 1994, Brinker's market cap dropped by 61 percent to a more reasonable P/E ratio in the high teens.

FINANCIAL CRISES

Financial crises and bubbles aren't the same. Bubbles are the rise and fall of the market value of company shares. Unlike debt, equities don't have maturity dates or covenants that can allow the holder to immediately demand cash from the company. Therefore, when bubbles burst they don't have a drastic effect on the economy (unless they're accompanied by large amounts of debt).

Financial crises, on the other hand, do have a dramatic and far-reaching effect on the real economy, because they're brought about by excessive financial leverage, which has a negative domino effect when the value of the underlying assets falls and those who owe the debt can no longer service it. First the debt crisis causes an economic downturn, which then causes the stock market to decline.

As we discussed in Chapter 3, the financial crisis of 2007–2009 was caused by consumers buying illiquid homes with adjustable-rate debt, and banks and investors financing the purchase of illiquid mortgage-backed debt with short-term debt. Then the stock market decline in 2008 mostly occurred after the collapse of Lehman Brothers and the bad news about the health of other major banks. By the way, it was not unlike the stock market's reactions in prior recessions, and one could even argue that it reacted too late.*

---

*Richard Dobbs and Timothy Koller, "The Crisis: Timing Strategic Moves," *McKinsey on Finance* (Spring 2009), 1–5.

Indeed, the aggressive use of leverage is one key factor that ties together most major financial crises over the past 50 years. In particular, crises arise when companies, banks, or investors use short-term debt to buy long-lived, illiquid assets. What typically happens is that some event triggers an unwillingness among lenders to refinance the short-term debt; since the borrower doesn't have enough cash on hand to repay the short-term debt, he or she must sell some assets. The assets are illiquid and other borrowers are trying to do the same, so the price the borrower can realize isn't enough to repay the debt. In other words, the borrower's assets and liabilities are mismatched.

In the past 30 years there have been at least six financial crises that were largely due to companies and banks financing illiquid assets with short-term debt. In the United States in the 1980s, savings and loan institutions aggressively expanded, funding that expansion with short-term debt and deposits. When it became clear that their investments (typically real estate) were not worth their liabilities, lenders and depositors refused to lend more to them. In 1989, the U.S. government bailed out the industry.

In the mid-1990s, the fast-growing economies in East Asia—such as Thailand, South Korea, and Indonesia—fueled their investments in illiquid plants and equipment with short-term debt (often denominated in U.S. dollars). When global interest rates rose, and it also became clear that the companies had built too much capacity, they were unable to pay or refinance their debt. The crisis destabilized the local economies.

Other examples of financial crises fueled by too much short-term debt include the Russian government default in 1998; the collapse of Long-Term Capital Management, also in 1998; the U.S. commercial real estate crisis in the early 1990s; and the Japanese financial crisis that began in 1990 and, some argue, continues to this day.

In all these cases, the financial crisis led to an economic downturn, often severe. Stock market bubbles that were not accompanied by massive amounts of debt have never caused such severe damage to the economy.

BUBBLES REINFORCE NEED TO FOCUS ON LONG-TERM VALUE CREATION

Although rare and short-lived, there are stock market bubbles. Markets can indeed be inefficient in the sense that prices sometimes deviate from fundamentals, but this doesn't make the core-of-value principle and discounted cash flow valuation superfluous or irrelevant—not by a long shot.

Paradoxically, given such market deviations, it's even more important for corporate managers and investors to understand the true, intrinsic value of companies. This allows them to exploit any market deviations if and when they occur, for example, by using shares to pay for acquisitions when those shares are overvalued by the market, or repurchasing shares when the market value is too low.

Two caveats are important to note in these examples. First, we wouldn't recommend basing decisions to issue or repurchase stock, divest or acquire businesses, or settle in cash or shares for transactions based exclusively on a perceived difference between market value and intrinsic value. Instead, these decisions should be grounded in a sound strategic and business rationale that is expected to create value for shareholders. Market deviations are more relevant as tactical considerations related to the timing and execution of strategic decisions—that is, when to issue additional capital or how to pay for particular transactions.

Second, managers should be critical of analyses claiming to find market deviations for a company's shares. After careful analysis, most of the alleged deviations that we've encountered in our client experience turned out to be insignificant or even nonexistent. Market deviations are typically rare and short lived. Thus, the evidence for deviations should be compelling before managers act on it. They should be significant in both size and duration, given the cost and time to execute strategic decisions.

As long as your company's share price will eventually return to its long-run, intrinsic discounted cash flow (DCF) value, you should rely on using the DCF approach for making strategic decisions. What matters is the long-term behavior of your company's share price, not whether it's 5 or 10 percent undervalued this week.

9

Earnings Management

Companies will go to great lengths to achieve a certain earnings per share (EPS) number or smooth out their earnings, but this is mostly wasted energy. The evidence shows that these efforts aren't worth it, and they may actually hurt the company. Instead, senior executive time is better spent on decisions that fundamentally grow the company's revenues or increase its returns on capital.

For decades, companies have been struggling with how to manage earnings and whether to try and smooth them out. In 1974, the *Wall Street Journal* published an editorial lamenting the narrow focus many executives have on EPS:

> A lot of executives apparently believe that if they can figure out a way to boost reported earnings, their stock prices will go up even if the higher earnings do not represent any underlying economic change. In other words, the executives think they are smart and the market is dumb . . . The market is smart. Apparently, the dumb one is the corporate executive caught up in the earnings-per-share mystique.

In a recent survey, Graham, Harvey, and Rajgopal interviewed 400 chief financial officers and asked about the actions their companies would take to meet their quarterly earnings target.* The results, summarized in Exhibit 9.1, show that fully 80 percent of the CFOs were willing to reduce such discretionary expenditures as marketing and product development to meet their short-term earnings target—even

* John R. Graham, Cam Harvey, and Shiva Rajgopal, "Value Destruction and Financial Reporting Decisions," *Financial Analysts Journal* 62 (2006): 27–39.

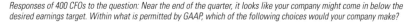

EXHIBIT 9.1 **Short-Term CFO Actions to Hit Earnings Target**

Responses of 400 CFOs to the question: Near the end of the quarter, it looks like your company might come in below the desired earnings target. Within what is permitted by GAAP, which of the following choices would your company make?

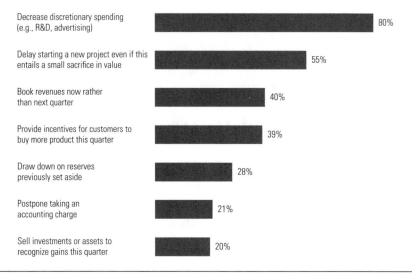

Action	%
Decrease discretionary spending (e.g., R&D, advertising)	80%
Delay starting a new project even if this entails a small sacrifice in value	55%
Book revenues now rather than next quarter	40%
Provide incentives for customers to buy more product this quarter	39%
Draw down on reserves previously set aside	28%
Postpone taking an accounting charge	21%
Sell investments or assets to recognize gains this quarter	20%

Source: John R. Graham, Cam Harvey, and Shiva Rajgopal.

though they knew it would hurt the company's longer-term performance. Almost 40 percent would provide incentives for customers to shift their purchases to an earlier quarter. The researchers also found that many CFOs would pass up or delay value-creating projects if they reduced short-term earnings.

To be clear, we won't argue that earnings are irrelevant. Earnings are an important measure of economic performance and an indicator of cash flow generation. In fact, reported earnings will equal cash flow over the life span of a company. The question is, how far should companies go to manage their short-term earnings?

Earlier we made the case that the market values of companies are ultimately driven by sophisticated investors. These investors understand that the world is not smooth; there are many drivers of earnings that can't be predicted or controlled by management, such as exchange rates or oil prices. For these investors (who read the footnotes in accounting statements), excessive smoothness raises concerns. They know when results are up because the company sold a subsidiary for a gain, even though operating results were flat. They know if the company changed accounting policies in a way that increased profits.

Sophisticated investors don't act based on reported earnings per share; they dissect the earnings information. Were there any unusual items, such as gains on asset sales or tax windfalls? What was the impact of exchange rates? Did all units meet their targets, or did some units outperform to make up for other underperforming units? And, of course, sophisticated investors pay attention to future earnings drivers, such as new products in the pipeline and geographic expansion.

Many of these items might not make it into the press or sell-side analyst reports, and some investors may actually prefer this practice because it gives them an edge over less sophisticated investors. When sophisticated investors favor a company's long-term outlook, they often view short-term earnings shortfalls and potential overreaction by unsophisticated investors as an opportunity to buy shares at a lower price.

Sophisticated investors also know that outsiders can't figure out all the vicissitudes of what the company might be doing to manage earnings. Outsiders can't figure out when a company gives discounts to customers to accelerate purchases from next quarter to the current quarter. They can't immediately figure out that a company is starving product development and passing up long-term growth to meet current earnings. But sophisticated investors know that lack of fuel for R&D will eventually slow the growth engine.

The inability of outsiders to know all the decisions management makes means that companies can fool even the sophisticated investors and the market as a whole for a period of time. But is this worth it? Despite conventional wisdom, the evidence shows that there is a small or nonexistent impact for meeting or missing consensus earnings estimates, reducing earnings volatility, and improving earnings through accounting changes. To us, it doesn't seem worth the try.

CONSENSUS ESTIMATES DON'T MATTER

Suppose you're the CEO of a large company. The quarter is shaping up a little worse than expected by the analysts who cover you because industry growth has slowed a bit—so you're not likely to meet expected earnings. What do you do? (a) Nothing, (b) Offer special incentives to customers to accelerate purchases from next quarter to this quarter, or (c) Cut your advertising budget just enough to make up for the earnings shortfall.

If you pursue (a), do nothing, you know that your share price will likely decline, at least in the short term. If you do (b) or (c), your share price might not change or might go up with the earnings announcement, but what are the medium-term ramifications?

Let's suppose the industry is experiencing a structural slowdown that's likely to persist. If you believe you can make up for the shortfall in the next several quarters, it will be tempting to go ahead with (b) or (c). But are you kidding yourself—is the shortfall really just a one-quarter problem or has something more fundamental changed?

As we said, you can fool the market in the near term because investors don't have enough details to see what you're actually doing. You can get away with it for a while, but eventually, even sooner rather than later, the market will come to understand what you are doing. So why erode your credibility?

Much smoothing behavior is based on a desire to meet consensus estimates, which seems misplaced because analyst forecasts aren't particularly prescient. Exhibit 9.2 shows the trend of consensus earnings forecasts for the S&P 500. Each line represents a single year's earnings, and the end point is the actual earnings for the year. The line preceding it represents the consensus estimate at points up to three years before the actual results are known.

The consensus forecasts aren't very good. Some observations: out of the 25 years we examined, the consensus forecast in January for the upcoming year (e.g., January 2008 forecast for calendar year 2008), is within 5 percent of actual only 7 of the 25 years. Of the years the consensus was off by more than 5 percent, there were 16 years in which the consensus was too high relative to actual, versus only two years in which it was too low relative to the actual.

In general, analysts' earnings estimates are not accurate; they tend to be too optimistic, and they almost never identify inflection points (changes in the direction of earnings from increase to decrease or vice versa). In fact, in 12 of the 25 years, one would have been closer than the analysts by simply forecasting that the upcoming year's earnings would equal last year's earnings.

Analysts' estimates for five-year periods are even less useful. When they're asked, they usually give some number, often around 10 percent for a five-year, rolling-earnings growth forecast. For companies in the S&P 500, Exhibit 9.3 compares rolling five-year projected earnings growth with actual five-year earnings growth. Not only are the

EXHIBIT 9.2 **Aggregate EPS Forecast for S&P 500 Index**

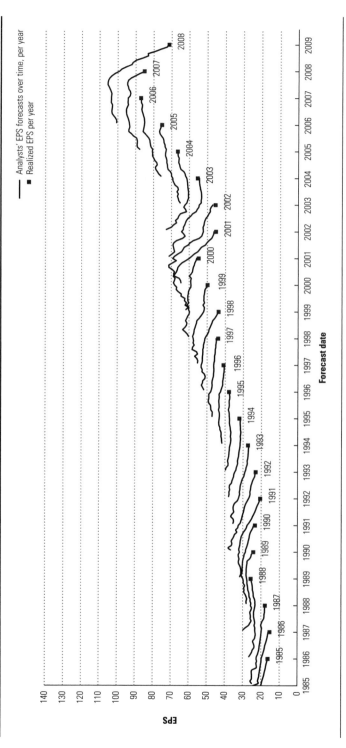

Source: Institutional Brokers' Estimate System, McKinsey Corporate Performance Center analysis.

EXHIBIT 9.3 **Long-Term Earnings Growth: Forecasted vs. Actual**

Five-year rolling earnings growth, percent

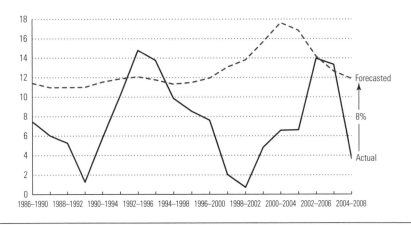

Source: Institutional Brokers' Estimate System, McKinsey Corporate Performance Center analysis.

five-year growth rates almost always overestimated, but the estimated rates exceed 10 percent for every period.

We examined similar statistics at the industry and individual company levels, and found similar results.

The fact that consensus earnings estimates are constantly revised raises the question of how to define an *earnings surprise*, which the press likes to talk about. Because companies rarely meet the consensus earnings one year out, there's no element of surprise there. In common usage, an earnings surprise refers to the difference between the actual earnings and the consensus estimate just before the announcement of the actual results. In other words, a surprise is the difference between actual and expected earnings just days or weeks before the announcement of earnings.

Not surprisingly, the analysts are much more accurate here. Furthermore, companies typically provide information or explicit guidance to investors and analysts about their upcoming results. So a surprise says as much about management's internal controls and accounting systems as its operating performance.

Think of it this way. On December 31, a company announces that its sales for the quarter are better than expected; then analysts raise their earnings forecast for the year. Two weeks later, the company announces its earnings, which reflect that the better than expected sales announced on December 31 didn't lead to better than expected earnings. The surprise is that management didn't clue analysts in on December 31 that the earnings wouldn't go up with unexpected sales, and investors are left to question why management didn't tell them more. They may speculate that the company's information systems weren't good enough to let even the company know what to expect.

Given that surprises are so short term, it only follows that the actual impact of earnings misses is much smaller than conventional wisdom might indicate. Researchers have shown that earnings surprises explained less than 2 percent of share-price volatility in the four weeks surrounding announcements.* In fact, more than 40 percent of companies with positive (or negative) earnings surprises actually had a negative (or positive) return *in the opposite direction.*

There's also strong evidence that the market looks beyond the short-term surprise in assessing earnings announcements. We analyzed the share-price reaction to the profit announcements of the 595 largest European companies for 2007. We divided the companies along two dimensions: (1) Was the company's earnings announcement a positive or negative surprise? and (2) Did analysts' expectations for earnings two years out increase or decrease?

Not surprisingly, in the cases in which both dimensions were positive or negative, the stock price reaction was similarly positive or negative, as shown by Exhibit 9.4. For instance, when companies beat the consensus earnings estimate in the current period and analysts raised expected earnings two years out, the median share price went up by 2.4 percent. However, when the companies beat the consensus and analysts lowered expected earnings two years out, the median share price declined by 0.6 percent. Conversely, when companies fell short on current earnings but analysts increased expected earnings two years out, the median share price went up by 1.5 percent.

Whether analysts raised or lowered expected earnings two years out was a more critical factor driving the share price than whether or not the company met analyst expectations in the current period.

---

*W. Kinney, D. Burgstahler, and R. Martin, "Earnings Surprise 'Materiality' as Measured by Stock Returns," *Journal of Accounting Research*, 40(5) (December 2002): 1297–1329.

EXHIBIT 9.4 **Long-Term Performance Expectations Drive Share Price**

Median abnormal return[1] on 595 announcements of fiscal-year earnings for 2007 by European companies, percent

		Negative	Positive
Change in long-term expectations (change in expected EPS for 2009)	Increase	1.5	2.4
	Decrease	−0.5	−0.6

Short-term surprise
(actual EPS 2007 relative to
expected EPS for 2007)

[1] Excess return over market return measured over a three-day interval following the earnings announcement.

Source: Bloomberg, McKinsey Corporate Performance Center analysis.

There is some evidence that the market places a premium value on companies that consistently surprise the market positively, but only when those companies surprise positively for several years in succession.* It takes more than one lucky shot in terms of an earnings surprise to gain a premium in the stock market. Firms that repeatedly exceed earnings expectations also show superior business performance in terms of profitability and growth in subsequent years.†

However, the longer a company surprises the market with its earnings, the harsher the market reacts once the pattern is broken. Although any premium in a company's valuation appears to build up gradually over a prolonged succession of positive earnings surprises, the premium is very rapidly lost when the market's confidence in ongoing outperformance evaporates.

The market turns out to be quite sophisticated in interpreting earnings announcements. For instance, markets don't respond favorably to earnings increases accompanied by high accruals: subsequent to

---

* R. Kasznik and M. McNichols, "Does Meeting Earnings Expectations Matter? Evidence from Analyst Forecast Revisions and Share Prices," *Journal of Accounting Research* 40, no. 3 (June 2002): 727–759.
† E. Bartov, D. Givoly, and C. Hayn, "The Rewards to Meeting or Beating Earnings Expectations," *Journal of Accounting and Economics* 33(2) (June 2002): 173–204.

such earnings reports, shareholder returns are poor relative to peers. The contribution of high accruals to earnings typically indicates that a company has reached a turning point and is facing lower earnings in the future.[*]

When you add it all up, the evidence points to companies spending too much senior management time trying to meet analyst earnings expectations, when they should be focused on the implications of short-term earnings for the long-term performance of the company. That said, companies shouldn't give investors the impression that internal controls and information flows are weak. We favor transparency about the drivers of performance gaps versus expectations. Think of it this way: if the investors could see what you are doing to meet the expectations number, would they approve?

EARNINGS VOLATILITY IS INEVITABLE

Conventional wisdom is that investors prefer smooth earnings growth and avoid companies with volatile earnings. Executives regularly cite stable earnings growth as a reason for strategic actions—such as when the CEO of Conoco justified its pending merger with Phillips Petroleum in part by asserting that the merger would offer greater earnings stability throughout the commodity price cycle. If investors really preferred smooth earnings, you would expect that companies with smooth earnings growth would generate higher TRS and have higher valuation multiples, everything else equal.

Using different techniques, company samples, and time frames, all the studies we examined reached the same conclusion:[†] There is no meaningful relationship between earnings variability and TRS or valuation multiples.

To illustrate these findings, Exhibit 9.5 compares the TRS of 135 companies with above-average earnings volatility to the TRS of

---

[*] K. Chan, L. Chan, N. Jegadeesh, and J. Lakonishok, "Earnings Quality and Stock Returns," *Journal of Business* 79(3) (2006): 1041–1082.

[†] See B. Rountree, J. Weston, and G. Allayannis, "Do Investors Value Smooth Performance?" *Journal of Financial Economics* 90(3) (December 2008): 237–251; J. McInnis, "Earnings Smoothness, Average Returns, and Implied Cost of Equity Capital," *Accounting Review* (January 2010); R. Barnes, "Earnings Volatility and Market Valuation: An Empirical Investigation," LBS Accounting Subject Area Working Paper ACCT 019 (2003).

EXHIBIT 9.5 **Earnings Volatility and TRS Not Linked**

Distribution of TRS[1] by earnings-growth-volatility[2] category, number of companies as a percentage of sample

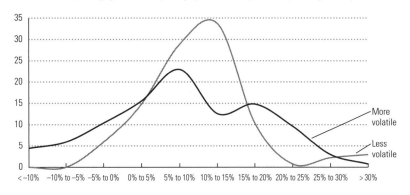

[1] 1997–2007 CAGR.
[2] Volatility is measured by the difference between the second-highest growth and the second-lowest growth during the 10-year period.
Source: McKinsey Corporate Performance Center analysis.

135 companies with below-average volatility. Although the median return of the low-volatility companies is higher than the high-volatility companies, the statistical significance of the difference disappears when we factor in growth and ROIC. More interesting, though, is the observation that there are plenty of low-volatility companies with low TRS, just as there are plenty of high-volatility companies with high returns. You can also see that there are more extreme TRS results with the high-volatility companies.

We believe investors realize the world of corporate performance isn't smooth. How could a company with 5 different businesses in 10 different countries achieve 10 percent earnings growth each year for years? The chances of unexpected positive results in one area exactly offsetting unexpected negative results are slim. The chances that each business performs exactly as planned are even slimmer.

Smooth earnings growth is a myth, as there are almost no companies that deliver this. Exhibit 9.6 shows five U.S. companies that are among the lowest 10 percent of all large companies in earnings growth volatility from 1998 to 2007. The first company is Walgreens, with remarkably stable earnings. From 2001 through 2007, Walgreens' annual earnings growth rate varied between 14 and 17 percent—seven

EXHIBIT 9.6 **Earnings Growth of Least Volatile Companies:**[1] **Not So Smooth**

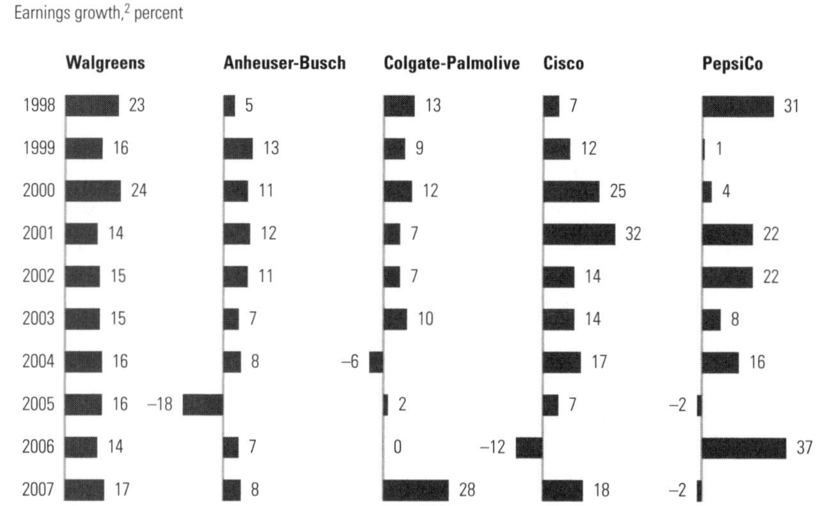

Earnings growth,[2] percent

	Walgreens	Anheuser-Busch	Colgate-Palmolive	Cisco	PepsiCo
1998	23	5	13	7	31
1999	16	13	9	12	1
2000	24	11	12	25	4
2001	14	12	7	32	22
2002	15	11	7	14	22
2003	15	7	10	14	8
2004	16	8	−6	17	16
2005	16	−18	2	7	−2
2006	14	7	0 −12		37
2007	17	8	28	18	−2

[1] These five least-volatile companies are drawn from the 500 largest, nonfinancial U.S. companies.
[2] Earnings is defined as net income before extraordinary items, adjusted for goodwill impairment.

Source: McKinsey Corporate Performance Center analysis.

years of virtually steady growth. But Walgreens is the only example. We looked at 500 other large companies and couldn't find a single one with seven years of such steady earnings growth. In fact, we could only find a handful of cases where earnings growth was steady for four or more years.

Most low-volatility companies follow patterns similar to the other four companies in Exhibit 9.6. Look at Anheuser-Busch, for example, which had four years of steady growth around 12 percent from 1999 to 2002. Then after 7 to 8 percent growth in 2003 and 2004, the company's earnings dropped 18 percent in 2005. This pattern is common. Of the 500 companies we examined, 460 of them had a least one year of earnings decline during the period.

Investors expect natural volatility associated with the industry in which a company participates. In some cases, like gold mining companies, they actually want exposure to changing gold prices. Companies, therefore, shouldn't try to reduce natural volatility, especially if it means reducing expenses like marketing and product development.

ACCOUNTING TREATMENT WON'T CHANGE UNDERLYING VALUE

Companies sometimes go to great lengths to secure a favorable accounting treatment, as evidenced by the battles over goodwill and employee stock options. But as we've established, sophisticated investors don't take reported earnings at face value; instead they try to ascertain the underlying economic performance of the company. Although we can't prove a negative (that accounting treatment doesn't matter) directly, we can show specific examples of how investors have seen through accounting results and focused on underlying economic performance.

One piece of evidence comes from companies that report different accounting results for different stock markets. Non-U.S. companies that have securities listed in the United States, for example, are required to report equity and net profit under U.S. Generally Accepted Accounting Principles (GAAP), which can differ significantly from the equity and net profit reported under their domestic accounting standards. If stock prices are truly based on reported earnings, which would investors choose—the earnings reported under U.S. GAAP or domestic accounting standards? To the market, it shouldn't matter. The market isn't interested in accounting choices; investors care about underlying performance.

To test this, we analyzed a sample of 50 European companies that began reporting reconciliations of equity and profit to U.S. GAAP after obtaining U.S. listings between 1997 and 2004. The differences between net income and equity under U.S. and local accounting standards were often quite large: in over half of the cases, the deviation was more than 30 percent.

Many executives probably worried that lower earnings under U.S. GAAP would translate directly to a lower share price, but this didn't materialize. Even though two-thirds of the companies in our sample reported lower earnings following U.S. disclosure, the stock market reaction to their disclosure was positive. Evidently, increased disclosure outweighed any artificial accounting effects.

Since 2001 under U.S. GAAP, and since 2005 under International Financial Reporting Standards (IFRS), goodwill is no longer amortized on the income statement according to fixed schedules. Instead, companies must write off goodwill only when the goodwill is impaired based on business valuations by independent auditors. What effect did changes in accounting for goodwill have on share prices? To answer this question, we looked at this accounting change's impact on share price in two ways.

First, we investigated the share-price reactions for companies that stopped amortizing significant amounts of goodwill. These companies would show an increase in reported EPS after this change, since goodwill amortization was no longer charged to the income statement.

We analyzed the share-price reaction for a sample of 54 U.S. companies with significant goodwill on the day of the announcement (July, 2001) that goodwill amortization in the United States would be abolished. Although these companies experienced a small initial boost in their share prices, the effect lasted less than two weeks. Furthermore, the initial share-price reaction was not related to the relative amount of goodwill amortization for these companies, and for about one-third of the sample the share price actually declined upon the announcement.

Second, we also looked at 54 companies in the United States and Europe that wrote off significant amounts of impaired goodwill against their profit since January 2002. We didn't find a statistically significant drop in share prices on the day of the write-off announcement. Why? The markets already had anticipated the lower benefits from past acquisitions and had reduced the stock price by an average of 35 percent in the six months preceding the write-off announcement.

As for the debate over whether employee stock options should be expensed in the income statement, much of the concern centers on whether the negative earnings impact would drive stock prices lower. From a capital market perspective, the answer is clear: as long as investors have sufficient information on the amount, terms, and conditions of the options granted, new expensing rules will not drive down share prices. In fact, according to a recent study, companies that voluntarily began expensing their employee options *before* it became mandatory experienced positive share-price reactions when they announced their intentions to expense options, despite the negative impact on reported earnings.*

The price reaction was especially strong when companies said they were expensing their options to boost transparency. The same researchers found that when sufficient information about the options

* D. Aboody, M. Barth, and R. Kasznik, "Firms' Voluntary Recognition of Stock-Based Compensation Expense," *Journal of Accounting Research*, 42(2) (December 2004): 251–275.

is disclosed, the stock market includes the options' values in its valuation of the companies, even when these values are not explicitly expensed in the income statement.*

Companies would save significant time and energy if they assume that investors are just as smart as they are, and do not try to smooth earnings.

---

* D. Aboody, M. Barth, and R. Kasznik, "SFAS No. 123 Stock-Based Compensation Expense and Equity Market Values," *Accounting Review*, 79(2) (2004): 251–275.

Part Three

Managing Value Creation

10

Return on Capital

As we've been discussing, return on capital is one of the two core drivers of value creation. Yet it's surprising to us how often executives can't identify the one or two factors that most influence their company's ROIC—namely, what is the business's competitive advantage and how is it affected by the industry's structure and competitive behavior? These companies are likely missing value creation opportunities.

This chapter explores how competitive advantage, industry structure, and competitor behavior drive ROIC: why some companies earn 10 percent returns while others earn 50 percent returns. We also provide a historical context for ROIC trends, such as how they vary across industries and how they fluctuate or persist over time.

To illustrate, let's go back to the height of the tech boom with two newcomers at the time, eBay and Webvan, a California-based grocery delivery company. In November 1999, eBay's market capitalization was $23 billion, while Webvan's was $8 billion. eBay continued to prosper while Webvan disappeared. Analyzing the potential competitive advantage in their strategies would have shown that eBay was destined for success and Webvan was doomed.

Let's look at eBay's strategy. Its core business is online auctions that collect a small amount of money for each transaction between a buyer and a seller. The business requires little capital for managing its web site and facilitating transactions, needing just some computers but no inventories or accounts receivable.

Once started, as long as the site works well and the fees are modest, potential buyers and sellers have incentives to use it. As more buyers use eBay, it attracts more sellers, which in turn again attracts more buyers. In addition, the marginal cost of each additional buyer or seller is close to zero.

Once eBay's business got going and it was providing good service at a reasonable price, customers had little reason to switch to a new entrant. Therefore, eBay maintains a substantial competitive advantage and, not surprisingly, earns returns on capital exceeding 50 percent.

eBay is an example of an increasing returns to scale business that we described in Chapter 1. In such a business, the first competitor to get big often attracts the bulk of revenues and profits (the winner take all effect). Webvan and others assumed that they, too, could benefit from increasing returns to scale by getting big before their competitors. Webvan quickly spent more than $1 billion building warehouses and buying trucks. But increasing returns to scale didn't apply to Webvan's business, so it couldn't earn the high ROIC that eBay earned.

Here's why. The Webvan business model was capital intensive with substantial warehouses, trucks, and inventory. On top of this, Webvan was selling the very same thin-margin products found in local grocery stores, so it had to keep its prices in line with those stores. When it began, Webvan provided free delivery for orders over $50 and charged only $4.95 for smaller orders. But given the high cost of delivering to customers in specific locations during specific time frames, Webvan eventually raised its threshold for free delivery to $100 and raised fees for smaller orders. In the end, the higher costs of delivery, including picking and packaging, more than offset the savings from not having physical stores.

Finally, Webvan's business wasn't economically scalable, especially compared with a company like eBay, which adds new customers at a near zero cost. Although Webvan may not have needed to add more warehouses as they added customers, the company did need more food pickers, trucks, and drivers to meet increased demand.

So where was the competitive advantage? Webvan hoped to deter other grocery delivery businesses from entering the market by establishing itself first, and its planned competitive advantage was based on this deterrence. But other delivery companies weren't its primary competitors, while other grocery stores were. Webvan couldn't price its service high enough to cover its substantial operating costs without losing customers to the grocery stores.

While eBay created both an attractive industry structure and a capital efficient business that permitted high returns, Webvan entered an industry with a highly competitive industry structure—grocery retailing—that was bound to keep returns on capital modest. Webvan had no competitive advantage versus the grocery stores. This example highlights just how difficult it is to escape poor industry structure, and just how damaging the millstone of high capital intensity can be.

WHAT DRIVES RETURN ON CAPITAL?

We'll use a simple formula to show the linkage between strategy and ROIC in the context of an industry's structure and behavior. If one thinks about the ROIC for a business on a per-unit basis, one can define it as follows:

$$\text{Return on Capital} = \frac{\text{Operating Profit}}{\text{Capital}} = \frac{\text{Price} - \text{Cost}}{\text{Capital}}$$

A company that has a competitive advantage earns a higher ROIC because it either charges a price premium or it produces its products more efficiently (having lower costs or capital per unit)—or both. Between the two, price premiums offer the greatest opportunity to achieve an attractive ROIC, but price premiums are more difficult to achieve than cost efficiencies.

Because providing a general strategy framework is beyond the scope of this book, we'll focus on characterizing the most common examples of competitive advantage (and high ROIC). The strategy model that drives this thinking is the Structure-Conduct-Performance (SCP) model, originally developed in the 1930s by Edward Mason but not widely influential in business until Michael Porter published *Competitive Strategy* in 1980 along with his *five forces*.* Although there have been extensions of the model since then, the core framework is probably still the most widely used way of thinking about strategy.

The SCP model says that the structure of an industry influences the conduct of the competitors, which in turn drives the performance of

---

* John Stuckey, "Perspectives on Strategy" (McKinsey staff paper, no. 62, April 2005); Michael Porter, *Competitive Strategy: Techniques for Analyzing Industries and Competitors* (New York: Free Press, 1980).

the companies in the industry. The structure of the industry is defined by the five forces: barriers to entry, substitution threat, buyer power, supplier power, and rivalry determinants (such as industry concentration, switching costs, barriers to exit, fixed/variable cost structures, and others). The behavior (conduct) of the competitors is the final driver of performance.

The importance—and stickiness—of industry structure is demonstrated by Exhibit 10.1, which displays the median returns on capital for 29 industries, as well as the 25th and 75th percentiles.

The high-ROIC industries tend to be those with attractive industry structures.* For example, household and personal products companies have developed long-lasting brands that make it difficult for new competitors to gain a foothold. The companies also tend to compete for shelf space on factors other than just price.

The low-ROIC industries, such as paper products, are those with undifferentiated products, high capital intensity, and fewer opportunities for innovation (in paper everyone uses the same paper machines). This makes it difficult at best for any competitor to charge a price premium or to build a sustainable cost advantage.

Although industry structure is probably the most important driver of competitive advantage and returns on capital, the difference in company returns within the same industry shows that companies can sometimes create competitive advantages in low-return industries; it also shows that companies can operate at a competitive disadvantage in high-return industries.

For instance, automakers have been plagued for years with overcapacity because new entrants aren't deterred by the industry's low returns (think Korea's entry into the U.S. market), and because unionized plants don't close easily. Nevertheless, Toyota has managed to stand out because of its efficiencies, and because its reputation for quality allows it to charge a price premium in the U.S. market relative to domestic manufacturers.

The auto industry demonstrates that competitive advantage is often market specific. Toyota and the other Japanese producers can charge price premiums in the United States, where they compete with

---

* Some of the variation in returns is due to data limitations because many of the companies are in multiple subindustries, and the definitions are broad. But there are examples of companies earning attractive returns in industries where the median return is low (e.g., Wal-Mart and Intel), and vice versa.

EXHIBIT 10.1 **ROIC Variations across and within Industries**

ROIC, without goodwill (percent)

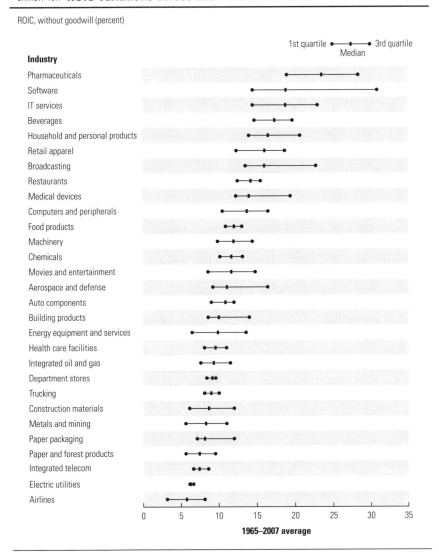

Source: Compustat, McKinsey Corporate Performance Center analysis.

American producers, but not in Japan, where they compete only with each other.

Finally, industry structure and competitive behavior aren't fixed; they're subject to shocks of technological innovation, changes in government regulation, and competitive entry—any or all of which can affect an entire industry or just individual companies. This is why the software industry might consistently earn high returns, but the leading companies may not be the same in 20 years, just as the leaders today were not major players 20 years ago.

The other construct to keep in mind is that we're really talking about specific business units, product lines, and market segments—not companies at large—because this is the only way to gain traction in strategic thinking. Even a business like soup or dog food might have subsegments with very different competitive dynamics.

That said, price-premium advantages can be disaggregated into five subcategories, and cost and capital efficiency advantages can be disaggregated into four subcategories, as summarized in the table that follows.

Price Premium	Cost/Capital Efficiency
Innovative products—Difficult-to-copy or patent-protected products, services, or technologies. **Quality**—Real or perceived difference in quality over and above competing products or services. **Brand**—Brand price premium over and above any innovation or quality differences. **Customer lock-in**—Difficult for customers to replace a product or service with a competing product or service. **Rational price discipline**—Transparent behavior by industry leaders in capacity management and pricing policy.	**Innovative business methods**—Difficult to copy business methods that contrast with established industry practice. **Unique resources**—Unique location (e.g., geological, transport) characteristics or unique access to a raw material(s). **Economies of scale**—Scale in targeted activities or local markets. **Scalability/Flexibility**—Adding customers and increasing or redirecting capacity at negligible marginal cost.

Innovative Products/Services

Innovative products and services that yield high returns on capital are either protected by patents or are difficult and expensive to copy, or both. Without at least one of these protections (patented or difficult to copy), even an innovative product won't do much to enable persistently high returns.

Pharmaceutical companies earn high returns because they produce innovative products that, even if easy to copy, are protected by patents for up to 20 years. These companies can charge premium prices, reflecting their innovations, until generic suppliers enter with lower prices at the time of patent expiry.

Apple's iPod is a good example of a difficult to copy product that isn't patent protected (at least not the core technology). MP3 players had been on the market for many years before Apple introduced its line of iPod products, which have captured more than a 70 percent share of the MP3 market. Even though the core MP3 technology is the same for all competitors, the iPod has been successful because of its appealing design, ease of use, user interface, and integration with Apple's music store, iTunes.

Quality

A term as broadly used as *quality* requires definition first. In the context of competitive advantage and ROIC, quality is the real or perceived difference between one product or service and another, and the willingness of customers to pay a higher price for it. In the car business, BMW enjoys a price premium due to the perception among customers that its cars handle and drive better than comparable products that cost less. Yet the cost to provide the extra quality is much less than the price premium. This is one of the reasons why BMW has earned higher returns than most other carmakers.

Sometimes the perception of quality lasts significantly longer than the reality does, as is the case with Toyota and Honda relative to General Motors, Ford, and Chrysler. Although today American and Japanese cars are comparable in terms of quantifiable quality measures, such as the JD Power survey, companies like Toyota still extract a price premium for their products.* Even though the American and Japanese sticker prices on similar vehicles might be the same, American manufacturers are often forced to sell at $2,000 to $3,000 below sticker price.

Brand

Price premiums based on brand are often highly correlated with price premiums based on quality. Although the quality of a product may

---

* At the time of writing, we don't know whether the negative publicity in early 2010 about Toyota's gas pedals will have a longer-term effect.

matter more than its established branding, sometimes the brand itself is what matters more, especially when the brand has persisted for a very long time (for instance, Coca-Cola, Perrier, Mercedes-Benz).

Packaged food is a good example of where branded products are important. In some categories like breakfast cereal (think Cheerios), customers are very loyal to their brands, but in other categories, like meat, branding hasn't been successful. As a result, cereal companies earn returns on capital greater than 30 percent, while most meat processors earn returns of less than 15 percent. You might expect that brands would be more important with meat, because meat quality is more variable than cereal quality, but this is not the case.

Similarly, teens are willing to pay higher prices for clothes with logos like Abercrombie & Fitch and Juicy Couture, despite the fact that they can buy clothes with similar quality and style at lower prices.

Once developed, brand loyalty can last a long time. The father of one of this book's authors had been loyal to General Motors for over 50 years, despite acknowledging its declining quality relative to Japanese brands. It took until 2005 for him to switch and purchase a Japanese brand (Nissan's Infiniti).

Customer Lock-In

When it is costly or inconvenient for customers to replace your product or service with another one, your company can charge a price premium—if not for the initial sale, then at least for additional units, or for subsequent generations and iterations of the original product.

A medical device like a stent, for instance, can achieve customer lock-in because it takes doctors time to become trained and proficient with the device. Once doctors are up to speed on a particular stent, they won't switch to a competing product unless there is a very compelling reason for making that new investment, such as improved patient outcomes.

Although basically an older technology, Bloomberg financial terminals lead the market because of high switching costs. Bankers and traders have invested considerable time learning how to work with the Bloomberg terminals and are reluctant to learn another system. An installed base like Bloomberg's presents a difficult challenge for competitors.

Rational Price Discipline

In commodity industries with many competitors, the laws of supply and demand work to drive down prices and returns on capital. This applies not just to conventional commodities like chemicals and paper, but also to such commodities as airline seats. It would only take an increase in airline ticket prices of 5 to 10 percent to turn the industry's aggregate losses to an aggregate profit, but each competitor is tempted to get an edge in filling seats by refusing to raise prices, even when costs like fuel go up for all competitors.

Every once in a while, we find an industry that is able to overcome the forces of competition and set prices at a level to earn reasonable returns (but rarely more than 15 percent) without resorting to illegal methods. For example, for many years, almost all real estate agents in the United States charged a six percent commission on the price of the homes they sold. In other cases, disciplined pricing is sanctioned by the government through its regulatory structure. For example, until the 1970s, airline fares in the United States were high because competitors were restricted from entering each other's markets. Prices collapsed with deregulation in 1978.

Rational, legitimate price discipline typically works when one competitor acts as the leader and the others quickly replicate its price moves. In general, disciplined competitive behavior only works when there are few competitors, typically four or fewer. In addition, there must be barriers to new entrants, and each competitor must be large enough so that price wars reduce the profit on their existing volume more than the extra volume from any new sales. If the smaller competitors have more to gain in volume than lose from lower prices, it's very difficult for the industry to maintain price discipline. Finally, it helps if prices are transparent to all competitors, so everyone knows when someone attempts to undercut prices.

Most attempts at disciplined price behavior fail. Take the paper industry for example. Returns on capital have averaged less than 10 percent from 1965 to 2007. The industry creates its own problem because the companies all tend to expand at the same time (after demand and prices have risen). As a result, a large block of new capacity comes on line at the same time, upsetting the supply-demand balance and forcing down prices and returns.

One strategy researcher summed up the question of how many competitors matter as follows, "Industries with only two competitors avoid damaging competition; industries with six or more competitors might as well have twice that number because they will have great difficulty behaving cooperatively; industries with three to five competitors can go either way, and that way will vary over time."[*]

Even cartels (which are illegal in most of the world) find it difficult to maintain discipline. OPEC members continually cheat on their quotas leading to periodic price declines. Without the discipline of Saudi Arabia, the largest producer, the cartel would find it even more difficult to maintain oil prices.

Innovative Business Methods

A company's business method is the combination of its production, logistics, and how the product or service is delivered to the customer. Most production methods can be copied, but some are difficult to copy quickly enough. For example, early in its life Dell put together a new way of making and distributing personal computers, when competitors like HP and Compaq led the market selling through retailers. Instead, Dell made its machines to order with virtually no inventory, also receiving payments from customers as soon as products shipped, thereby enabling it to operate with little invested capital. Dell was successful in large part because all the big competitors were already beholden to their retail distribution business models, that is, they built ahead of time, then sold to their resellers. Given this, they couldn't easily switch to a direct sales model without angering their retailers.

But the success formula in today's PC market has shifted away from the clear advantage Dell once had, because notebook computers (instead of desktops) now dominate. Dell's build-to-order model was more advantageous when assembling machines with standardized parts that could be purchased from different suppliers at different times at very low cost. Notebook computers, by contrast, are built to much tighter part specifications, often via vendors that make the parts specifically for Dell. Since everything has to fit together just right, Dell in turn needs more support from its vendors and can't pressure them and switch them out so easily on the basis of cost alone.

The best business-method innovations make it difficult for existing competitors to adapt. Ultraviolet pool cleaning, for instance, has the potential to substantially reduce the cost of cleaning pools and nearly

---

[*] John Stuckey, "Perspectives on Strategy" (McKinsey internal staff paper, July 2005).

eliminates the need for chlorine. Existing competitors (pool cleaners, chlorine makers) will have difficulty adjusting to the new way that ultraviolet cleaning streamlines the water treatment process.

Unique Resources

Sometimes a company has access to a unique resource that can't be replicated, which gives it a significant cost advantage. A typical example would be a mine whose ore is richer than most other ore bodies. Take two nickel mining companies, Norilsk Nickel, which produces nickel in northern Siberia, and Vale, which produces nickel in South America. Norilsk Nickel has significantly higher precious metal content (e.g., palladium) in its nickel ore compared with Vale's. In other words, it gets not only nickel from its ore but also some high-priced palladium. As a result, Norilsk earned a pretax return on capital of 67 percent in 2007 compared with Vale's 25 percent on its nickel business. (Note that 2007 was a year of high nickel prices.)

Geography often plays a role when it comes to unique resources. In general, whenever the cost of shipping a product is high relative to the value of the product (e.g., cement or salt), producers near customers have a unique advantage.

Economies of Scale

This notion is often misunderstood, as there are no automatic economies that come with size. Scale can be important, but usually only insofar as it operates at the local level, not the national or global level. For example, if you're a retailer, it's much more important to be large in one city than to be large across the country because warehousing and local advertising costs (and other costs) are fixed at the local level. Buying airtime ad space in Chicago is the same whether you have 1 store or 10.

A profitability driver for health insurers in the United States is their ability to negotiate prices with providers (hospitals and doctors), who tend to operate locally rather than nationally. The insurer with the highest market share in a local market will be in a position to negotiate better prices, regardless of its national market share. In other words, it's better to be number one in 10 states, than to be number one nationwide but number four in every market.

Size or scale can work against you as well. In the 1980s, UPS was attacked by RPS, another package delivery service that differentiated its business and pricing, offering significant discounts for commercial customers in highly populated areas. Meanwhile, UPS only offered modest volume discounts, charging generally the same for each of, say, 10 packages delivered to an office building as it did for delivering one package to a residence. In essence, RPS was picking off high-margin business from UPS, and UPS's grand scale did little to prevent this. RPS teaches that what matters is having the right scale in the right market.

Scalability/Flexibility

A business is scalable or flexible when the cost to serve additional customers is very low, and usually this entails the delivery of products and services through the use of information technology.

Consider ADP, which provides payroll-processing and related services to small- and medium-sized businesses. All customers are on the same computers and software, so adding additional customers involves negligible cost—a highly scalable business model that allows margins to increase as ADP grows. Likewise, such companies as eBay and products like Microsoft Office add customers at miniscule incremental cost.

Other examples of scalable businesses include media companies that make and distribute movies or TV shows. Making the movie or show requires spending for the crew, sets, actors, and so on. But those costs are fixed regardless of how many people end up viewing (and paying for) the show. There may be some incremental advertising costs, and very small costs associated with putting the movie on a DVD (or streaming it), but, overall, costs don't rise as customers increase.

This isn't to say that all IT-based or IT-enabled businesses are scalable. Many operate more like consulting firms (which are not scalable), whereby they incur costs to service each specific contract with clients, and these costs mount as the number of clients increases. For example, many companies that maintain data centers do so on a cost-plus basis by adding people, equipment, and facilities as they add new clients.

RETURN ON CAPITAL SUSTAINABILITY

Central to value creation is understanding the sustainability of ROIC. The longer a company can sustain a high ROIC the more value it will

EXHIBIT 10.2 **Persistence of Industry ROICs**

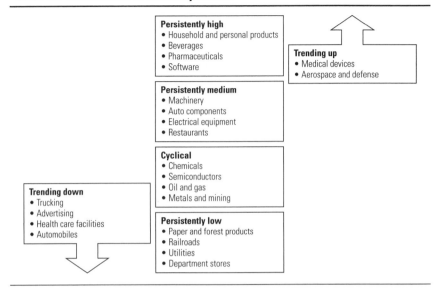

create. In a perfectly competitive economy, returns on capital over the cost of capital eventually get competed away. But in real economies, high-, medium- and low-ROIC companies (and industries) tend to remain so, even over longer time frames.

We ranked the returns on capital across industries over the past 45 years and found that most industries stayed in the same group (high, medium, and low) over that period, as shown by Exhibit 10.2.

Persistently high-return industries included household and personal products, beverages, pharmaceuticals, and software. As you'd expect, these industries have consistently high returns because they're protected by brands or patents, or they're scalable (software). We also see persistently low returns in paper and forest products, railroads, utilities, and department stores. These are commodity industries in which price premiums are difficult to achieve (because of low entry barriers, commodity products, or returns that are regulated). Yes, department stores behave like commodity industries with little price differentiation and, therefore, realize persistently low returns as a rule. Some industries are cyclical, with returns up at certain times and down at others, but overall these industries don't demonstrate a clear trend up or down over time.

As theory would suggest, we did find a number of industries where there was a clear downward trend in returns. These included trucking, advertising, health care facilities, and automobiles. Competition in trucking, advertising, and automobiles has increased substantially over the past five decades. For-profit health care facilities have had their prices squeezed by the government, insurers, and competition with nonprofits.

Industries with returns on capital clearly trending up are rare. Two clear examples are medical devices and aerospace/defense. Innovation in medical devices has led the industry toward higher value-added, differentiated products like stents and artificial joints, and away from more commoditized products like syringes and forceps. We wouldn't expect aerospace and defense to have increased returns on capital, but upon deeper examination, we found that companies in this sector have reduced capital intensity as they've gained more contracts for which the government provides up-front funding. So the higher ROIC has been driven by a lower capital base.

In general, advantages that rise from brand and quality on the price side, and scalability on the cost side, tend to have more staying power than those rising from more temporal sources of advantage, like innovation (which tends to be surpassed by newer innovations). Also, we have to add the factor of product life cycle into our thinking; although Cheerios isn't as exciting as some innovative, new technology, the likelihood of obsolescence for the culturally-engrained, branded cereal is low. After a new technology is obsolete or replaced, Cheerios will remain a stalwart brand.

Along these lines, a unique resource can be a durable source of advantage if it's related to a long product life cycle, but not as advantageous if it isn't. Similarly, a business model that locks customers into a product with a short life cycle is far less valuable than one that locks customers in for a long time.

There's also evidence of sustainability of return differentials at the company level. The transition probabilities in Exhibit 10.3 measure the probability that a company will stay in the same ROIC group or migrate to another group in 10 years. Reading across the chart, of the companies that earned less than 10 percent ROIC in 1995, 57 percent earned less than 10 percent 10 years later, 28 percent earned 10–20 percent, and 15 percent earned more than 20 percent.

These results show that high-ROIC companies tend to maintain their high returns, and low-ROIC companies tend to retain their low returns. We've looked at this over earlier time periods as well and found similar results, except that fewer of the lower-return companies

EXHIBIT 10.3 **ROIC Transition Probability, 1995–2005**

Probability that company's ROIC will be in given group in 2005, percent

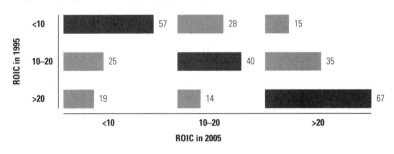

Source: Compustat, McKinsey Corporate Performance Center analysis.

improved to a higher group. The 1995–2005 period may be unusual in that the median company increased its return on capital, a phenomenon we'll discuss in more detail in the next section.

If a company finds a strategy that earns an attractive ROIC, there's a good chance it will earn that attractive return over time and through changing economic, industry, and company conditions, especially if it has longer rather than shorter product life cycles. The converse is also true (if a company earns a low return on capital, that will persist too).

Although competition clearly plays a major role in driving ROIC, managers can extend the persistence of returns by anticipating and responding to changes in the environment better than competitors do. Procter & Gamble has a strong record of continuing to introduce successful new products like Swiffer, Febreze, and Crest Whitestrips. It also anticipated the strong growth in beauty products with a number of acquisitions that increased its revenues in the area from $7.3 billion to $19.5 billion, and advanced it from the owner of just one billion-dollar brand (sales) in 1999 to eight in 2008.

TRENDS IN RETURNS ON CAPITAL

As you would expect in a competitive economy, median returns on capital are close to the cost of capital. The median ROIC for large U.S.-based companies from 1963 to 2008 was about 10 percent. Stripping out the high-inflation years, that's about two percentage points higher than the median cost of capital for these companies. Competition has done

EXHIBIT 10.4 **U.S.-Based Nonfinancial Companies: ROIC, 1963–2008**

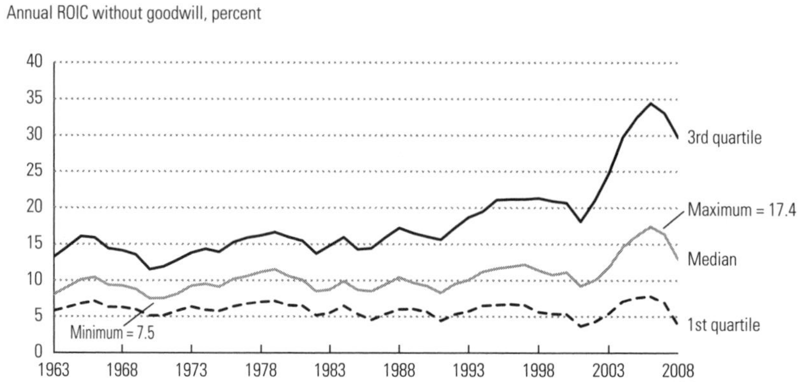

Annual ROIC without goodwill, percent

Source: Compustat, McKinsey Corporate Performance Center analysis.

its job of wringing out much of the economic surplus from companies for the benefit of consumers.

Median returns were stable until about 2004, as shown by Exhibit 10.4. Until 2004, a company had to earn a return greater than 10 percent to be in the top half and above 18–20 percent to be in the top quartile. In recent years, however, a company had to earn a return greater than 17 percent to be above the median, and a return above about 25 percent to be in the top quartile.*

Exhibit 10.5 looks at this trend in ROIC from a different perspective. Here we look at the distribution of companies across different ROIC ranges for three points in time, in the 1960s, the 1990s, and the 2000s. As you can see from Exhibit 10.5, most companies earned between 5 and 20 percent returns over the past 50 years. What has changed recently, however, is the number of companies earning very high returns. In the 1960s only one percent of companies earned returns greater than 50 percent, whereas, in the 2000s, 14 percent of companies earned such high returns.

The increase in companies with high ROIC raises the questions about whether the new higher median reflects a permanent shift in the economics of companies, or whether it merely reflects the temporary

---

* The numbers in the section are based on U.S. companies because longer-term data for non-U.S. companies isn't readily available. In recent years, the global distribution of returns and the U.S. distribution have been very similar.

EXHIBIT 10.5 **Distribution of ROIC: Shifting to the Right**

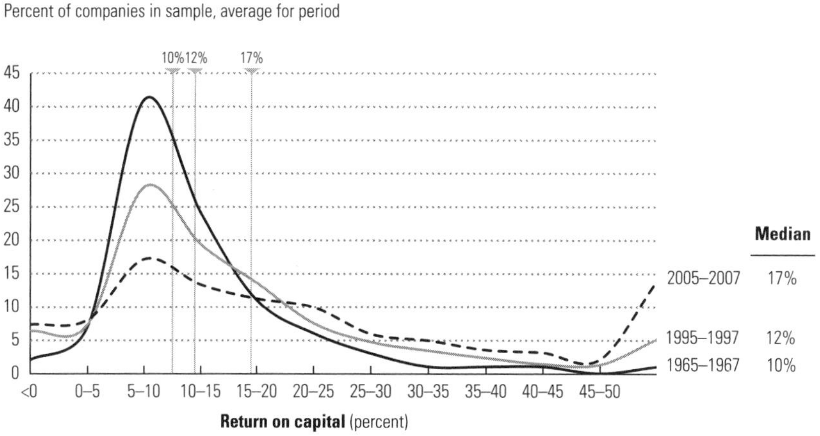
Percent of companies in sample, average for period
10% 12% 17%
45
40
35
30
25
20
15
10
5
0
<0
0–5
5–10
10–15
15–20
20–25
25–30
30–35
35–40
40–45
45–50
Return on capital (percent)
Median
2005–2007 17%
1995–1997 12%
1965–1967 10%

Source: Compustat, McKinsey Corporate Performance Center analysis.

strength of the economy in the mid-2000s. We can get some clues about the answer by examining how the returns have changed by industry as shown in Exhibit 10.6.

Although many industries have increased their ROIC in recent years, some of the increases are probably cyclical and not sustainable. Commodity price-driven industries like energy, metals, mining, and chemicals have all benefited from high commodity prices in the mid-2000s that subsequently declined in the recession.

Other industries however, particularly those at the top of the list, may have experienced fundamental increases in returns. We already mentioned the reasons for increasing returns in medical devices, and in aerospace and defense. But the increase in ROIC for pharmaceutical companies could be threatened as sophisticated customers exercise more bargaining power and as health care reform downwardly pressures prices. In addition, software and IT services might be able to keep their high returns because they tend to have low capital requirements and are often scalable businesses.

The extent to which companies are in capital-light industries (like software) will tend to keep the overall median ROIC high, but this will be offset by declines in commodity-oriented industries and health care. In any case, companies need to think about where returns will settle

EXHIBIT 10.6 **ROIC Trends across Industries**

Industry median ROIC without goodwill, percent

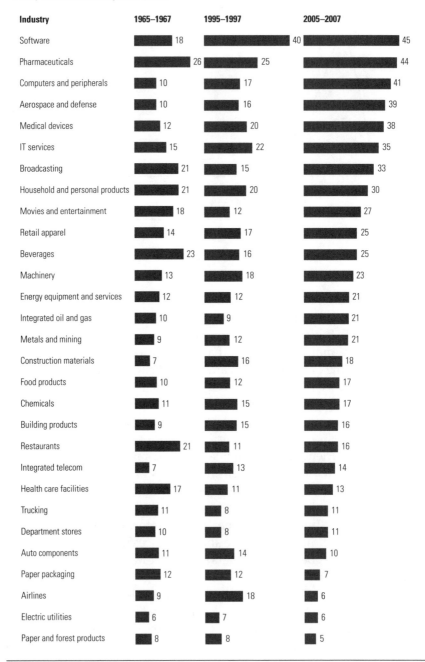

Industry	1965–1967	1995–1997	2005–2007
Software	18	40	45
Pharmaceuticals	26	25	44
Computers and peripherals	10	17	41
Aerospace and defense	10	16	39
Medical devices	12	20	38
IT services	15	22	35
Broadcasting	21	15	33
Household and personal products	21	20	30
Movies and entertainment	18	12	27
Retail apparel	14	17	25
Beverages	23	16	25
Machinery	13	18	23
Energy equipment and services	12	12	21
Integrated oil and gas	10	9	21
Metals and mining	9	12	21
Construction materials	7	16	18
Food products	10	12	17
Chemicals	11	15	17
Building products	9	15	16
Restaurants	21	11	16
Integrated telecom	7	13	14
Health care facilities	17	11	13
Trucking	11	8	11
Department stores	10	8	11
Auto components	11	14	10
Paper packaging	12	12	7
Airlines	9	18	6
Electric utilities	6	7	6
Paper and forest products	8	8	5

Source: Compustat, McKinsey Corporate Performance Center analysis.

for their industries so they can set the right targets and make the right investments.

Another trend in return on capital is the impact of acquisitions. When a company acquires another company, the difference between the price it pays and the value of its underlying assets (property, plant and equipment, and working capital) is recorded as an asset called *goodwill*. Of course, goodwill is not an asset in the sense that you can touch it or sell it. Goodwill merely reflects part of the price paid on which the acquiring company needs to earn a return.

We're often asked whether to include goodwill when computing a company's ROIC. Our answer is that you need to use both measures because they give you insights on different aspects of company performance. ROIC excluding goodwill reflects the underlying economics of an industry or company. ROIC including goodwill reflects whether management has been able to extract value from acquisitions.

Exhibit 10.7 shows the ROIC with and without goodwill for more than 4,000 nonfinancial companies. Although returns without goodwill have been increasing remarkably, returns with goodwill have been flat, suggesting that these companies haven't been able to extract much value from their acquisitions. This isn't to say that they haven't improved the performance of the acquired businesses. In fact, when we look deeper we see significant realized synergies. However, these companies paid high prices for their acquisitions, so most of the value

EXHIBIT 10.7 **ROIC with Goodwill Is Flat**

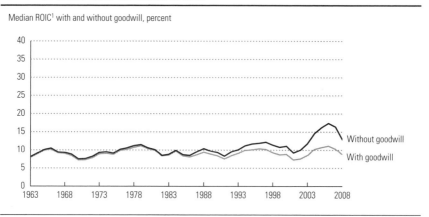

Median ROIC[1] with and without goodwill, percent

[1] For large nonfinancial companies.

Source: Compustat, McKinsey Corporate Performance Center analysis.

creation was transferred to the shareholders of the target company. (We discuss acquisitions and value creation more in Chapter 13.)

RETURN ON CAPITAL IS STILL RELEVANT

Some have argued that return on capital has become irrelevant because the economy has shifted to businesses without much physical capital. We now have an economy where access to talent and intellectual property is more important than access to capital. It's true that access to capital often isn't a scarce resource, even in the tight credit environment. If you've got a good idea, it's relatively easy to raise the money you need to start your business.

But it's not access to capital that matters (maybe it mattered before 1960); it's competition that matters. Just as it did in the 1960s, competition still puts downward pressure on ROIC. During the period 1963 to 2008, worker productivity increased 3.5 times in the United States and even faster outside the country. The reason returns haven't increased is because competition shifts the benefits of innovation and productivity to consumers in the form of lower prices, and to workers in the form of higher wages. As a result, fully 60 percent of companies still earned less than 20 percent ROIC in the boom years of 2005–2007.

Given that return on capital does still matter, it's important to develop a point of view about what your company can and should earn, according to its competitive position and strategy. Are returns stable, increasing, or decreasing in the industry as a whole? What is the outlook for the industry and for your company, given your strategy and given what you know about your competitors?

11

Growth

The business world is obsessed with growth. There's a sense that to thrive, a company has to grow—and there's some truth to this. For example, slower-growth companies may generate fewer opportunities for people and may, therefore, have difficulty attracting and retaining talent. Slow growing companies are much more likely to be acquired than faster growing companies. Over the past 25 years, 340 companies have left the S&P 500 index, most because they were swallowed up by larger companies.

But growth doesn't lead to higher value creation, as we discussed in Chapter 2, unless returns on capital are adequate. For example, among 64 companies with low ROIC, those that grew at above-average rates but didn't improve their ROIC, earned 4 percent lower shareholder returns per year over 10 years than companies that grew below average but improved their ROIC.*

Growth is undeniably a critical driver of value creation, but different types of growth come with different returns on capital and, therefore, create different amounts of value. For example, growth from creating whole new product categories tends to create more value than growth from pricing and promotion tactics to gain market share from peers. Just as executives need to understand whether their strategies will lead to high returns on capital, as we discussed in Chapter 10, they also need to know which growth opportunities will create the highest value.

* Bin Jiang and Timothy Koller, "How to Choose between Growth and ROIC," *McKinsey on Finance*, no. 25 (Autumn 2007): 19–22.

DIFFERENT GROWTH CREATES DIFFERENT VALUE

Revenue growth comes in four types: market-share increases, price increases, growth in an underlying market, and acquisitions.* Each type can be further broken down into subtypes; for instance, you can increase market share by either lowering prices or improving efforts to market and sell your product or service. Additionally, the competitive structure and behavior of an industry will affect the value created from each type of growth. So the variations of growth types and their value impact can be enormous.

A useful way to assess the value creation potential from a specific type of growth is to examine who loses when a company grows revenues, and how the losers can respond or retaliate.

For example, attempts to increase market share through price competition comes at the expense of competitors. If those competitors are strong enough to retaliate, or even just hang on for the duration of the price war, then the growth associated with the increased market share probably won't create much value; if price discounting becomes the norm, this may even reduce value. On the other hand, increasing market share by more effective marketing or sales will create more value if the competitors can't retaliate in kind.

Similarly, price increases by all competitors come at the expense of customers, pressuring them to either reduce consumption or look for substitute products. Therefore, price increases, like market share increases, won't create much value unless customers don't have a good option to reduce consumption or find substitutes.

Of all growth categories, high growth in the underlying product market tends to create the most value because it comes at the expense of companies in other industries, which might not even know to whom they're losing share. These companies have the least ability to retaliate.

The value of growth from acquisitions tends to be low because the underlying value of the growth is offset by the acquisition price as we discuss more in Chapter 13.

In Exhibit 11.1 we rank different types of growth in a greater level of detail, but they still fall into the four basic buckets. This ranking

---

* Patrick Viguerie, Sven Smit, and Mehrdad Baghai, *The Granularity of Growth: How to Identify the Sources of Growth and Drive Enduring Company Performance* (Hoboken, NJ: John Wiley & Sons, 2008).

EXHIBIT 11.1 **Value of Different Types of Growth**

Value created[1]	Type of growth	Rationale
↑ Above average ↓	• Create new markets through new products • Convince existing customers to buy more of a product • Attract new customers to the market	• No established competitors; diverts customer spending • All competitors benefit; low risk of retaliation • All competitors benefit; low risk of retaliation
↑ Average ↓	• Gain market share in fast-growing market • Make bolt-on acquisitions to accelerate product growth	• Competitors can still grow despite losing share; moderate risk of retaliation • Modest acquisition premium relative to upside potential
↑ Below average ↓	• Gain share from rivals through incremental innovation • Gain share from rivals through product promotion and pricing • Make large acquisitions	• Competitors can replicate and take back customers • Competitors can retaliate quickly • High premium to pay; most value diverted to selling shareholders

[1] Per dollar of revenue.

may not be exactly the same for all industries, but it works well as a starting point.

At the very top are variations of fast-growing markets that take revenues from distant industries, not direct competitors or customers, usually entailing some form of innovation that creates entirely new product categories. For example, the coronary stent reduced the need for surgery, lowering both the risk and cost of treating cardiac problems. Traditional treatments and surgery could not retaliate. Another example is the way consumers have shifted from television viewing to Internet usage and video games. Traditional television cannot compete with the interactivity of the Internet and video games.

The next highest value created is getting current customers to buy more of a product or related products. For example, if Procter & Gamble convinces customers to wash their hands more frequently, the market for hand soap will accelerate—and direct competitors won't retaliate because they benefit as well. The ROIC associated with the additional revenue is likely to be high because the manufacturing and distribution systems can typically absorb the additional sales at little additional cost. But the benefit might not be as large if the company has to increase costs substantially to get those sales. For example, getting bank customers to buy insurance products requires an entirely new sales force because the products are more complex than the list of products the bankers are already selling.

Attracting new customers to a market can also create substantial value. For example, consumer packaged goods companies, such as Unilever (with its Axe brand) and Johnson & Johnson (with its Neutrogena Men brand), increased the growth of skin care products by convincing men to use them. Once again, competitors didn't retaliate because they also experienced higher growth. But men's skin care products aren't that different from women's, so much of the R&D, manufacturing, and distribution could be shared. The major incremental cost was marketing and advertising.

The value created from market-share increases depends both on the rate at which the underlying product market grows and the way market share is gained. For example, when a company gains share through aggressive advertising in a fast-growing market, competitors may still grow absolute revenues at an attractive rate, so they may not retaliate.

Gaining share in a mature market, however, is more likely to result in retaliation by competitors. Unless you fundamentally change a product or create an entirely new market category, competitors will copy your incremental innovations very quickly, so not much value will be created. For example, hybrid and electric vehicles aren't fundamentally different for customers than gas or diesel vehicles; electric vehicles can't command much of a premium price beyond their higher costs. Plus competitors quickly copy each other's innovations. Because the total number of vehicles sold won't increase, if one company gains market share for a while, competitors will try to take it back. All in all, we can't expect much value creation for the auto companies from hybrid or electric vehicles.

Gaining share from rivals via pricing/promotion/marketing in a mature market rarely creates much value, if any. For example, Huggies and Pampers dominate the disposable diaper market, and both brands are financially strong, so they can easily retaliate if the other tries to gain share through aggressive increases in marketing and advertising. As Amazon continued expanding into the U.S. consumer electronics retail market in 2009, Wal-Mart retaliated with price cuts on such key products as top-selling video games and game consoles, even though

Amazon's $20 billion in sales in 2008 were a fraction of Wal-Mart's $406 billion sales in the same year.

In concentrated markets, share battles often lead to a cycle of market share gives and takes, but rarely a permanent share gain for a competitor unless that competitor changes the product or its delivery substantially enough to effectively create a new product. The exception is when share is gained from small, weak competitors who are forced out of the market entirely.

Although price increases, over and above cost increases, create value if volume declines are minimal, they tend not to be repeatable. If a company or group of competitors gets away with an extra price increase this year, they are unlikely to get an extra increase next year as well. Further, the extra increase this year could be eroded in future years. For evidence, if companies would regularly increase prices faster than costs, you would observe sustainably increasing profit margins, a rare phenomenon. One exception we found was packaged goods companies in the 1990s. They passed on commodity cost increases to customers but did not lower prices when their commodity costs subsequently declined. They haven't been able to do this since.

Because product market growth tends to create the most value, companies should aim to be in the fastest-growing product markets so they can achieve growth that consistently creates value. If a company is in the wrong markets and can't easily get into the right ones, it may do better by sustaining growth at the same level as its competitors while finding ways to improve and sustain its ROIC. But that's easier said than done.

GROWTH IS DIFFICULT TO SUSTAIN

Sustaining high growth is much more difficult than sustaining high ROIC. The math is simple. Suppose your core product markets are growing at the rate of GDP (say 5 percent nominal growth), and you currently have $10 billion in revenues. Ten years from now, assuming you grow at 5 percent per year, your revenues will be $16.3 billion. But let's assume you aspire to grow organically at 8 percent per year, so in 10 years your revenues will need to be $21.6 billion, $5.3 billion more than if you were growing at 5 percent per year. If your product markets are growing at only 5 percent, where are you going to find that magnitude of growth?

In light of this major hurdle, many companies have unrealistic growth targets. We know of one already large company with sales in excess of $5 billion that announced growth targets of more than 20 percent per year for the next 20 years. Because annual world economic growth is typically less than 4 percent in real terms, and many companies are competing for their share of the growth, revenue targets need to be more realistic.

Exhibit 11.2 shows the real revenue growth distribution for the top 500 nonfinancial companies globally from 1997–2007. The median revenue growth rate was 5.9 percent, with about one-third of the companies growing revenues faster than 10 percent (including the effect of acquisitions, so fewer companies grew faster than 10 percent organically).

Exhibit 11.3 presents real revenue growth rates between 1965 and 2008 for the 500 largest nonfinancial companies in the United States. The median annual, real revenue growth rate was 5.4 percent. Although this median revenue growth rate fluctuates between 1 and 9 percent with the health of the economy, there is no upward or downward trend.

EXHIBIT 11.2 **Distribution of Growth Rates**

Inflation-adjusted 1997–2007 revenue growth rate distribution, percent

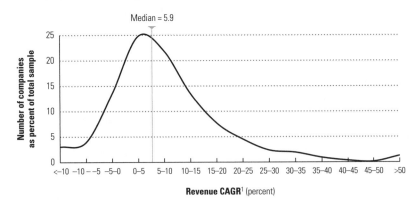

1 Compound annual growth rate.

Source: Compustat, McKinsey Corporate Performance Center analysis.

EXHIBIT 11.3 **Long-Term Revenue Growth for Nonfinancial Companies**

3-year revenue growth rate,[1] adjusted for inflation, percent

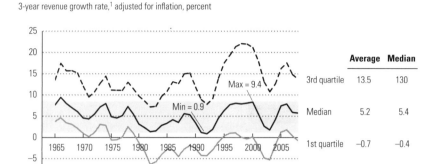

	Average	Median
3rd quartile	13.5	130
Median	5.2	5.4
1st quartile	−0.7	−0.4

[1] Compound annual growth rate.

Source: Compustat, McKinsey Corporate Performance Center analysis.

You should also note that beginning in the mid-1970s, one quarter of all these large companies actually shrank in real terms in a given year. Thus, although most companies publicly project healthy growth over the next five years, history suggests that many mature firms will shrink in real terms.

During this same period (1965–2008), median GDP growth for the United States was 3.2 percent, meaningfully lower than the revenue growth rate for the companies. How can these companies in the aggregate grow faster than the economy? The biggest driver is that U.S. companies have been globalizing, which means their revenues from outside the United States have been growing much faster than revenues from inside the United States; by 2008, 48 percent of revenues from these large companies were derived from outside this country.

In addition, some value chains have broken up, leading to double counting of revenues. For example, when a company outsources its information technology operations, the original company's revenues don't change, but the second company's revenues grow. So the fact that revenues from the largest 500 companies are a greater share of GDP now doesn't mean that those companies are actually producing more of the GDP.

Exhibit 11.4, which reports the transition probabilities from one grouping to another, shows that maintaining high growth is uncommon. Only 25 percent of high-growth companies maintained 15 percent

EXHIBIT 11.4 **Revenue Growth Transition Probability**

Probability that company's growth rate[1] will be in given group from 2004 to 2007, percent

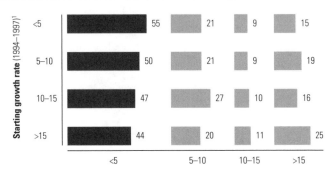

Ending growth rate (2004–2007)[1]

[1] Compound annual growth rate.

Source: Compustat, McKinsey Corporate Performance Center analysis.

real growth 10 years later, most of which was probably driven by acquisitions. Also see that 44 percent of companies growing faster than 15 percent in 1994–1997 grew at real rates below 5 percent 10 years later.

GROWTH REQUIRES CONTINUAL SEARCH FOR NEW MARKETS

Sustaining growth is difficult because most products have natural life cycles. The market for a product—meaning the market for a narrow product category sold to a specific customer segment in a specific geography—typically follows an S-curve until maturity, as shown by Exhibit 11.5. The left side shows a stylized S curve, while the right side shows the growth curves for various real products, scaled to their relative penetration of U.S. households.

First a product has to prove itself with early adopters. Growth then accelerates as more people want to buy the product, until it reaches its point of maximum penetration. After this point of maturity, and depending on the nature of the product, either sales fall back to the same rate of growth as the population or the economy, or sales may start to shrink. To illustrate, autos and packaged snacks have continued to grow in line with economic growth for half a century or more, while

EXHIBIT 11.5 **Variation in Growth over Product Life Cycle**

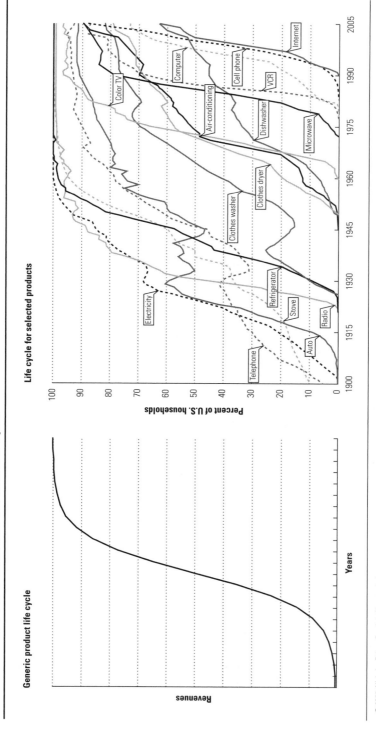

Generic product life cycle

Life cycle for selected products

EXHIBIT 11.6 **Wal-Mart and eBay: Growth Trajectories**

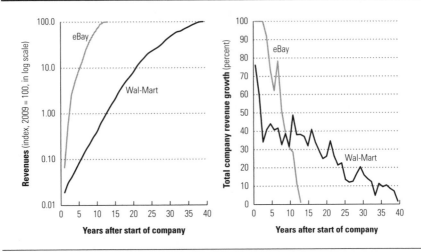

Source: McKinsey Corporate Performance Center analysis.

videocassette recorders lasted less than 20 years before they declined and disappeared.

Although the pattern is typically the same, the size and pace will vary with each product. Exhibit 11.6 compares Wal-Mart and eBay. While both have some activities outside their core product, they are largely one product companies.

Wal-Mart's growth didn't dip below 10 percent until the end of the 1990s, some 35 years after it was founded. In contrast, eBay saw its growth fall to below 10 percent after only 12 years, having grown very rapidly to reach maturity early. Because eBay is an Internet-based auction house, it doesn't need to add many more staff members to grow. In contrast, Wal-Mart, a physical retailer, has to add people as quickly as it adds stores and sales—so the speed at which Wal-Mart can hire and train people limits its rate of growth relative to eBay.

Also, Wal-Mart's core market is much larger than eBay's, having generated $406 billion of revenues in 2008, most of which came from its discount and supercenter stores. On the other hand eBay's core market is much smaller, having generated about $8.5 billion of revenues in 2008.

Sustaining high growth presents major challenges for companies of virtually any size. Given the natural life cycle of products, the only way to achieve high growth is to continually find new products,

EXHIBIT 11.7 **The Challenge of Sustaining High Growth**

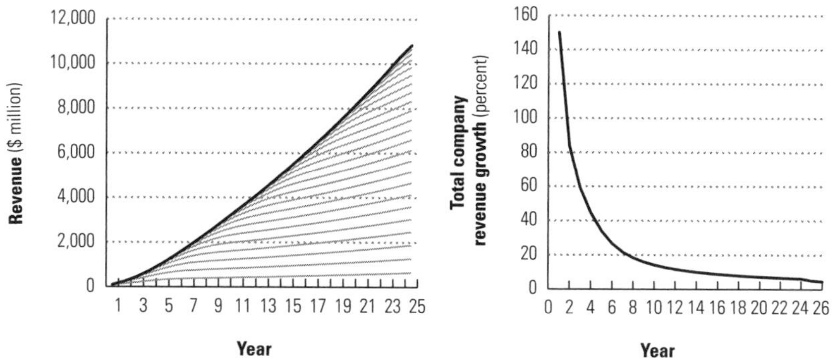

Source: McKinsey Corporate Performance Center analysis.

geographic markets, or customer segments in which to compete, entering those markets early enough to enjoy their more profitable high-growth phase. Exhibit 11.7 illustrates this by showing the cumulative sales for a company that introduces one new product, or opens one new geographic market or customer segment, in each year. All the new products, geographies, or segments are identical in terms of sales volume and growth; their growth rates are very high in the beginning and eventually slow to 3 percent once the market is fully penetrated.

Although the company continues to launch new products that are just as successful as their predecessors, aggregate sales growth slows down rapidly as the company gets bigger. In the long term, growth approaches 3 percent, equal to the long-term growth rate of the markets for the company's products.

Ultimately, the size and growth of a company are constrained by the size of its product markets and the number of product markets in which it competes. Exxon Mobil, for instance, derived most of its 2009 revenue of $310 billion from two products in large markets: crude oil and natural gas. Procter & Gamble, on the other hand, reached its 2009 revenue of $79 billion by competing in hundreds of smaller product markets.

Regardless of constraints, growth still varies considerably across companies in the same industry, as shown by Exhibit 11.8.

To sustain high growth, companies need to overcome the *portfolio treadmill* effect: for each product that matures and declines in revenues,

EXHIBIT 11.8 **Considerable Variation in Revenue Growth**

Industry growth, inflation-adjusted, percent

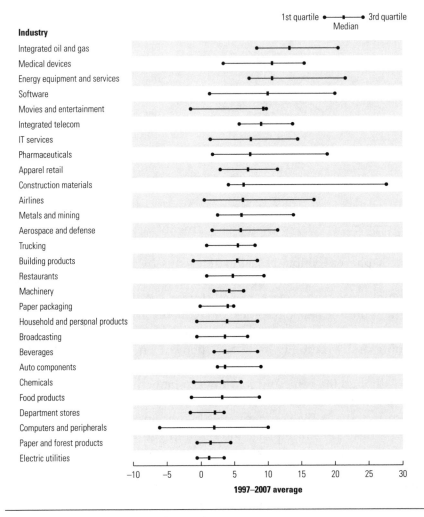

Source: Compustat, McKinsey Corporate Performance Center analysis.

the company needs to find a similar-sized replacement product to stay level in revenues—and even more to continue growing. But finding sizeable new sources of growth requires more experimentation and a longer time horizon through which many companies are not willing to invest. General Electric's GE Capital business was a side business in 1981, when it generated about eight percent of GE's profits. Only after

26 years of consistent investment did it reach 50 percent of GE's profits in 2005.

Although the importance of growth is undeniable, large companies need to have patience and discipline—patience to nurture new growth platforms over many years and discipline to distinguish the types of growth that will create the most value.

12

The Business Portfolio

Deciding what businesses to be in is clearly one of the most important decisions executives make. In fact, to a large extent, the businesses a company is in represent its destiny. For example, a company that produces commodity chemicals is unlikely to ever earn as much return on capital as a branded breakfast cereal company can.

Kaplan, Sensoy, and Strömberg use the analogy of whether to bet on the horse or the jockey.[*] They analyzed small start-up companies financed by venture capital firms, tracking whether they eventually grew large and successful enough to go public. Their finding was that it was better to have a competitive advantage (horse) than to have a good management team (jockey). With a competitive advantage, the venture capitalists could always replace a weak management team, but even the best management team might not be able to salvage a weak business. In other words, bet on the horse, not the jockey.

Warren Buffett said it in his compelling way: "When a management team with a reputation for brilliance joins a business with poor fundamental economics, it is the reputation of the business that remains intact."

Although the best management team may not be able to salvage a poor or declining business, different owners or management teams may extract different levels of performance from a given business. This is the best-owner principle that we discussed in Chapter 5.

[*] Steven N. Kaplan, Berk A. Sensoy, and Per Strömberg, "Should Investors Bet on the Jockey or the Horse? Evidence from the Evolution of Firms from Early Business Plans to Public Companies," *Journal of Finance*, 64(1) (February 2009): 75–115.

But even if one company is the best owner of a business today, that doesn't mean the company will be the best owner in the future. At different stages of an industry's or company's life span, resource decisions that once made economic sense can become problematic. For instance, the company that invented a ground-breaking innovation may not be best suited to exploit it.

Similarly, as demand falls off in a mature industry, long-standing companies are likely to have excess capacity. If they don't have the will or ability to shrink assets and people along with capacity, then they're not the best owner of the business anymore. At any time in a business's history, one group of managers may be better equipped to manage the business than another. At moments like these, acquisitions and divestitures are often the best or only way to sensibly allocate resources.

This means that companies need to regularly assess whether they should continue to own each of the businesses in their portfolios. There may be businesses that should be divested because they no longer fit with the rest of the portfolio, even though they once were the foundation of a company's success. Companies also need to be on the constant lookout for new businesses to own and develop either through acquisitions or start-ups.

A McKinsey study of 200 large U.S. companies over a 10-year period showed that companies with a passive portfolio approach—those that didn't sell businesses or only sold poor businesses under pressure—underperformed companies with an active portfolio approach.* The best performers systematically divested as well as acquired companies. The process is natural and never ending. A divested unit may very well pursue further separations later in its lifetime, especially in dynamic industries undergoing rapid growth and technological change.

United States defense company General Dynamics provides an interesting example of an active portfolio approach that created considerable value. At the beginning of the 1990s, General Dynamics faced an unattractive industry environment. According to forecasts at that time, U.S. defense spending would be cut significantly, and this was expected to hurt General Dynamics since it was a diversified supplier of weapons systems.

---

* J. Brandimarte, W. Fallon, and R. McNish, "Trading the Corporate Portfolio," *McKinsey on Finance* (Fall 2001): 1–5.

When CEO William A. Anders took control in 1991, he initiated a series of divestitures. Revenues were halved in a period of two years, but shareholder returns were extraordinary: an annualized rate of 58 percent between 1991 and 1995, more than double the shareholder returns of General Dynamics' major peers. Then, starting in 1995, Anders began acquiring companies in attractive subsectors. Over the next seven years, General Dynamics' annualized return exceeded 20 percent, again more than double the typical returns in the sector.

The ideal multibusiness company is one in which each business earns an attractive ROIC with good growth prospects, where the company helps each business achieve its potential, and where executives are continually developing or acquiring similarly high-ROIC businesses and disposing of businesses that are in decline.* Although this idealized world doesn't exist, using it as a benchmark can help companies manage their business portfolios better.

This disciplined approach leads companies to focus strategically on three activities: (1) Defining why and how they are the best (or at least better) owners of the businesses in their portfolio, (2) continually pruning businesses that are losing their innate attractiveness or best-owner status, and (3) searching for new businesses with innate attractiveness or opportunities for the company to add value.

BEST OWNER: CORPORATE VALUE ADDED

In Chapter 5 we talked about the ways that a company can be the best owner of a business. As a reminder, we identified five sources of best (or better) ownership:

1. Unique links across businesses within a portfolio
2. Distinctive skills that the company can bring to all or at least most of its business units
3. Better insight/foresight
4. Better governance
5. Distinctive access to talent, capital, government, suppliers, and customers

---

* A handful of companies might create value a different way, namely by improving the performance of companies regardless of their ROIC level.

As economies, capital markets, and companies mature and become more sophisticated, some sources of value are becoming more rare. Therefore, we've seen a clear trend toward companies becoming more focused and less diversified, and we expect this trend to continue.

Starting at the bottom of the list, distinctive access to talent, capital, government, suppliers, and customers is largely irrelevant for developed economies. The benefits of such access are now largely limited to emerging markets. For example, in emerging markets you may still find that well-known, large, multibusiness companies are attractive employers for managerial talent. The reverse is often the case in developed economies, where managers and functional experts, like researchers and marketing specialists, feel stifled by conglomerate parents.

Regarding access to capital, it may still be available only to those with the right connections in emerging markets, but capital is plentiful in developed economies.

Government purchasing and regulation tends to be more rule based rather than relationship based in developed economies, making government access less important. The U.S. government has actually gone even further, favoring smaller companies over larger companies for government contracts. We expect that as economies like China and India develop, this source of best ownership will decline for those markets as well, although that could be many decades into the future.

Finally, regarding suppliers and customers, those in developed markets are more sophisticated and often prefer to deal with more specialized companies. Customers will shop around for the best products and services, regardless of broader corporate-wide relationships.

The next source of best ownership is better governance, which tends to be limited to situations in which stock market ownership or ownership by a large company has failed to maximize value creation. As a result, better governance will always be a source of value added, but as a make-or-break source it tends to be temporary. A private equity firm or company identifies a poorly governed company, takes it over, improves its governance and performance, and then refloats it or sells it to another company.

Large companies in developed economies usually can only rely on finding value added from the first three sources of best ownership: unique linkages, distinctive skills, or better insight/foresight. Most of these value-added sources are attributes of underlying business characteristics. It's logical that a company producing hand soap might also produce dish soap, even though they may be marketed under different brands, because they share common technologies, and they are sold through the same retail channels with common customers and distribution needs. Similarly, a telecommunications company might be able to use a single network to provide voice and data services that will serve both commercial and residential customers.

Wherever there are common customers, technologies, or shared assets (like telecommunications networks), it's natural to look for linkages insights, or skills that can be applied across businesses. But the important words to add to these sources of best ownership are *unique* links, *special* insights, and *distinctive* skills. Without them, it's unlikely that the parent company adds value. As markets mature and become more sophisticated, it's become increasingly difficult for companies to justify owning businesses without well-defined unique links, distinctive skills, or special insights.

We examined the 50 largest U.S.-based companies ranked by 2009 profits. Of these 50, only three are traditional conglomerates with a wide range of unconnected businesses: General Electric, United Technologies, and Berkshire Hathaway. Another seven could be considered moderately diversified (Walt Disney, 3M, Johnson & Johnson, Abbott Laboratories, Bank of America, JP Morgan Chase, and Hewlett-Packard), where more than one-fourth of profits does not come from a single, narrowly defined industry or customer.*

Most large companies are highly focused. For example, IBM focuses entirely on providing service and products to corporate IT departments. It no longer sells any consumer products and has said it will stay out of that market. Procter & Gamble's products are mostly branded consumer products in the areas of health, beauty, and household care—and these products are mostly sold through discount stores, grocery stores, and drug stores (P&G has a few exceptions with pet foods and Pringles potato chips).

Another way companies have become more focused is by moving away from vertical integration, a process that's been under way now for more than a hundred years. As raw materials and semifinished goods markets have become more liquid and sophisticated, companies can more easily focus on only a narrow part of the value chain where they can be distinctive. Automakers, for instance, stopped making their own tires and steel a long time ago, and more recently they've stopped making their own brakes and seats. Paper companies no longer own

---

* We considered Hewlett-Packard moderately diversified because it serves both business IT needs and consumers. IBM, on the other hand, focuses entirely on business IT needs.

forests. Magazines don't do their own printing anymore. Many technology companies, like Apple, contract out all their actual manufacturing, focusing on design and marketing.

Although the trend is toward portfolio focus and vertical disintegration, we've learned that, almost by definition, unique situations bucking the trend are sometimes where opportunities for value creation reside. For example, the major western oil companies originally produced, refined, and marketed oil in an integrated chain—hence the term *integrated oil companies*. Because there wasn't a liquid market in crude oil, companies strived to achieve a "balance" between their oil production and refining capacity. But now the market for crude oil is one of the most deep and liquid of any commodity, so the rationale for vertical integration has disappeared and refineries source crude broadly. However, there are certain crude oils from Alaska with unique characteristics that are more profitable when vertically integrated with dedicated refineries in California, so this is an exception to the rule of waning vertical integration.

DIVESTITURES: REGULAR PRUNING

The logic for systematic divestitures is the same clear reason that apple farmers prune their groves. Smart apple farmers saw off dead and weakened branches to keep their trees healthy. They also cut back a number of vigorous limbs—those that are blocking light from the rest of the tree or otherwise hampering its growth. Only through such careful, systematic pruning does an orchard produce its highest possible yield. Like the annual pruning of apple trees, regularly divesting businesses—even some good healthy ones—ensures that remaining units reach their full potential and that the overall company grows stronger.*

The Costs of Keeping Businesses

The desire to hold on to businesses, particularly successful ones, is strong. A business may generate substantial cash flows. Or an important part of its identity may entail strong sentimental attachments to the

---

* Lee Dranikoff, Tim Koller, and Antoon Schneider, "Divestitures: Strategy's Missing Link," *Harvard Business Review*, 80(5) (May 2002): 74–83.

company among employees. Selling a business can seem like treason to some. When Jack Welch sold GE's housewares unit, he got angry letters from employees accusing him of destroying the company's heritage.*

But whatever the pain of divesting, holding on to a unit too long also imposes substantial if less apparent costs, often far outweighing the benefits of keeping the unit. Let's look at three of these costs.

Costs to the Parent   Well-established, mature businesses provide a company with stability and cash flows, but this stability can be a mixed blessing. The culture of the mature business unit may become incompatible with the culture that the parent company wants to create. Also, mature units are often relatively large and may absorb a significant share of scarce management time that might be better spent on pursuing growth opportunities. Pactiv (producer of specialty packaging products) sold its aluminum business in 1999, despite the fact that the unit had strong cash flow. According to management, the aluminum business was using resources and management time that could have been more usefully deployed elsewhere.

Conflicts of interest between business units can also distort decision making and be a reason to pursue divestment. During the early 1990s, Lucent—at that time a business unit of AT&T and a successful maker of telecom equipment—was selling its products to many of AT&T's competitors. To avoid conflict and to ease possible customer concerns, AT&T arranged to spin off Lucent in 1996.

Costs to the Unit   A business unit's performance may be hampered by poor fit with the parent company, not just in strategy but also in terms of the parent company's core capabilities and top management capacity. Earlier, and in Chapter 5, we described the life cycle of better owner capabilities, and the fact that business portfolios may evolve away from what a corporation considers its core.

In his autobiography, *Jack: Straight from the Gut*, Jack Welch tells an illuminating story about how divestitures can liberate business units and their employees. He recounts how a general manager of an air-conditioning business that GE had sold told him about the sale's salutary effects: "Jack, I love it here. When I get up in the morning and come to work, my boss is thinking about air-conditioning. He thinks

---

* Jack Welch, *Jack: Straight from the Gut* (New York: Warner Books, 2001).

it's wonderful. Every time I talked to you on the phone, it was about some customer complaint or my margins. You hated air-conditioning. Jack, today we're all winners and we all feel it. In Louisville, I was the orphan."

According to Tyco's CFO, one of the benefits of its bold breakup was that it spun off such units as health care (now Covidien) to attract talent that would have hesitated to join a diversified industrial. "They now see [the spun-off business] as a health care company with a very defined strategy, where people can advance while remaining in health care and playing a very significant role."

Depressed Exit Prices   The final cost of postponing divestitures is the direct impact on the company's value. A well-timed divestiture can increase value and a poorly timed one can destroy it. Unfortunately, when it comes to managing business units, most corporations fail to "Buy low, sell high." Rather, they unload a unit only after several years of poor performance—at fire-sale prices. Although some industries are so turbulent that managers simply can't foresee market peaks and troughs, in many cases companies do understand the trajectories of their units but choose to look the other way until it's too late.

Timing the market perfectly isn't possible, of course. But a simple rule of thumb can improve a company's timing considerably: sell sooner. For the vast majority of divestitures we've studied, it's clear that an earlier sale would have generated a much higher price.

Evidence Supports Earlier Divestitures

When companies do divest, they almost always do so too late, reacting to some kind of pressure. If you doubt this, gather your own data. Pick a week at random and tally all the divestitures that are noteworthy enough to be reported in a leading newspaper. For each one, check to see how analysts and journalists explain its rationale.

Invariably, you'll find that the majority of divestitures are done under some sort of pressure—perhaps the divested business is losing money, or the parent has an onerous debt burden. We studied 50 large divestitures and found that more than three-quarters of them were reactive. And most happened only after long delays, when problems became so obvious that action became unavoidable. A study by David Ravenscraft and F. M. Scherer shows that divested businesses had below-average profits (versus peers) for seven years prior to their sale.* Other researchers have confirmed that parent companies tend to hold on to underperforming businesses for too long.† So how can one counteract the inertia?

First, get over the concern for appearances. Executives are often concerned that divestitures look like an admission of failure, make their company smaller, and reduce their stock market value. Yet the research shows that, on the contrary, the stock market consistently reacts positively to divestiture announcements.‡ The divested business units also benefit. Research has also shown that spun-off businesses tend to increase their profit margins by one-third during the three years after the transactions are complete.§

Second, don't worry about dilution. It's true that divestitures will reduce a company's earnings per share (if you sell a business with a lower P/E than the remaining businesses). However, the share price of the company typically increases, which means that the P/E of the company (what remains) increases. The P/E of the unit sold is lower than the rest of the company because it has lower growth and ROIC potential. So once that unit is gone, the company as a whole will have higher growth and ROIC potential and be valued at a higher P/E. By the way, the math works out regardless of whether the proceeds from the sale are used to pay down debt or repurchase shares.

Third, ignore the impact on the size of your company. Executives and boards often express concerns that divesting will reduce the size of the company, which will also lead to a lower value in the capital markets. There does seem to be a misconception that larger companies are valued more highly than smaller companies, but there is no evidence to back this up, except for some academic studies showing that companies with less than $500 million market capitalization might have slightly higher costs of capital.**

---

* L. Lang, A. Poulsen, and R. Stulz, "Asset Sales, Firm Performance, and the Agency Costs of Managerial Discretion," *Journal of Financial Economics* 37 (1994): 3–37.
† D. Ravenscraft and F. Scherer, *Mergers, Sell-Offs, and Economic Efficiency* (Washington, DC: Brookings Institution, 1987), 167; and M. Cho and M. Cohen, "The Economic Causes and Consequences of Corporate Divestiture," *Managerial and Decision Economics* 18 (1997): 367–374.
‡ J. Mulherin and A. Boone, "Comparing Acquisitions and Divestitures," *Journal of Corporate Finance* 6 (2000): 117–139.
§ P. Cusatis, J. Miles, and J. Woolridge, "Some New Evidence That Spinoffs Create Value," *Journal of Applied Corporate Finance* 7 (1994): 100–107.
** Robert S. McNish and Michael W. Palys, "Does Scale Matter to Capital Markets?" *McKinsey on Finance* (Summer 2005): 21–23.

A value-creating approach to divestitures may result in pruning good and bad businesses at any stage of their life cycles. Clearly, divesting a good business is often not an intuitive choice and may be difficult for managers. Therefore, it makes sense to enforce some discipline in active portfolio management; one way to do this is to hold regular, dedicated business exit review meetings, ensuring in the process that the topic remains on the executive agenda and that each unit receives a *date stamp*, or estimated time of exit. This practice has the advantage of obliging executives to evaluate all businesses as their sell-by dates approach.

ADDING TO THE PORTFOLIO

One of the most difficult tasks for executives is identifying new businesses to add to their portfolios, either by starting them from scratch or through acquisitions. The track record of most companies isn't good, which is why 50% of the Fortune 500 drop off the list every 10 years. Companies typically reach the size of a Fortune 500 company on the strength of one or several key businesses or products, but then those products or businesses mature and they are unable to find the next source of major growth (this is compounded by the fact that the next source of growth must be larger to have a meaningful impact on the already large company).

Unlike making divestitures from a relatively small universe of possibilities, finding new business opportunities is more like searching for a needle in a haystack. There are so many places to look, so where do you focus?

It's far beyond our scope to tell you how to find the next big opportunity for your company. Every company needs to design its own approach to hunting for new ideas that is tailored to its unique circumstances. Much of the literature in this area argues that companies are not systematic enough in their search.

For example, our former colleagues Mehrdad Baghai, Stephen Coley, and David White argue that "most managers are preoccupied with their existing businesses. They must learn to focus their attention as much on where they are heading as on where they are today."* They

---

* Mehrdad Baghai, Stephen Coley, and David White, *The Alchemy of Growth: Kickstarting and Sustaining Growth in Your Company* (London: The Orion Publishing Group), 1.

argue that building and managing a continuous pipeline of business creation is the central challenge of sustained growth. One way to maintain that pipeline is to ensure that a company explicitly manages growth opportunities across three horizons of development:

- Horizon 1 businesses are those that currently generate the bulk of a company's profits and cash flow. They are modestly growing.
- Horizon 2 businesses are the emerging stars of the company with modest revenues and profits, but it will be at least four to five years before they contribute a significant amount of profits and cash flows to the company.
- Horizon 3 businesses are the research projects, test-market pilots, alliances, minority stakes, and memoranda of understanding that are currently under way and that will be significant contributors, if successful, in a decade or more.

The key is to make sure that the company pays sufficient attention to activities in each of the three horizons. In the next chapter, we discuss different acquisitions strategies for adding to a company's portfolio of businesses.

BUSINESS PORTFOLIO DIVERSIFICATION

A perennial question in corporate strategy is whether companies should hold a diversified portfolio of businesses. The idea of diversification should have been dropped by the 1970s, yet some executives still say things like "It's the third leg of the stool that makes a company stable." Our perspective is that diversification is intrinsically neither good nor bad; it depends on whether the parent company adds more value to the businesses it owns than any other potential owner could, making it the best owner of those businesses under the circumstances.

Over the years, different reasons have been floated to encourage or justify diversification, but these have largely fallen out of favor in developed markets. Most rest on the idea that different businesses have different business cycles, so cash flows at the peak of one business's cycle will offset the lean cash years of other businesses, thereby stabilizing a company's consolidated cash flows. If cash flows and earnings are smoothed in this way, the reasoning goes, then investors will pay higher prices for the company's stock.

The facts refute this argument, however. First, we haven't found any evidence that diversified companies actually generate smoother cash flows. We examined the 50 companies from the S&P 500 with the lowest earnings volatility from 1997 to 2007. Fewer than 10 could be considered diversified companies, in the sense of owning businesses in more than two distinct industries. Second, and just as important, there is no evidence that investors pay higher prices for less volatile companies (see Chapter 9). In our regular analyses of diversified companies for our clients, we almost never find that the summed values of a diversified company's business units is substantially different from the market value of the consolidated company.*

A second argument is that diversified companies with more stable cash flows can safely take on more debt, thus getting a larger tax benefit from debt. Although this may make sense in theory, we've never come across diversified companies that systematically used more debt than their peers.

Finally, a more nuanced argument is that diversified companies are better positioned to take advantage of different business cycles in different sectors. They can use cash flows from their businesses in sectors at the top of their cycle to invest in businesses in sectors at the bottom of their cycle (when their undiversified competitors cannot).

Once again, we haven't found diversified companies that actually behave that way. In fact, we typically find the opposite: the senior executives at diversified companies don't understand their individual business units well enough to have the confidence to invest at the bottom of the cycle, when none of the competitors are investing. Diversified companies tend to respond to opportunities more slowly than less diversified companies.

Although any benefits from diversification are elusive, the costs are very real. Investors can diversify their portfolios at lower cost than companies, because they only have to buy and sell stocks, something they can do easily and relatively cheaply many times a year. But substantially changing the shape of a portfolio of real businesses involves considerable transaction costs and disruption, and it typically takes many years. Moreover, the business units of diversified companies often don't perform as well as those of more focused peers, partly because of added complexity and bureaucracy.

---

* This assumes that the values of business units are based on peer businesses with similar performance.

Of course, diversification can be value creating when the parent company is the best owner for all the businesses in its stable. Danaher, for example, has one of the most diversified portfolios of all U.S. corporations, with more than 40 wide-ranging businesses and combined revenues of more than $12 billion. Danaher buys companies that can benefit from its proven system (Danaher Business System) for controlling quality, delivery, and cost, and for spawning innovation.

However strategically valid a company's portfolio of businesses, whether diversified or not, the ultimate test is whether the company can effectively operate each company in the portfolio. There are no simple rules of thumb. Danaher may be able to effectively apply a set of management systems to 40 different businesses. Conversely, the retail industry requires such hands-on management that there are very few successful multiformat retailers. Grocers run grocery chains, department stores run department store chains, hardware stores run hardware store chains. Even clothing store chains rarely have more than a handful of store formats or brands.

It's not enough to own businesses that *should* have linkages; it's figuring out how to make them *actually work together* that has tripped up seemingly logical strategies. One need only look at the many failed attempts to see how difficult it is to combine banking and insurance companies with their theoretical cross-selling opportunities, or even the failed attempts to take retail concepts across national borders.

SIZE AND SCALE

Another perennial question for executives pondering their portfolio of businesses is whether the absolute size and/or scale of the company confers benefits—either in the way the stock market values companies or in the way companies actually perform regarding growth and ROIC.

Some pundits have led executives to believe that larger companies are valued more highly by the stock market. One argument for this is that larger companies' shares are in greater demand by investors because they get more coverage from stock analysts and the press, and there is more demand from institutional investors. Another argument is that larger companies have lower costs of capital because they are less risky, or because their shares are more liquid. Higher demand or lower cost of capital should lead to higher valuation multiples.

There may be some truth to these arguments, but only for companies on the smaller end of the scale. The cut-off level at which companies are at a disadvantage in the way they are valued in the market is probably in the range of a market capitalization of $250 million to $500 million. Below this level there is some evidence of higher cost of capital, for example. When you get above that range, however, whether a company has a market capitalization of $1 billion, $5 billion, or $25 billion, there is no evidence that size matters in its valuation.*

Gaining clarity about whether size affects a company's growth or ROIC is muddled by a key notion that students learn in their earliest business or economics classes: the concept of economies of scale. At its simplest, economies of scale means that as a company gets larger it can spread its fixed costs over a larger volume of sales, so its cost per unit will decline, leading to higher profit margins and ROIC.

It's true that companies do experience economies of scale, but only in certain circumstances. One issue is that large (and often medium-sized) companies have already frequently benefited from all or most of the economies of scale in an industry. Take the example of package-delivery companies like FedEx or UPS. You might think that adding more packages might not have much additional cost (the planes and trucks are already in place, so it doesn't cost anything to add extra packages). But the reality is more complex.

First, the networks of these companies are finely tuned and optimized to minimize unused capacity, so increasing volume by 10 percent might in fact require 10 percent more planes and trucks. In our experience, many companies have already captured all the economies of scale available to them. Second, not all economies of scale are the same, so the type of scale matters. In the case of package delivery companies, adding more packages from existing customers has lower costs than adding the same amount of packages from new customers.

Achieving scale advantages in products like ice cream or bread can also be very challenging due to the reality of local nuances. Customers in different regions and places have different tastes and preferences for these products—and such activities as marketing, advertising, and distribution have to be locally purchased and deployed. Just because a company is the largest globally doesn't mean its market share in individual countries, regions, or localities is high.

---

* Robert S. McNish and Michael W. Palys, "Does Scale Matter to Capital Markets?" *McKinsey on Finance* (Summer 2005): 21–23.

Size and scale, just like diversification, don't automatically confer benefits to a company's performance or value in the stock market. In fact, the opposite may occur. Large size can beget complexity and diseconomies of scale. As companies get large, they add business units and expand geographically, the chains of command get longer, and more people are involved in every decision. It's not unusual for smaller, more nimble companies to have lower costs than larger companies. As with many other strategic issues, whether size helps or hurts, whether it generates scale economies or diseconomies, depends on the unique circumstances of each company.

13

Mergers and Acquisitions

Acquisitions are both an important source of growth for companies and an important element of a dynamic economy. Acquisitions that put companies in the hands of better owners or managers, or that reduce excess capacity, typically create substantial value both for the economy as a whole and for investors.

You can see this effect in the increased combined cash flows of the many companies involved in acquisitions. However, despite the fact that acquisitions overall create value, the distribution of any value they create tends to be lopsided, with the selling companies' shareholders capturing the bulk.

Although it's true that, statistically, most acquisitions don't create value for the acquirer's shareholders, that's largely irrelevant for the executive trying to decide whether to proceed with an acquisition. The challenge for executives is to ensure that their acquisitions are in the minority that *do* create value for their shareholders.

MEASURING VALUE CREATION

The conservation-of-value principle helps us explain how to create value from acquisitions (see Chapter 3). Acquisitions create value when the cash flows of the combined companies are greater than they would have otherwise been. Some of that value will accrue to the acquirer's shareholders if it doesn't pay too much for the acquisition.

The value created for an acquirer's shareholders equals the difference between the value received by the acquirer and the price paid by the acquirer. The value received by the acquirer equals the intrinsic value of the target company as a stand-alone company run by its former management team, plus the present value of any performance improvements to be achieved after the acquisition, which will show up as improved cash flows for the target's business or the acquirer's business. The price paid is the market value of the target plus any premium required to convince the target's shareholders to sell its shares.

Exhibit 13.1 shows an illustrative acquisition. Company A buys Company B for $1.3 billion, a transaction that includes a 30 percent premium over its market value. Company A expects to increase the value of B by 40 percent through various operating improvements, so the value of B to A is $1.4 billion. Subtracting the purchase price of $1.3 billion from the value to A of $1.4 billion leaves $100 million of value creation for A's shareholders.

In the case where the stand-alone value of the target equals its market value, the acquirer only creates value for its shareholders when the value of improvements is greater than the premium paid. Examining this equation, it's easy to see why most of the value creation

EXHIBIT 13.1 **Acquisition Evaluation Framework**

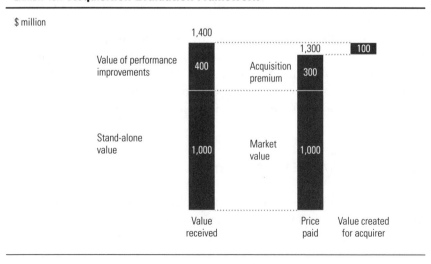

EXHIBIT 13.2 **Value Creation for Given Performance Improvements and Premium Paid**

Value creation as percent of deal value

Premium paid as percent of stand-alone value	10	20	30	40	50
0	10	20	30	40	50
10	0	9	18	27	36
20	−8	0	8	17	25
30	−15	−8	0	8	15
	10	20	30	40	50

Value of performance improvements as percent of stand-alone value

from acquisitions goes to the seller's shareholders: If a company pays a 30 percent premium, then it must increase the value of the target by at least 30 percent to create any value.

Exhibit 13.2 shows the value created for the acquirer's shareholders relative to the amount invested in acquisitions at different levels of premiums and operating improvements. For example, if Company A, mentioned earlier, paid a 30 percent premium for Company B and improved B's value by 40 percent, then the value created for the acquirers' shareholders would represent 8 percent of the amount Company A invested in the deal.

If we further assume that Company A was worth about three times Company B at the time of the acquisition, this major acquisition would be expected to increase Company A's value by only 3 percent—$100 million of value creation (see Exhibit 13.1) divided by A's value of $3.0 billion. As this example shows, it's difficult for an acquirer to create a substantial amount of value from acquisitions.

Although a 40 percent performance improvement sounds steep, that's what acquirers often achieve. Exhibit 13.3 presents an estimate of the value creation from four large deals in the consumer products sector. To estimate the gross value creation, we discounted the announced actual performance improvements at the company's cost of capital. The performance improvements were substantial, typically over 50 percent

EXHIBIT 13.3 **Selected Acquisitions: Significant Improvements**

percent

	Year	Present value of announced performance improvements as a percent of target's stand-alone value	Premium paid as a percent of target's stand-alone value	Net value created from acquisition as a percent of purchase price
Kellogg/Keebler	2000	45–70	15	30–50
PepsiCo/Quaker Oats	2000	35–55	10	25–40
Clorox/First Brands	1998	70–105	60	5–25
Henkel/National Starch	2007	60–90	55	5–25

of the target's value. In addition, Kellogg and PepsiCo paid unusually low premiums for their acquisitions, allowing them to capture more value.

EMPIRICAL RESULTS

The question of whether acquisitions create value has been studied by academics and other researchers for decades. Not surprisingly, given the benefits of acquisitions described in this chapter's introduction, researchers have shown that acquisitions collectively do create value for the shareholders of both the acquirer and the acquired company. According to McKinsey research on 1,415 acquisitions from 1997 through 2009, the combined value of the acquirer and target increased by about four percent on average.[*]

However, the evidence on returns is also overwhelming that acquisitions don't create much, if any, value for the acquiring company's shareholders. Empirical studies examining the reaction of capital markets to M&A announcements find that the value-weighted average deal lowers the acquirer's stock price between one and three percent.[†] Stock returns following the acquisition are no better. Mark Mitchell and Erik Stafford find that acquirers underperform comparable companies on TRS by five percent during the three years following the acquisitions.[‡]

[*] Werner Rehm and Carsten Buch Sivertsen, "A Strong Foundation for M&A in 2010," *McKinsey on Finance* 34 (Winter 2010): 17–22.

[†] S. B. Moeller, F. P. Schlingemann, and R. M. Stulz, "Do Shareholders of Acquiring Firms Gain from Acquisitions?" (NBER working paper no. W9523, Ohio State University, 2003).

[‡] M. L. Mitchell and E. Stafford, "Managerial Decisions and Long-Term Stock Price Performance," *Journal of Business* 73 (2000): 287–329.

Another way to look at the question is to estimate what percentage of deals create any value at all for the acquiring company's shareholders. McKinsey research found that one-third created value, one-third did not, and for the final third, the empirical results were inconclusive.* These studies typically examine the stock market reaction to an acquisition within a few days of its announcement. Research has shown that the initial market reactions are persistent (on average) and indicate future performance quite accurately.[†]

Nevertheless, although studies of announcement effects give useful results for large samples, the same approach cannot be applied to individual transactions. Although the market correctly assesses the results of transactions on average, that doesn't mean that its initial assessment of a single transaction will always be correct. Another problem with studying announcement effects is that the analysis doesn't work for strings of small acquisitions in which no single deal is large enough to affect the parent's share price.

Researchers have also tried to identify specific factors that differentiate deals that are good for acquirers from those that are not. This research points to three characteristics that matter, none of which are surprising.

1. *Strong operators are more successful.* According to empirical research, acquirers whose earnings and share price grow at a rate above industry average for three years before the acquisition earn statistically significant positive returns on announcement.[‡]

2. *Low transaction premiums are better.* Researchers have found that acquirers paying a high premium earn negative returns on announcement.[§]

* Werner Rehm and Carsten Buch Sivertsen, "A Strong Foundation for M&A in 2010," *McKinsey on Finance* 34 (Winter 2010): 17–22.

[†] Mark Sirower and Sumit Sahna, "Avoiding the Synergy Trap: Practical Guidance on M&A Decisions for CEOs and Boards," *Journal of Applied Corporate Finance* 18, 3 (Summer 2006): 83–95.

[‡] R. Morck, A. Shleifer, and R. Vishny, "Do Managerial Objectives Drive Bad Acquisitions?" *Journal of Finance* 45 (1990): 31–48. Another study found similar results using the market-to-book ratio as a measure of corporate performance: H. Servaes, "Tobin's Q and the Gains from Takeovers," *Journal of Finance* 46 (1991): 409–419.

[§] M. L. Sirower, *The Synergy Trap* (New York: Free Press, 1997); and N. G. Travlos, "Corporate Takeover Bids, Methods of Payment, and Bidding Firms' Stock Return," *Journal of Finance* 42 (1987): 943–963. The result was statistically significant in Sirower but not significant in Travlos.

3. *Being the sole bidder helps.* Several studies have found that acquirer stock returns are negatively correlated with the number of bidders; the more companies attempting to buy the target, the higher the price.*

It's just as important to identify the characteristics that don't matter. There's no evidence that the following acquisition dimensions indicate either value creation or destruction as a result:

- Size of the acquirer relative to the target
- Whether the transaction is EPS accretive or dilutive
- The P/E ratio of the acquirer relative to the target
- The relatedness of the acquirer and target

This empirical evidence makes it clear: In M&A, as in most areas of management, there is no magic formula to apply. Like any other business process, acquisitions aren't inherently good or bad, just as marketing or research and development aren't inherently good or bad. Each deal must have its own strategic logic and, in our experience, successful acquirers have well-articulated, specific value creation ideas going into each deal. The strategic rationales for less successful deals tend to be vague, such as to "pursue international scale," fill in portfolio gaps, build a third leg of the portfolio, or, at last resort, shallowly calling the deal "strategic."

VALUE-CREATING ACQUISITION ARCHETYPES

The empirical analysis comes up short in its ability to identify specific acquisition strategies that create value. In the absence of empirical research, our suggestions for strategies that create value are based on our acquisitions work with companies. In our experience, the strategic rationale for an acquisition that creates value typically fits one of the following five archetypes:

1. Improve the target company's performance.
2. Consolidate to remove excess capacity from an industry.

---

* R. Morck, A. Shleifer, and R. Vishny, "Do Managerial Objectives Drive Bad Acquisitions?" *Journal of Finance* 45 (1990): 31–48; and D. K. Datta, V. K. Narayanan, and G. E. Pinches, "Factors Influencing Wealth Creation from Mergers and Acquisitions: A Meta-Analysis," *Strategic Management Journal* 13 (1992): 67–84.

3. Accelerate market access for target's or buyer's products.

4. Acquire skills or technologies faster or at a lower cost than they can be built.

5. Pick winners early and help them develop their businesses.

If an acquisition doesn't fit one or more of these archetypes, it's unlikely to create value. The strategic rationale should be a specific articulation of one of these archetypes, not a vague concept like growth or strategic positioning. Although growth and strategic positioning may be important, they need to be translated into something more tangible. Furthermore, even if your acquisition conforms to one of the archetypes, it still won't create value if you overpay or don't deliver on the value creation plan.

Improve the Target Company's Performance

Improving the performance of the target company is one of the most common sources of value creation. Put simply, you buy a company and radically reduce costs to improve margins and cash flows. In some cases, the acquirer may also take steps to accelerate revenue growth.

Delivering this is what the best private equity firms do. Acharya, Hahn, and Kehoe studied successful private equity acquisitions in which the target company was bought, improved, and sold with no additional acquisitions along the way.[*] They found that the operating profit margins of the acquired businesses increased by an average of about 2.5 percentage points more than peer companies during the private equity firm ownership period. That means many of the transactions increased operating profit margins even more (and some less, of course).

Keep in mind that it's easier to improve the performance of a company with low margins and low ROIC than it is to improve the performance of a company with high margins and high ROIC. Consider the case of buying a company with a 6 percent operating profit margin. Reducing costs by 3 percentage points from 94 percent of revenues to 91 percent of revenues increases the margin to 9 percent, and could lead to a 50 percent increase in the value of the company. In contrast, if the company's operating profit margin is 30 percent, increasing value

* Viral V. Acharya, Moritz Hahn, and Conor Kehoe, "Corporate Governance and Value Creation: Evidence from Private Equity" (working paper, February 4, 2010).

by 50 percent requires increasing the margin to 45 percent. Costs would need to decline from 70 percent of revenues to 55 percent, a 21 percent reduction in the cost base. That expectation might be unreasonable.

Consolidate to Remove Excess Capacity from an Industry

As industries mature, they typically develop excess capacity. In chemicals, for example, companies constantly look for ways to get more production out of their plants while new competitors continue to enter the industry. Saudi Basic Industries Corporation (SABIC), which began production in the mid-1980s, grew from 6.3 million metric tons of value-added commodities in 1985 to 56 million tons in 2008. Now one of the world's largest petrochemicals concerns, SABIC expects continued growth, estimating its annual production to reach 135 million tons by 2020.

The combination of higher production from existing capacity and new capacity from new entrants often generates more supply than demand. It is in no single competitor's interest to shut a plant, however. Companies often find it easier to close plants across the larger combined entity resulting from an acquisition than, absent an acquisition, to close their least productive plants and end up with a smaller company.

Reducing excess capacity in an industry is not limited to shutting factories, but can extend to less tangible forms of capacity. Consolidation in the pharmaceutical industry, for instance, has significantly reduced sales-force capacity as merged companies' portfolios of products change and this changes how they interact with physicians. Pharmaceutical companies have also significantly reduced their R&D capacity as they've found more productive ways to conduct research and, accordingly, pruned their portfolios of development projects.

Accelerate Market Access for Target's or Buyer's Products

Often, relatively small companies with innovative products have difficulty reaching the entire potential market for their products. For instance, small pharmaceutical companies typically don't have advanced abilities for launching products or the large sales forces required to reach physicians. But larger pharmaceutical companies have the sales and product management capacity to radically accelerate the sales growth of the smaller companies' products.

IBM has pursued this strategy in its software business. From 2002 to 2009, IBM acquired 70 companies for about $14 billion. By pushing the products of these companies through IBM's global sales force, IBM estimates it increased the revenues of these businesses by almost 50 percent in the first two years after each acquisition, and by an average of more than 10 percent in the next three years.*

In some cases, the target can also help accelerate the acquirer's revenue growth. In Procter & Gamble's acquisition of Gillette, the combined company benefited because P&G had stronger sales in some emerging markets and Gillette had a bigger share of others. Working together, they were able to introduce their products into new markets much more quickly.

Acquire Skills or Technologies Faster or at a Lower Cost Than They Can Be Built

Cisco Systems has used acquisitions to assemble a broad line of network solution products and to grow very quickly from a single product line into the key player in Internet equipment. Strategically acquiring from without rather than building from within, from 1993 to 2001, Cisco acquired 71 companies at an average price of approximately $350 million. Cisco's sales increased from $650 million in 1993 to $22 billion in 2001, with nearly 40 percent of its 2001 revenue coming directly from these acquisitions. By 2009, Cisco had more than $36 billion in revenue and a market capitalization of approximately $150 billion.

Pick Winners Early and Help Them Develop Their Businesses

The final winning acquisition strategy involves making acquisitions early in the life cycle of a new industry or product line, long before it's apparent to most others that the industry will become large. Johnson & Johnson pursued this strategy in its early acquisitions of medical device businesses. When Johnson & Johnson bought device manufacturer Cordis in 1996, Cordis had $500 million in revenues. By 2007, its revenues had increased to $3.8 billion, reflecting a 20 percent annual growth rate. J&J also purchased orthopedic device manufacturer DePuy in 1996 when DePuy had $900 million in revenues. By 2007,

---

* 2010 IBM Investor Briefing, May 12, 2010.

Depuy's revenues had grown to $4.6 billion, also at an annual growth rate of 20 percent.

This acquisition strategy requires a disciplined approach by management in three dimensions. First, you must be willing to make investments early, long before your competitors and the market see the industry's or company's potential. Second, you need to make multiple bets and expect that some will fail. Third, you need the skills and patience to nurture the acquired businesses.

MORE DIFFICULT STRATEGIES FOR CREATING VALUE FROM ACQUISITIONS

Beyond the five main acquisition strategies already outlined, executives often justify acquisitions by choosing from a much broader menu of strategies, including rollups, consolidating to improve competitive behavior, entering into transformational mergers, and buying cheap. Although these strategies can create value, we find that they do so rarely, in large part because they're difficult to successfully execute. Therefore, value-minded executives should cast a critical eye toward deals based on these strategies.

Rollup Strategy

Rollup strategies consolidate highly fragmented markets in which the current competitors are too small to achieve scale economies. Beginning in the 1960s, Service Corporation International, for instance, grew from a single funeral home in Houston to more than 1,400 funeral homes and cemeteries in 2008. Similarly, Clear Channel Communications rolled up the U.S. market for radio stations, eventually owning more than 900.

This strategy works when the businesses as a group can realize substantial cost savings or achieve higher revenues than individual businesses. Service Corporation's funeral homes in a single city can share vehicles, purchasing, and back-office operations, for example. They can also coordinate advertising across a city to both reduce costs and realize higher revenues.

Size per se is not what creates a successful rollup; what matters is the right kind of size. For example, for Service Corporation, multiple locations in individual cities have been more important than many branches spread over many cities, because the cost savings (such as sharing vehicles) can be realized only if the branches are near one another.

Because rollup strategies are hard to disguise, they invite copycats. As others tried to copy Service Corporation's strategy, prices for some funeral homes were eventually bid up to levels that made additional acquisitions uneconomic.

Consolidate to Improve Competitive Behavior

Many executives in highly competitive industries hope that consolidation will lead competitors to focus less on price competition, thereby improving the industry's ROIC. However, the evidence shows that unless an industry consolidates down to just three or four competitors and can keep entrants out, competitor pricing behavior doesn't change; smaller businesses or new entrants often have an incentive to gain share through lower prices. So in an industry with, say, 10 competitors, many deals must be done before the basis of competition changes.

Enter into a Transformational Merger

A frequently mentioned reason for an acquisition or merger is to transform one or both companies. Transformational merger successes are rare, however, because the circumstances have to be just right, and the management team needs to execute the strategy well.

The best way to describe a transformational merger is by example. One of the world's leading pharmaceutical companies, Switzerland's Novartis was formed in 1996 by the $30 billion merger of Sandoz and Ciba-Geigy. But this merger was much more than a simple combination of businesses: under the leadership of the new CEO, Daniel Vasella, Sandoz and Ciba-Geigy were transformed into an entirely new company. Using the merger as a catalyst for change, Vasella and his management team not only captured $1.4 billion in cost savings but also redefined the company's mission and strategy, portfolio, organization, and all key processes from research to sales. In every area, there was no automatic choice for either the Ciba or the Sandoz way of doing business; instead, a systematic effort was made to find the best way of doing business.

Novartis shifted its strategic focus to innovation in its life sciences business (pharmaceuticals, nutrition, and agricultural) and spun off the $7 billion Ciba Specialty Chemicals business in 1997. Organizational changes included restructuring R&D worldwide by therapeutic rather than geographic area, enabling Novartis to build up a world-leading oncology franchise. Across all departments and management layers, Novartis created a strong performance-oriented culture, supported by a change from a seniority-based to a performance-based compensation system for its managers.

Buy Cheap

The final way to create value from an acquisition is to buy cheap—in other words, at a price below the target's intrinsic value. In our experience, however, opportunities to create value by buying cheap are rare and relatively small.

Although market values revert to intrinsic values over longer periods, there can be brief moments when the two fall out of alignment. Markets, for instance, sometimes overreact to negative news, such as the criminal investigation of an executive or the failure of a single product in a portfolio of many strong products. Such moments are less rare in cyclical industries, where assets are often undervalued at the bottom of a cycle. Comparing actual market valuations with intrinsic values based on a "perfect foresight" model, we found companies in cyclical industries could more than double shareholder returns (relative to actual returns) if they acquired assets at the bottom of a cycle and sold at the top.[*]

Although markets do offer up occasional opportunities for companies to buy below intrinsic value, we haven't seen many cases. To gain control of the target, the acquirer must pay the target's shareholders a premium over the current market value. Although premiums can vary widely, the average premiums for corporate control have been fairly stable, near 30 percent of the preannouncement price of the target's equity.

For targets pursued by multiple acquirers, the premium rises dramatically, creating the so-called winner's curse. If several companies evaluate a given target and all identify roughly the same synergies, the one who overestimates potential synergies the most will offer the highest price. Because the offer price is based on an overestimate of value to be created, the winner overpays and is ultimately a loser.[†]

---

[*] T. Koller and M. de Heer, "Valuing Cyclical Companies," *The McKinsey Quarterly* no. 2 (2000): 62–69.
[†] K. Rock, "Why New Issues Are Underpriced," *Journal of Financial Economics* 15 (1986): 187–212.

FOCUS ON VALUE CREATION, NOT ACCOUNTING

Many managers focus on the accretion and dilution of earnings represented by an acquisition, rather than on the value it could create. They do so despite numerous studies showing that stock markets pay no attention to the effects of an acquisition on accounting numbers; markets react only to the value that the deal is estimated to create. Focusing on accounting measures is, therefore, dangerous and can easily lead to poor decisions.

By 2005, both International Financial Reporting Standards (IFRS) and U.S. Generally Accepted Accounting Principles (U.S. GAAP) eliminated amortization of goodwill. As a result, many, if not most, acquisitions paid for with cash are now earnings accretive regardless of whether they will create value. It doesn't take much for an acquisition to be earnings accretive, as the example in Exhibit 13.4 shows. The acquirer pays $500 million in cash for the target, financing the purchase by borrowing $500 million at a 6 percent interest rate (with an effective cost of 3.9% after taxes). To see the earnings accretion, add the target's earnings of $30 million to the acquirer's $80 million of earnings and subtract the after-tax interest expense on the debt of $19.5 million. The acquirer's earnings will now be $90.5 million, a 13 percent increase over its prior earnings.

The acquirer's earnings will increase as long as the income from the target exceeds the after-tax interest expense on the new debt. In this example, the earnings of the target are 6 percent of the acquisition price, while the interest on the debt is only 3.9 percent after tax. While earnings accretive, there is no way to tell if this deal will create value. In fact, based on the information presented, it appears as if the deal destroys value, because the acquirer's shareholders are earning a return on their capital of only 6 percent, far below the cost of capital for most

EXHIBIT 13.4 **EPS Accretion with Value Destruction**

	Total ($ million)	Per share	
Net income of acquirer	80.0	2.00	
Net income of target	30.0	0.75	◀─ 6.0% after-tax return on acquisition price of $500 million
Additional after-tax interest expense	(19.5)	(0.49)	◀─ 3.9% after-tax interest expense on acquisition price
Net income of acquirer after acquisition	90.5	2.26	

EXHIBIT 13.5 **Market Reaction to EPS Impact of Acquisitions**

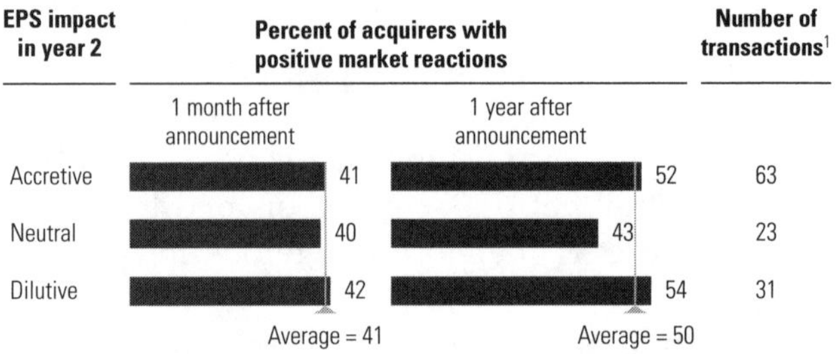

EPS impact in year 2	Percent of acquirers with positive market reactions		Number of transactions[1]
	1 month after announcement	1 year after announcement	
Accretive	41	52	63
Neutral	40	43	23
Dilutive	42	54	31
	Average = 41	Average = 50	

[1] The sample set included 117 transactions greater than $3 billion by U.S. companies between January 1999 and December 2000.

Source: Thomson, analyst reports, Compustat, McKinsey Corporate Performance Center analysis.

companies. It may be that improvements in performance in future years will make this a value-creating deal, but there's no way to determine that from the earnings accretion.

Financial markets understand the priority of creating real value over accounting results. In a study of 117 U.S. transactions, we found that earnings accretion or dilution resulting from the deals was not a factor in the market's reaction (Exhibit 13.5).* Regardless of whether the expected EPS was greater, smaller, or the same two years after the deal, about 41 percent of the acquirers saw a positive market reaction.

The question of whether a transaction will create value cannot be reduced to a crude metric like accounting earnings accretion or dilution. The only relevant measure is whether the acquisition increases the cash flow of combined entity over the longer term (though short-term markers like cost savings and revenue enhancements are helpful indicators). Further, although the different archetypal acquisition strategies can be helpful in identifying acquisitions that might create value, in the end, every deal creates or destroys value based on its own unique ability to increase cash flow under specific industry and market circumstances.

* Richard Dobbs, Billy Nand, and Werner Rehm, "Merger Valuation: Time to Jettison EPS," *McKinsey on Finance*, Spring (2005): 17–20.

14

Risk

The economic crisis that began in 2007 alerted many executives to the gaps in their understanding and management of risk. As a result, many have taken actions to improve their risk management, some of which will be beneficial, but many of which serve merely to mollify their boards of directors.

Risks can be categorized in many ways. For our purpose, a useful distinction is between (1) internal risks that the company can be expected to control (such as employee and customer safety, pollution, and employee malfeasance), (2) natural disasters (such as hurricanes or earthquakes), and (3) external economic risks (such as recession, inflation, interest rate changes, commodity price changes, shifts in consumer demand and preferences, technological change, and competitor actions).

Internal risks and natural-disaster risks are typically one-directional, downside risks that can result in major crises but do so infrequently. Companies need to weigh how much they are willing to invest to reduce these risks. For example, heavy industries with real safety risks like oil production need to decide how much to invest in training and building a safety culture, while industries like gaming or securities trading need to decide how to effectively monitor employee behavior.

Our focus in this chapter is on external economic risks. Decisions about how to manage these risks are complex because they're often two-sided risks (economic changes can be beneficial or harmful), and reducing these risks may not be feasible at a reasonable cost.

Suppose it's 2005 as you read this. You run a high-tech company, and somehow you know there's a high probability that U.S. housing prices will decline, leading to a major recession sometime in the next one to five years. What could you do? You could make sure you don't have too much debt on your balance sheet so you can weather the recession without too much difficulty and, perhaps, improve your competitive position relative to weaker competitors. That would be wise and relatively low cost.

In addition, you could cut back on product development and slow the building of your sales force. But you would risk losing market share that would be difficult to regain. Or you could try to buy some hedges in the financial markets. But what financial instruments would you buy? Because you don't sell a traded commodity, you can't buy a direct hedge. About the only thing you could buy are equity index contracts that would pay off if the value of an equity index were to fall (e.g., the S&P 500), but the movements in the index will be at best loosely linked to the operating performance of your company. You're probably best off to just be prepared by having a plan for what to do when the economy does start to fall.

RISK AFFECTS COMPANIES AND INVESTORS DIFFERENTLY

As executives decide how to tackle risk management, they need to consider that investors in their companies view risk differently than they do, and their boards of directors may have a third perspective on risk. Investors typically have only a portion of their portfolio in a single company so they may prefer companies to undertake investments with large potential payoffs, even if there is a low chance of success. Managers may be reluctant to commit to the same investments because failure will damage their careers. Boards of directors may be more interested in limiting downside risk rather than taking chances on large upside potential.

These different perspectives lead to a nonintuitive relationship between the amount of risk in a company and the price of that risk. Think of the amount of risk as the range of uncertainty about a company's future cash flows. The price of risk is the rate that investors use when valuing a company's cash flows (also called the cost of capital, the

EXHIBIT 14.1 **Volatility of Portfolio Return: Declining with Diversification**

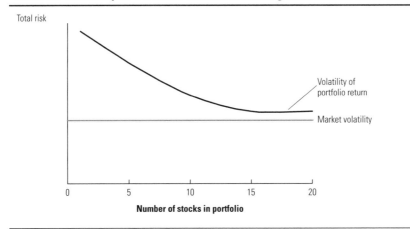

discount rate, or the expected return to investors).* What's not intuitive is that the price of risk is often unrelated to the amount of risk; diversification by investors breaks the link between the amount of risk and the price of risk.

Stock market investors, especially institutional investors, typically have hundreds of different stocks in their portfolios; even the most concentrated institutional investors have at least 50. As a result, their exposure to any single company is limited. Exhibit 14.1 shows what happens to the total risk of a portfolio of stocks as more shares are added to the portfolio. The total risk declines because companies' cash flows are not correlated. Some will increase when others decline.

One of the insights of academic finance that has stood the test of time concerns the effect of diversification on the price of risk (cost of capital). If diversification reduces risk to investors and it's not costly to diversify, then investors won't demand a return for any risks they take that they can easily eliminate through diversification. They require compensation only for risks they can't diversify.

---

* The cost of capital to a company equals the minimum return that investors expect to earn from investing in the company. That is why the terms *expected return to investors* and *cost of capital* are essentially the same. The cost of capital is also called the discount rate, because you discount future cash flows at this rate when calculating the present value of an investment.

The risks they can't diversify are those that affect all companies—for example, exposure to economic cycles. However, because most of the risks that companies face are diversifiable, most risks don't affect a company's cost of capital.

The cost of equity capital in early 2010 for a large nonfinancial company was in the range of 8–10 percent. That's about 4–5 percent more than the returns on government bonds (safe governments like U.S. or Germany) and only 2 to 3 percent higher than BBB-rated corporate bonds.

The cost of equity range is narrow, despite encompassing companies with predictable cash flows like Campbell Soup, as well as less predictable companies like Google. The range is narrow because investors diversify their holdings. If the range were broader, we would also see a wider range of P/E ratios, but we don't. Most large companies have P/Es between 12 and 20. If the cost of capital varied from 6 to 15 percent instead of 8 to 10 percent, many more companies would have P/Es below 8 and above 25.

Whether a company's cost of capital is 8 percent or 10 percent, or somewhere in between, is hotly debated in the finance field. For decades, the standard model for measuring differences in costs of capital has been the capital asset pricing model (CAPM), which has been criticized by academics and practitioners for not adequately reflecting the empirical data on stock performance. But those criticisms have, in turn, been criticized for their own data issues. In any case, emerging competing theories don't lead to a wider spread of costs of capital across companies than the CAPM. So even if new approaches supplant the CAPM, the practical impact for business decision making will be small or nil. When returns on capital across companies vary from less than 5 percent to more than 30 percent, a one or two percentage point difference in the cost of capital seems hardly worth arguing about.

MEASURING RISK

Risk management isn't possible without measuring the risks a company faces. As we saw with the banks in 2008, measuring risk requires thoughtfulness, not necessarily complex models. In the case of the banks, we saw that their complex models had plenty of math and statistics, but little economic analysis.

The pitfalls of risk measurement are many. For example, individual risks may interact in complex and subtle ways. Consider the impact of new carbon regulations on an aluminum producer.* A simplistic analysis suggests that company profits would get squeezed if the government imposed a tax on carbon emissions. The logic is that their costs would increase because they would need to pay more either for their own carbon emissions or for the goods they purchase. Furthermore, they would not be able to pass on their higher costs to customers.

However, in aluminum, different producers are likely to be affected differently. In the U.S. Midwest, there is much more demand than supply, so the price of aluminum is heavily influenced by the cost of getting aluminum to the region. High carbon taxes will increase transportation costs to the region. But a producer with a smelter in the region will not incur these additional costs, so that producer may actually benefit from high carbon taxes.

Another effect might be to increase the demand for aluminum. With high carbon emission taxes, automobile manufacturers might shift more of an automobile's content from steel to aluminum to reduce weight and improve fuel efficiency. The effect of certain risks may not be obvious and are sometimes counterintuitive.

Risk quantification can also be hindered by the use of apparently sophisticated models that typically rely on short-term historical data (assuming that the past several years are representative of the future), rather than on fundamental economic analysis. For example, a model of Greece's interest rates, based on its volatility since the introduction of the Euro in 1999, would lull you into a sense of complacency. Fundamental analysis of the economy would have shown that a debt crisis was brewing and that the potential volatility would be much higher than in the recent past. Such an analysis would have included a look at productivity and innovation in the private sector, pension obligations, and the proportion of people dependent on government for their income (either pension recipients, government employees, or welfare recipients). In this case, a simple qualitative analysis might have been more insightful than a sophisticated statistical analysis based on irrelevant parameters.

---

* Example adapted from Eric Lamarre and Martin Pergler, "Risk: Seeing Around the Corners," *McKinsey on Finance* 33 (Autumn 2009): 2–7.

A final problem is the attempt by companies to reduce an entire company's risk to a single measure, such as value at risk (for financial institutions) or cash flow at risk (for nonfinancial companies). Take cash flow at risk, which is typically measured as the potential decline in cash flow for one year with some level of confidence. For example, a company might calculate that there is less than a 5 percent probability that cash flow for the year will be more than $1 billion below the base case. Although this cash flow at risk number might reassure a management team with $2 billion of excess cash that they can survive the 5 percent probability case, it doesn't tell them what they should do about the risks they do face.

We believe there is a more useful approach that, if done well, will help companies overcome most of the common pitfalls in risk measurement. The approach must be more granular, specifying the magnitude of upside/downside value impact, cash-flow impact, and probabilities—as illustrated in Exhibit 14.2—for each individual risk a company faces. For example, a new product developed by this hypothetical company has a 50 percent chance of failure, but the impact of failure on both value and cash flows over the next three years is only $100 million. The new product has a 20 percent chance of success, with a value of $1.8 billion, and $500 million of extra cash flow over the next three years.

Note also that for this company, the impact of volatile interest rates is minor, though its probability is fairly high, whereas a safety breach is costly but low probability. The company is probably better

EXHIBIT 14.2 **Example of Risk Measurement**

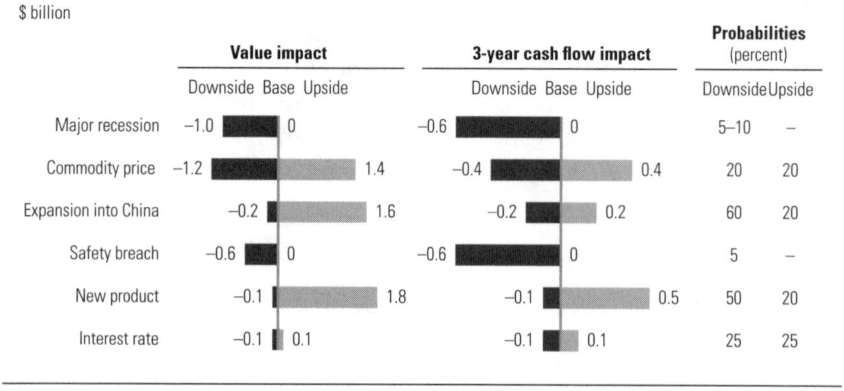

$ billion

	Value impact			3-year cash flow impact			Probabilities (percent)	
	Downside	Base	Upside	Downside	Base	Upside	Downside	Upside
Major recession	−1.0	0		−0.6	0		5–10	–
Commodity price	−1.2		1.4	−0.4		0.4	20	20
Expansion into China	−0.2		1.6	−0.2		0.2	60	20
Safety breach	−0.6	0		−0.6	0		5	–
New product	−0.1		1.8	−0.1		0.5	50	20
Interest rate	−0.1	0.1		−0.1	0.1		25	25

off by putting resources into even further reducing the probability of a safety breach, rather than trying to manage the high probability but low impact of volatile interest rates.

COMPANIES SHOULD RETAIN SOME RISKS

Executives shouldn't jump to the conclusion that all risks should be reduced. There may be some risks that the company should take on, because that's what is best for its investors. For example, investors in gold mining companies and oil production companies buy those stocks to gain exposure to often volatile gold or oil prices. If gold and oil companies hedge their revenues, that effort merely complicates life for their investors, who then have to guess how much price risk is hedged by the company and how and whether management will change its policy in the future.

Moreover, the maximum time that large hedges are available is typically only one or two years. But a company's value includes the cash flows from subsequent years at fluctuating market prices. So although hedging may reduce short-term cash flow volatility, it will have little effect on the company's valuation based on long-term cash flows.

The decision about which risks to accept and which to minimize is highly situation specific, even among companies in the same industry. Consider the effect of currency risk on Heineken, the global brewer. For marketing purposes, Heineken produces its flagship brand, Heineken, in the Netherlands and ships it around the world, especially to the United States. Most other large brewers, in contrast, produce most of their beer in the same national markets in which they sell. So for most brewers, an exchange-rate change affects only the translation of their profits into their reporting currency.

For most brewers, a 1 percent decline in the value of the currency of one of their nonhome markets translates into a 1 percent change in revenues from those markets, and a 1 percent change in profits as well. The effect on revenues and profits is the same because all the revenues and costs are in the same currency. There is no change in the operating margin.

Heineken's picture is different. Consider Heineken's sales in the United States. When the exchange rate changes, Heineken's revenues in euros are affected, but not its costs. If the dollar declines by 1 percent, Heineken's euro revenues also decline by 1 percent. But since its costs are in euros, they don't change. Assuming a 10 percent margin with which to begin, a 1 percent decline in the dollar will reduce Heineken's margin to 9 percent, and its profits reported in euros will decline by a whopping 10 percent.

Because Heineken's production facilities are in a different country than its sales, its foreign exchange risk is much larger than that of other global brewers. Hedging might be critical to Heineken's survival, whereas the other global brewers probably wouldn't benefit from hedging because the impact of exchange rate changes isn't material for them.

FINANCIAL MARKETS ARE OF LIMITED HELP IN REDUCING ECONOMIC RISKS

Once you've measured your risks and decided which ones to take on, you need to consider what ways there are to reduce risks. Let's say you're an auto producer making cars in Japan and selling them into the U.S. market. Much of your costs, labor, engineering, design, and some raw materials are yen-denominated. If the dollar declines and you can't raise your prices in the U.S. market (because your competitors are producing in the United States or Europe), your yen revenues will decline, reducing your yen profits (potentially significantly).

Theory suggests that an auto company could hedge against this risk in the currency markets. But that assumes that the currency markets are deep enough to provide long-term hedges. In reality, they aren't that deep. The size of hedges required by an auto manufacturer would swamp the currency markets and at best would protect the company for 12 to 18 months. As a practical matter, the only way to reduce currency risk is to either shift production to the U.S. market, so revenues and costs are aligned (which most of the Japanese and German manufacturers have been doing), or ensure you have enough financial strength to absorb any adverse currency movements for several years, or both.

Even when you can hedge in the financial markets, the true costs of hedging can be large. Financial hedging transactions typically require that a company post a significant amount of capital that is pledged against potential losses. Let's suppose you expect to receive 100 billion yen in one year and you want to lock in the dollar equivalent. The current exchange rate is 100 yen to the dollar, so the current value of the receivable is $1 billion. You enter into a one-year, $1 billion forward contract to purchase 100 billion yen at a rate of 100 yen to $1. The counterparty will want some assurance that you will have enough capital in one year to make the purchase, so they may ask you to set aside $100 million of cash or government bonds as collateral. During the course of the year, you cannot use that money to invest in your business or pay cash to your shareholders.

Another cost is lost upside; hedging to lock in current prices can cost more in forgone upside than the value of the downside protection. A large independent natural gas producer, for example, was evaluating a hedge for its production during the coming two years. The price of natural gas in the futures markets was $5.50 per million British thermal units (BTUs). The company's fundamental perspective was that gas prices in the next two years would stay within a range of $5.00 to $8.00 per million BTUs. By hedging production at $5.50 per million BTUs, the company protected itself from only a $0.50 decline in prices and gave up a potential upside of $2.50 if prices rose to $8.00.

Often the only practical ways to reduce macroeconomic risks, like currency and commodity price risks, is to either make structural changes to the company, like shifting production, or to simply make sure the company has enough of a financial cushion to absorb the risks.

HOW MUCH RISK TO ADOPT

From finance theory, we can derive that companies shouldn't take on risks that endanger the entire firm. Beyond that, however, finance theory doesn't provide guidance about how much risk to take on.

Consider Project A that requires an up-front investment of $20 million (Exhibit 14.3). If everything goes well with the project, the company earns $10 million per year forever. If not, the company gets zero. (Such all or nothing projects are not unusual.) To value Project A, finance theory directs you to discount the expected cash flow at the cost of capital. But what is the expected cash flow in this case? If there is a 60 percent chance of everything going well, the expected cash flows would be $6 million per year. At a 10 percent cost of capital, the project would be worth $60 million once completed. Subtracting the $20 million investment, the net value of the project before the investment is made is $40 million.

EXHIBIT 14.3 **Analysis of Project A**

$ thousands

	Success	Failure	Expected value
Probability of outcome (percent)	60	40	–
Cash flow per year	10,000	–	6,000
Cost of capital (percent)	10	10	10
Gross value of project	100,000	–	60,000
Initial investment	(20,000)	(20,000)	(20,000)
Net value of project	80,000	(20,000)	40,000

But the project will never generate $6 million per year. It will generate annual cash flows of either $10 million or zero. That means the present value of the discounted cash flows will be either $100 million or nothing, making the project net of the initial investment worth either $80 million or –$20 million. The probability of it being worth the expected value of $40 million ($60 million less the investment) is zero.

Rather than knowing the expected value, managers would be better off knowing that there is a 60 percent chance the project will be worth $80 million and a 40 percent risk of losing $20 million. Managers can then examine the scenarios under which each outcome prevails and decide whether the upside compensates for the downside, whether the company can comfortably absorb the potential loss, and whether they can take actions to reduce the magnitude or risk of loss. The theoretical approach of focusing on expected values, while mathematically correct, hides some important information about the range of particular outcomes.

How should a company think through whether to undertake the project with an upside of $80 million, a downside of –$20 million, and an expected value of $60 million? Theory says take on all projects with a positive expected value, regardless of the upside versus downside risk. But following the theory could be problematic.

What if the downside possibility would bankrupt the company? Consider an electric power company (Exhibit 14.4) with the opportunity to build a nuclear power facility for $15 billion (a rough estimate in 2009 for a facility with two reactors). Suppose the company is worth $32 billion before building the nuclear plant ($20 billion in existing debt

EXHIBIT 14.4 **Impact of Nuclear Plant on Company Value**

$ billion

	Company today	Company with nuclear plant		
		Plant successful	Plant unsuccessful	Expected value
Probability (percent)	–	80	20	–
Value of nuclear plant	–	28	–	22
Value of rest of company	32	32	32	32
Total value	32	60	32	54
Old debt	(20)	(20)	(20)	(20)
New debt	–	(15)	(15)	(15)
Equity value	12	25	(3)	19

and $12 billion in equity market capitalization). If the plant is success-fully constructed and brought on line, it will be worth $28 billion. But there is a 20 percent chance it will fail to receive regulatory approval and be worth zero. As a single project, the expected value is $22 billion, or $7 billion net of investment. Another way to put this is that there is an 80 percent chance the project will be worth $13 billion ($28 billion less $15 billion investment) and a 20 percent chance it will be worth –$15 billion.

Moreover, failure will bankrupt the company, because the cash flow from the company's existing plants will be insufficient to cover its existing debt plus the debt on the failed plant. In this case, the economics of the nuclear plant spill over onto the value of the rest of the company. Failure will wipe out all the equity of the company, not just the $15 billion invested in the plant.

We can extend the theory to say that a company shouldn't take on a risk that will put the rest of the company in danger. In other words, don't do anything that has large negative spillover effects. This caveat would be enough to guide managers in the earlier example of deciding whether to go ahead with Project A. If a $20 million loss would endanger the company as a whole, they should forgo the project, despite its $60 million expected value.

Just as companies have to carefully consider taking on risks that could spill over, they shouldn't be so conservative that they avoid risks that don't threaten their existence. For example, companies should not try to eliminate moderate volatility in earnings and cash flows. This means that companies shouldn't try to eliminate moderate exposure to macroeconomic risks, such as interest rate risk, currency risk, or commodity price risk—even though these introduce volatility into a company's reported earnings. We showed in Chapter 9 that investors don't penalize companies for moderate earnings volatility.

Furthermore, companies shouldn't necessarily pass up attractive but risky investment opportunities. Consider that hypothetical (though the example is based on a real situation) Company A has an opportunity to invest $1 billion in project S. There is a 40 percent chance the project will be worth $20 billion and a 60 percent chance the project will be a total failure, losing the entire $1 billion investment. The expected net present value (NPV) is $7 billion, or $7 for every $1 invested. The company currently generates about $1 billion per year of after-tax cash flow and has little debt, so even a total failure of the project wouldn't cause financial distress, though it would generate negative headlines.

The proposed investment would reduce the company's reported earnings by five percent for each of the next five years, and the success or failure of the project wouldn't be known for five years. Most investors would jump at this investment, yet many companies we know would not. First, the project might not even make it to the CEO or board because, even though its failure wouldn't come close to ruining the company, the careers of those proposing it might be damaged if it weren't to work out (so they might forego proposing it in the first place). Second, many companies wouldn't tolerate the short-term earnings reduction. Third, many companies would focus more on the potential loss of $1 billion than the possible gain of $20 billion.

RISK CULTURE

Companies frequently fall for three traps when it comes to risk management: (1) ignoring big risks (especially when it means countering a flawed status quo, as when banks were making mortgage loans to people who couldn't afford their houses unless house prices continued to rise), (2) paying high prices to reduce unimportant risks, like moderate earnings volatility, and (3) passing up high-return projects when their downside only results in relatively benign consequences on company value. Companies fall into these traps because of poor risk cultures, which we define as the inability of executives to openly discuss and act on risk.

For example, many companies have a practice of single-point projections, meaning that everything from capital expenditures to acquisitions to five-year strategies are boiled down to a single financial projection rather than multiple scenarios. Managers are reluctant to show any upside potential beyond the base case for fear it will become the demanded performance. Similarly, managers are reluctant to show any downside scenario for fear that the project will get rejected. That's why so many projects are just so-so, earning just enough over their cost of capital to get approved, but without getting hopes too high.

Companies sometimes fool themselves into thinking that they're more sophisticated because they use advanced statistical techniques, but they often misuse those techniques. We know one company that used sophisticated statistical techniques to analyze projects, but the results always showed that there was zero probability of a negative NPV project. The organization didn't have the ability to discuss failure but only varying degrees of success.

Simple techniques like scenario analysis can go a long way to improving risk management, but only if senior management demands both a broad enough range of scenarios (not plus or minus 10 percent) and encourages open discussion of both downside risk and upside potential.

15

Capital Structure

Capital structure decisions, including those related to dividends and share repurchases, are important—not because getting them right creates a significant amount of value, but because getting them wrong can destroy tremendous value. In 2006, for instance, a number of very large companies received proposals from investment banks to increase their debt levels considerably and pay out substantial amounts to shareholders (some as much as $50 billion)—with the idea that this would increase earnings per share (EPS) and share value. Fortunately, none of the companies decided to lever up in this manner; if they had, several of them would have found it difficult to survive the financial crisis that began in 2008.

The primary objective of a company's capital structure should be to make sure it has enough capital to pursue its strategic objectives and to weather any potential cash flow shortfalls along the way. If a company doesn't have enough capital, it will either pass up opportunities, or worse, fall into financial distress or bankruptcy (or need a government bailout). Having too much capital can always be remedied by increasing future distributions to shareholders.

Capital structure can be boiled down to three issues: (1) What is the right mix of debt and equity in a company's capital structure? (2) When should a company go beyond simple debt and equity and use complex capital structures (i.e., financial engineering)? (3) What combination of dividends and/or share repurchases should a company use to return cash to shareholders?

THE MIX OF DEBT AND EQUITY

Deciding on the mix of debt and equity is a balancing act. On the one hand, equity provides more flexibility for managers to work through unexpected downturns or take advantage of unforeseen opportunities (like acquisitions). On the other side, debt provides tax benefits and fiscal discipline.

It's important to distinguish between the real value-related effects of debt and its impact on the distribution of returns and risk across different classes of investors. Debt amplifies the returns for shareholders. For example, if a company earns a 10 percent return on capital, and can borrow half of its capital at 3 percent (after taxes), its equity holders can earn a 17 percent return. But that higher return doesn't create value because it comes at a cost of higher risk to the shareholders.

Exhibit 15.1 illustrates the risk. With no debt, the company can either earn a positive 10 percent or a negative 10 percent return. But if the company uses 50 percent debt/50 percent equity, the equity investors will earn is either a positive 16 percent or a negative 24 percent return. The debt amplifies the returns (increases risk) both ways, up and down. But, the downside risk is greater than the upside gain for the same amount of leverage.

Some investors may happily take on higher risk for expected higher returns, but that isn't value creation per se. Without debt, all the value creation or destruction accrues to the shareholders; with debt, it's shared between the shareholders and lenders, but the lenders get priority in exchange for a fixed return.

Debt is a double-edged sword: it can either create or destroy value via its effect on a company's cash flows. On the positive side,

EXHIBIT 15.1 **Effect of Leverage on Returns**

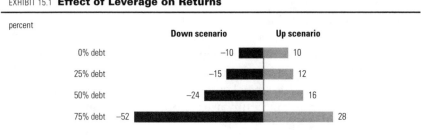

debt can increase a company's cash flows through the tax benefits it provides and the managerial discipline it imposes. On the negative side, debt can reduce a company's cash flows by reducing managerial flexibility and making the company a less reliable customer or supplier.

Debt increases cash flows by reducing taxes, because in most countries interest payments on debt are tax deductible whereas distributions to shareholders are not. Effectively, dividends and capital gains are taxed twice (at the corporate level and the investor level) because they're paid out of after-tax profits, while interest is only taxed at the investor level because it's paid out of pretax profits.

Although finance textbooks often show a theoretically high potential tax benefit from debt, in practice the benefit is much less significant for large investment-grade companies that have a small relevant range of capital structures. Exhibit 15.2 shows how this works in practice. Most companies with investment-grade debt ratings of BBB to A have interest coverage ratios of about 4.5 to 10 (EBITA divided by interest expense). Within that range, the difference in value between the 4.5 times coverage company and the 10 times coverage company is less

EXHIBIT 15.2 **Tax Benefit of Debt: Limited Impact on Enterprise Value**

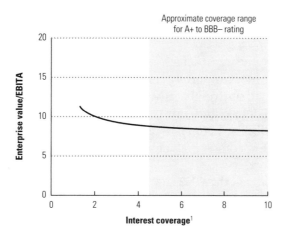

[1] EBITA/interest.

than 10 percent.* Although value curves up sharply once you drop below 4 times interest coverage, the company is also likely to drop into a below-investment-grade rating, which introduces restrictive covenants and other limitations on the company that typically overwhelm the tax benefits of debt.

Debt can also increase a company's cash flows by imposing discipline on its management. A company must make regular interest and principal payments, so it has less excess cash flow for pursuing frivolous investments or acquisitions that don't create value. Although this argument has been used over the years to support the high levels of debt in leveraged buyout transactions, it has a problem: a company needs to employ very large amounts of debt to get this discipline and, therefore, such debt is only useful for companies with very stable, predictable cash flows and limited investment opportunities.

We mentioned that debt reduces a company's cash flows in two ways. First, large amounts of debt reduce a company's flexibility to make value-creating investments, including capital expenditures, acquisitions, R&D, and sales and marketing. Second, large amounts of debt may make the company less desirable to do business with as a customer or a supplier, and less attractive as employer.

As an extreme, General Motor's and Chrysler's market shares declined considerably as consumers became concerned about buying a car from a company that might not be around in the near future. Similarly, suppliers typically demand up-front payment from retailers with heavy debt loads, which creates a negative cycle of lower inventories leading to lower sales, leading to even lower inventories, and so on downward.

In our view, the trade-off a company makes between flexibility and discipline is the most important consideration in determining its capital structure and far outweighs any tax benefits. Most large companies should target a debt-equity mix that gives them at least an investment-grade rating (BBB or better), because once you go below investment grade, debt often comes with significant covenants and, of course, a much higher cost.

Furthermore, as the 2008–2009 credit crisis demonstrated, below-investment-grade debt isn't always easy to obtain. Even refinancing existing debt that's coming due can be difficult, let alone obtaining

---

* Marc Goedhart, Tim Koller, Werner Rehm, "Marking Capital Structure Support Strategy," *McKinsey on Finance* 18 (Winter 2006): 12–17.

money for new investments or acquisitions. Most large companies follow this guideline with almost 90 percent of large nonfinancial companies having investment-grade debt ratings (BBB or better).[*]

Having a strong capital structure can make a big difference in some industries. In cyclical, capital-intensive industries like commodity chemicals and paper, investment spending typically follows profits. Companies invest in new manufacturing capacity when they have cash.[†] The pattern in such industries has been that all competitors invest at the same time leading to excess capacity and price pressure when all the plants come on line simultaneously. Over the cycle, a company could earn substantially more than its competitors if it developed a countercyclical strategic capital structure and maintained less debt than might otherwise be optimal. During bad times, it would have the ability to make investments when its competitors couldn't.

You can use sophisticated modeling techniques to hone your analyses, but ultimately you need to ask: what are my expected cash flows, what could go wrong, and what unexpected opportunities could arise? Set your debt level so that you can live through bad times in your industry while having the capacity to take advantage of unexpected opportunities.

COMPLEX FINANCIAL STRUCTURES AND FINANCIAL ENGINEERING

When it comes to financial structures, companies are best off following the advice of Albert Einstein: "Make everything as simple as possible but not simpler." In fact, most large companies tend to follow this advice, with just common equity and straight debt as sources of capital, not employing any complex features like convertibility or off-balance-sheet debt.

Complex financial instruments or structures rarely create value for large companies, but executives need to know why such complex features might or might not create value so they know if and when they are appropriate for their companies.

---

[*] Sample includes all nonfinancial companies with market capitalization greater than $5 billion at the end of 2009.
[†] Thomas Augat, Eric Bartels, and Florian Budde, "Multiple Choice for the Chemical Industry," *The McKinsey Quarterly* no. 3 (2003): 126–136.

In Chapter 3 we discussed the example of how separating hotel ownership from management creates substantial tax advantages. The hotels are owned by a tax pass-through entity like a REIT, but they're managed by a large hotel company such as Marriott. These deals are anything but simple because they need to ensure that the interests of the owner and management company are aligned. For example, they need to define in advance how they will make decisions about renovating the hotel, they need to define acceptable standards of customer service, and so on.

Financial engineering almost always generates such complexities, and things can go wrong when these complexities aren't managed well.* Consider what happened when the owners of Mervyn's, a clothing retail chain in the United States, tried to separate its real estate ownership from its operations.

In 2004, three private equity firms purchased Mervyns for $1.2 billion, then divided it into two separate companies, one owning all the real estate and one operating the stores. The store operator paid rent to the real estate company. Further complicating matters, the three private equity firms held different stakes in the two companies: one holding equal shares of both, one holding more of the real estate company, and one holding more of the operating company. Unfortunately, this meant that the interests of the owners were not aligned, as one was concerned more about the real estate company and wanted high rents, while the other wanted lower rents.

Although Mervyn's had plenty of other problems, this structure exacerbated the difficulty of improving the company's performance. Mervyn's filed for bankruptcy in 2008, and all of its stores were closed in 2009.

We'll use convertible debt to illustrate how to evaluate a complex instrument using the core-of-value and conservation-of-value principles. Convertible debt pays interest, and the debt can be converted to equity at a fixed price by the creditors. Because of the conversion feature, the creditors will accept a lower interest rate on the debt. About $150 billion of convertible securities were issued in 2007.

To illustrate, Company C issues convertible bonds with a face value of $1,000 at a 2 percent interest rate. The bonds can be converted by

---

* Emily Thornton, "What Have You Done to My Company?" *BusinessWeek*, December 8, 2008, 40–44.

the bondholder into equity at a price of $25 per share (for every $1,000 bond, the bondholder would get 40 shares: $1,000/$25). At the time of the bond issue, the shares are trading at $20, so the conversion price is at a 25 percent premium to the market value. Suppose that, three years later, the shares are trading at $35 per share, so the bondholders decide to convert, effectively paying $25 per share, a $10 discount to the share price at the time of conversion.

Here's how convertibles are marketed by bankers. The benefits to the company are that they pay a lower rate of interest than straight debt (2 percent in our example) and, if converted, the company receives a premium to the market value at the time of issue ($25 per share versus $20 per share). The benefit to the investors is that if the share price goes down, the investors still hold debt which, unless there is severe distress, won't go down much in value; but if the share price goes up enough, investors share in the gains (having the opportunity to buy shares at below-market prices). This positions convertibles as a win-win. Both investors and companies are better off than if the company issued straight debt or equity.

Sounds great, but the conservation-of-value principle tells us to look at the impact on cash flows. The total operating cash flows of the company do not change when the company issues convertible debt; only the distribution of those cash flows changes. So it can't be a good deal for both the company and the investors because they're dividing up the same pie.

Here's a better way to explain convertibles. For the company, if the share price goes up, the convertible owners will convert to equity at a *discount* to the market price at the time of the conversion (the bondholders pay $25 per share for shares worth $35 at the time of conversion). If the stock doesn't go up or goes down, the convertible owners will not convert, and the company will have to pay the full amount of the debt. So the company has to share the upside with the convertible holders when things go well, but the investors don't share the downside (unless the company defaults).

Convertible debt can make sense when investors or lenders differ from managers in their assessment of the company's credit risk.* When the discrepancy is great, it may become difficult or even impossible to

---

* See M. Brennan and E. Schwartz, "The Case for Convertibles," *Journal of Applied Corporate Finance* 1, no. 2 (1988): 55–64.

achieve agreement on the terms of credit. The key reason is that higher credit risk indeed makes the straight debt component of the convertible less attractive and the conversion component more attractive.

Another example of financial engineering is off-balance-sheet debt, which typically comes in the form of leases, securitization of assets, or project financing. Consider a company that currently owns its head-quarters building and sells that building to another party, which in turn leases the building back to the company (a sale leaseback arrangement). If the lease meets certain accounting requirements, the company can treat the transaction as a sale to the lessor, removing both the asset and the associated debt from its balance sheet. Sounds like a good deal, and it may be. But the company needs to consider that it no longer owns the asset, so it no longer shares in the appreciation of the building's value (or depreciation), and when the lease expires it must renegotiate the lease terms at then-market rates.

In addition, the company must disclose their obligations under the lease to investors and the credit rating agencies. Sophisticated investors and rating agencies treat these obligations as debt and add them back to the balance sheet when they evaluate the company.

With complex structures and financial engineering, always iden-tify the impact on a company's operating cash flows and the distri-bution of cash flows among investors. That will help you understand whether and how the structure might create value. And don't forget to identify potential unintended consequences that inevitably arise with complexity.

DIVIDENDS AND SHARE REPURCHASES

Most successful companies eventually find that they generate more cash flow than they can reinvest in their business at attractive returns on capital. Because building up unused cash on the balance sheet doesn't make sense, these companies need to return cash to their shareholders.

Some executives argue that returning cash to shareholders is a failure of management to find enough value-creating investments. We disagree, because returning cash is just algebra. Take a company with $1 billion in after-tax profits, a 20 percent ROIC, and projected revenue growth of 6 percent per year. To grow at 6 percent requires invest-ing about $300 million per year (over and above replacement capi-tal expenditures that we've assumed equal depreciation). This leaves

$700 million of additional cash flow available for investment or to return to shareholders.

Finding $700 million of value-creating new investment opportunities every year in most sectors of the economy is no simple task. Furthermore, at a 20 percent ROIC, the company would need to grow its revenues by 20 percent per year to absorb all of its cash flow. The company has no choice but to return a substantial amount of cash to shareholders.

A number of leading companies have adopted the sensible approach of regularly returning all cash they don't need, and using regular share repurchases to pay out the difference between the total payout and dividends. Although these companies don't have formal published policies, you can deduce their policies from their practices.

In the five years up through 2008, IBM for example generated $55 billion of free cash flow and returned $61 billion to shareholders.* Of the $61 billion IBM distributed to shareholders, $9 billion was distributed through dividends and $52 billion was distributed through share repurchases. As a side note, it's inconceivable that IBM could have successfully reinvested an additional $55 billion back into the business over those five years because it already spent $6 billion per year on R&D and more than $1 billion in advertising and promotion.

There are three ways to return cash: regular dividends, share repurchases, and special dividends. Special dividends are rarely used because they don't offer the flexibility for shareholders to decide whether they want to receive cash or increase their share of the company via repurchases, so we'll focus on regular dividends and share repurchases.†

As we mentioned in Chapter 3, until the early 1980s less than 10 percent of distributions to shareholders were share repurchases. Now, about 50 to 60 percent of total distributions are share repurchases. Why the shift? It's primarily about flexibility. Companies, especially in the United States, have conditioned investors to expect that they will cut dividends only in the most dire circumstances. From 2004 to 2008, only five percent of U.S.-listed companies with revenues greater than $500 million cut their dividend, and in almost every case the company faced a severe financial crisis. So companies are reluctant to establish a

---

* IBM could pay out more cash than it generated from operations because it also generated cash flow from divestitures, the exercise of employee stock options, borrowing, and reducing cash.

† In addition, most executive stock option plans don't adjust exercise prices for dividends, so executive stock options are worth more to executives when cash is returned via repurchases.

dividend level that they aren't confident of sustaining—opting, rather, to buy back shares.

Some investors also prefer repurchases because it allows them to choose whether to participate. For institutional investors, they can maintain their investment in a company without the transaction costs of reinvesting dividends. For individuals, by not participating in a share repurchase, they can defer taxes on the dividends, turning them into capital gains that will be realized potentially years in the future.

Theory says that share repurchases and dividend increases send signals from the managers of a company to investors, and this will drive a change in the company's share price. For share repurchases, there are three potential signals, two with positive implications for the company's value and one with negative implications.

The negative signal of a repurchase is that the company has run out of investment opportunities and can find nothing better to do with its cash than return it to shareholders. This assumes that stock market investors didn't already know that the company was generating more cash flow than it could reinvest. We've never seen a situation in which the stock market was surprised that the company couldn't reinvest its cash flow. Typically, investors are anticipating share repurchases long before managers make that decision, because there aren't many alternatives.

The first positive signal is that a share repurchase tells investors that management realizes it can't invest all its cash flow, and by returning cash to shareholders it won't squander the cash by investing in value-compromising opportunities. Sophisticated investors typically focus on this aspect of share repurchases.

A second positive signal is that management is more optimistic about the company's prospects and believes its shares are undervalued by the marketplace. There is some academic evidence to back up this idea, because share prices have historically risen upon repurchase program announcements. However, the increase isn't permanent. At best, the stock market recognizes the higher value of the company earlier than it otherwise would.

As share repurchases are now more regular for many companies, and with share repurchases now greater than dividends in the aggregate, we suspect that their signaling effect has declined. There haven't been any recent studies, however. Further, most companies tend to re-purchase shares when they have excess cash flow, which also tends to be when their share prices are high, so we don't expect that companies are able to systematically buy when their shares are undervalued.

Although share repurchases send a positive signal, so do dividend increases. Since managers only cut dividends as a last resort, increasing a dividend signals confidence that they can continue to pay the new higher dividend level. The signaling effect of dividends is probably stronger than share repurchases because it's a commitment to future payments, unlike share repurchases, which don't need to be repeated in future years.

An argument for share repurchases that doesn't hold up to scrutiny is that they increase value because they increase EPS. As we saw in Chapter 3, share repurchases do increase EPS mathematically, but that EPS increase will be offset by a P/E ratio decline, as the company is more risky as a result of the higher leverage. The net effect on share value is zero.

In summary, returning excess cash flow to shareholders is generally good, but it doesn't create value itself. A better way to think of returning cash to shareholders is that it prevents that cash from being invested in low-return projects.

A poorly managed capital structure can lead to financial distress and value destruction, but for companies whose leverage is already at reasonable levels, the potential to add value by "optimizing" capital structure is limited—especially relative to the impact of improvements in returns on capital and growth. Rather than fine tuning for the so-called optimal capital structure, managers should make sure the company has sufficient financial flexibility to support its strategy.

16

Investor
Communications

The value of investor communications can be difficult to determine. Some argue that it's a waste of management time and has no effect on a company's share price. Others have unrealistic expectations, assuming that your investor relations people can talk up your share price and, if they're really good, can tell you why your share price went down by 1.2 percent yesterday.

We fall somewhere in between. It's virtually impossible to interpret short-term price movements with any useful insights. And even if you could talk up your share price beyond its intrinsic value, you probably shouldn't. On the other hand, good investor communications can ensure that your share price doesn't get out of line with its intrinsic value, can build a base of loyal investors, and can ensure that executives don't make poor strategic decisions based on misunderstanding what investors are saying to them.

Often overlooked, the last point about listening to investors is a key reason we became interested in investor communications. We observed that companies do pay attention to investors and sometimes base important strategic decisions on what they believe investors want the company to do. Too often, however, executives don't know how to interpret what they are hearing from investors, often because they're listening to the wrong investors.

Good investor communications is as much about executives listening to the right investors as it is about telling investors about the company. It's about building relationships with the right kinds of investors and communicating to them at their level. It's also about not concerning oneself with investors who have a short-term orientation, carefully selecting which sell-side analysts to focus on, and not becoming overly occupied with the press, whose needs for a single simple headline get in the way of sophisticated analysis.*

OBJECTIVES OF INVESTOR COMMUNICATIONS

Good investor communications must be grounded in the right objectives, and achieving the highest possible share price through investor communications is not a wise objective. Instead, the overriding objective of investor communications should be to align a company's share price with management's perspective on the intrinsic value of the company.

A gap between a company's market value and its intrinsic value brings significant disadvantages to all the company's stakeholders. If the share price exceeds its intrinsic value, the price will eventually fall as the company's real performance becomes evident to the market. When that fall comes, employee morale will suffer, and management will have to face a concerned board of directors who may not understand why the price is falling so far so fast.

A share price that's too high may also encourage managers to keep it high by adopting short-term tactics, such as deferring investments or maintenance costs, that will hamper value creation in the long run. Conversely, a share price that is too low also has drawbacks, especially the threat of takeover. In addition, it makes paying for acquisitions with shares an unattractive option, and may demoralize managers and employees.

The second objective of investor communications is to develop support from a group of sophisticated intrinsic investors who thoroughly understand the company's strategies, strengths, and weaknesses—and who can better distinguish the shorter from the longer term.

The final objective is gaining intelligence about your customers, competitors, and suppliers. The best investors will be talking to your

---

*Special thanks to Robert Palter and Werner Rehm for their support and insights on this chapter. We drew heavily on their article "Opening Up to Investors," *McKinsey on Finance* (Spring 2009): 26–31.

customers, suppliers, and competitors, so they may be able to provide senior management with more objective insights.

INTRINSIC VALUE VERSUS MARKET VALUE

Any good strategy must begin with an honest assessment of the situation, and a strategy for investor communications is no different. It should start with an estimate of the size of the gap, if any, between management's view of the company's intrinsic value and the stock market value. In practice, we typically find that no significant gap exists, or that any gap can be explained by the company's historical performance relative to peers, or by the way the market is valuing the entire industry. Allow us to illustrate with a disguised example.

A large specialty chemicals company called Chemco has earned attractive returns on capital, but its product lines are in slow-growth segments. Consequently, Chemco's revenue growth has been low. Chemco recently adopted a strategy to buy small companies in faster-growing areas of the industry with higher ROICs—intending to apply its manufacturing and distribution skills to improve the performance of the acquired companies. Currently, 18 months since the company made its first acquisitions under this strategy, five percent of Chemco's revenues are from the fast-growth segments.

Chemco's managers were concerned that the company's P/E ratio trailed the P/Es of many companies against which it compared itself. They wondered whether such factors as the company's old-fashioned name or the small number of analysts covering the industry were the cause of the low value.

We began analyzing the apparent discrepancy by assessing Chemco's value relative to companies it considered peers. Some of the supposed peers were 100 percent focused on the fast-growth segments, far more than Chemco's five percent of revenues from fast-growth segments. Also, some of Chemco's peers were going through substantial restructurings, so current earnings were very low. When we segmented Chemco's peers, we found that its earnings multiple (enterprise value divided by earnings before interest, taxes, and amortization—EBITA) was in line with those of its close peers but behind those of the companies in the fast-growing segment (see Exhibit 16.1). A third set of companies had high multiples because of current low earnings due to restructuring. Exhibit 16.1 also shows that Chemco and its closest peers

EXHIBIT 16.1 **Chemco: Valuation in Line with Close Peers**

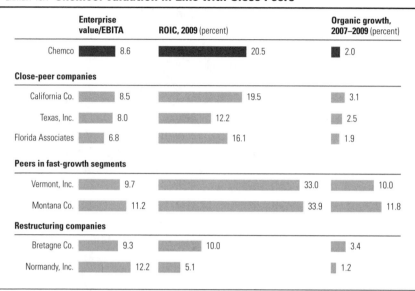

	Enterprise value/EBITA	ROIC, 2009 (percent)	Organic growth, 2007–2009 (percent)
Chemco	8.6	20.5	2.0
Close-peer companies			
California Co.	8.5	19.5	3.1
Texas, Inc.	8.0	12.2	2.5
Florida Associates	6.8	16.1	1.9
Peers in fast-growth segments			
Vermont, Inc.	9.7	33.0	10.0
Montana Co.	11.2	33.9	11.8
Restructuring companies			
Bretagne Co.	9.3	10.0	3.4
Normandy, Inc.	12.2	5.1	1.2

had lower ROICs and much lower growth rates than the other companies. Therefore, Chemco's value was aligned with its performance relative to its closest peers.

Next, we reverse engineered the share price of Chemco and its peers by building a discounted cash flow (DCF) model for each company and estimating what levels of future performance would be consistent with the current share price. We found that if Chemco increased its revenues at two percent per year and maintained its most recent level of margins and capital turnover, its DCF value would equal its current share price. This growth rate was in line with the implicit growth of its closest peers and lower than the companies in the fast-growing segment.

WHICH INVESTORS MATTER?

Does it matter who your investors are? It's not clear whether one investor base is better than another in helping align a company's intrinsic value with its share price. But understanding the company's investor base can give managers insights that might help them anticipate how the market will react to important events and strategic actions, as well as help managers improve the effectiveness and efficiency of their investor-relations activities.

In Chapter 7, we showed that traditional investor classification systems, like growth versus value, yield only a shallow understanding of how investors actually construct their portfolios. We showed that growth investors tended to invest in companies with high market-to-book ratios, not companies with faster revenue growth. (Remember, a slow-growing company can have a high valuation multiple if it has a high ROIC).

Perhaps a bigger problem is the erroneous belief by executives that they can increase their company's valuation multiple by marketing their shares better to growth investors, simply because growth investors tend to own shares with higher valuation multiples. We showed that, in fact, the causality runs in reverse: in our analysis of companies whose stock prices have recently increased enough to shift them from the value classification to the growth classification, an influx of growth investors is clearly not what precipitated the rise in market value. Rather, growth investors responded to higher multiples, moving into the stock only after the share price had already risen.

In Chapter 7 we also introduced an investor classification system based on differences among investors' portfolio-building strategies; this system offers a better understanding of which investors drive share prices. We identified four classes of investors: intrinsic, trading, mechanical, and closet indexers. The first two groups are the most important drivers of share prices, but in different ways. Trading investors buy and sell in anticipation of near-term events (quarterly earnings and product announcements, etc.). They generate a lot of trading volume, but because they're moving in and out over short horizons, their impact on long-term prices is minimal. In fact, they don't care whether the share price of a company is high or low, but merely whether it's likely to go up or down in the near term.

Intrinsic investors have the most influence on share price levels (except for short-term volatility triggered by company events). Compared with others, these investors typically have fewer companies in their portfolios, so they're able to do deeper and more detailed research on the intrinsic value of each of their investments. They also tend to have longer horizons, so they hold stocks for longer periods.

Based on their research, intrinsic investors form a view of what a stock is worth. If the price rises by a given margin above that value, the intrinsic investor will sell. If a stock's value falls well below what an intrinsic investor considers its real worth, this type of investor will buy in considerable volume, setting a floor to the price. The variation in views on company values held by different intrinsic investors tends to set the upper and lower limits of the trading range of particular stocks.

It's clear then that companies should focus their investor communications effort on intrinsic investors. If intrinsic investors view the value of your company consistent with your own view, then the market as a whole is likely to value your company as you do because of the role intrinsic investors play in driving share prices. Their understanding of long-term value creation also means that they're more likely than other investors to hold onto a stock through periods of short-term volatility (so long as they believe these periods don't reflect a material change in the underlying value of the company). These are also the investors to whom you should listen when you want to understand what the market thinks of your company.

A conundrum for companies is how to treat closet indexers, who may be some of a company's largest investors. Remember, closet indexers are likely to have more than 200 different companies in their portfolios, and most of their holdings are in proportion to the companies' sizes in an index such as the S&P 500. Examine whether the closet indexer is significantly over- or underweight in your company or industry. If yes, move them to the intrinsic category with respect to that company or industry. If not, keep them as closet indexers.

CEOs and CFOs have substantial demands on their time, and investors worry when executives spend too much time with investors instead of running the company. Just as a CEO has to decide which customers to personally spend time with, CEOs and CFOs must decide which investors will get their time. Our investor segmentation makes it clear that CEOs and CFOs should focus their time on a small set of intrinsic investors, and delegate interactions with trading investors and closet indexers to their investor relations executives. In fact, one of the key roles of the investor relations department should be to analytically determine which investors CEOs and CFOs should develop relationships with, facilitate those relationships, and be the gatekeeper for handling nonpriority investors on behalf of the CEO or CFO. The gatekeeper role may not be popular with investors, but it's essential.

Of course, CEOs and CFOs can't ignore the sell-side analysts, whose role has changed over time. Their job is to support their clients, and their most important clients are those who generate the most trading commissions: the trading-oriented investors. Many sophisticated trading (and intrinsic) investors are less concerned about whether the analyst has issued a buy or hold on a stock (sell recommendations are almost nonexistent), preferring to have up-to-date news about the company. Hence, sell-side analysts tend to focus on short-term events and near-term earnings so they can be first to pass that news on to their clients.

This said, there are often one to three sell-side analysts with deep understanding about the dynamics of the industry and the company's strategies, opportunities, and risks. These sell-side analysts are more like intrinsic investors in their approach. The logical way to treat sell-side analysts is to segment them into those whose interests and approach tends to mimic trading investors and those whose approach mimics intrinsic investors—then to pay more attention to the latter.

COMMUNICATING TO INTRINSIC INVESTORS

Intrinsic investors are sophisticated, and they've spent considerable effort to understand your business. They want transparency about results, management's candid assessment of the company's performance, and insightful guidance about the company's targets and strategies. Their role in determining stock prices makes it worth management's time to meet their needs for sophisticated communication that isn't oversimplified.

But many companies are reluctant to provide a detailed discussion of results, issues, and opportunities—arguing that it reduces their flexibility to manage reported profits, or that it will reveal sensitive information to competitors. In our experience, however, a company's competitors, customers, and suppliers already know more about any business than its managers might expect.

For example, there's a cottage industry of photographers dedicated to searching for and publicizing new car models that automotive manufacturers haven't yet formally acknowledged. In addition, a company's competitors will be talking regularly to the company's customers and suppliers, who won't hesitate to share information about the company whenever it's in their interest. So revealing details about yourself is unlikely to affect companies as adversely as you might expect, and you should assess the competitive costs and benefits of greater transparency with that in mind.

In some situations, companies might even be able to gain an advantage over their competitors via more transparency. Suppose a company has developed a new technology, product, or manufacturing process that management feels sure will give the company a lead over competitors. Furthermore, managers believe competitors will be unable to copy the innovation. At a strategic level, disclosing the innovation might discourage competitors from even trying to compete if they believe the company has too great a lead. From an investor's perspective, disclosure of the innovation could increase the company's share price relative to its competitors, thus making it more attractive to potential partners and key employees.

Sophisticated investors build up their view of a company's overall value by summing the values of its discrete businesses. So they're not much concerned with aggregate results: these are simply averages, providing little insight into how the company's individual businesses might be positioned for future growth and returns on invested capital. At many companies, management teams that desire a closer match between their company's market value and their own assessment might achieve this by disclosing more about the performances of their individual businesses.

How much detail is enough? Concerning financial data, it depends on whether the information is critical for assessing how much value a business can create. For instance, IBM discloses revenue growth in constant currency terms below the business unit level. Nestlé does so at a product and regional level. This kind of detailed financial information is very helpful to investors and gives competitors no insight into business models or sources of strategic advantage that they wouldn't already have learned from competitive intelligence and their own performance results.

As a rule of thumb, companies should provide a detailed income statement for each business unit, down to the level of earnings before EBITA, at least. They should also provide all operating items in the balance sheet—such as property, plant, and equipment (PP&E); accounts receivable; inventories; and accounts payable—reconciled with the consolidated reported numbers. Even companies with a single line of business can improve their disclosures without giving away strategically sensitive information. Whole Foods Market, a U.S. grocery chain, provides ROIC by age of store, shown by Exhibit 16.2. This gives investors deeper insights into the company's economic life cycle.

EXHIBIT 16.2 **Whole Foods: ROIC by Age of Store**

Comparable stores (Q1 2008)	Number of stores	Average size (square feet)	Growth (percent)	ROIC (percent)
Over 11 years old	64	28,300	5.4	78
Between 8 and 11 years old	28	33,400	4.0	55
Between 5 and 8 years old	41	33,900	8.3	41
Between 2 and 5 years old	41	44,600	11.7	22
Less than 2 years old (including 5 relocations)	15	58,100	37.7	−2

Source: Whole Foods Annual Report 2007, March 2008 investor presentation, and WholeFoods.com.

Concerning operational data, what to disclose depends on the key value drivers of a business or business unit. Ideally, these should be the metrics that management uses to make strategic or operational decisions. Companies in some industries, such as steel and airlines, likewise regularly disclose volumes and average prices, as well as the use and cost of energy, which are the key drivers of value in these sectors. Lowe's (the hardware retailer) provides helpful information about such value drivers as the number of transactions and the average ticket size, as shown in Exhibit 16.3.

To make sound investment decisions, intrinsic investors require executives to be honest in their public assessments of their company and its businesses. Yet executives typically approach public announcements less candidly. Most management presentations and publications

EXHIBIT 16.3 **Lowe's: Customer Transactions and Average Ticket Size**

Other metrics	2007	2006	2005
Comparable store sales (decrease)/increase (percent)	5.1	–	6.1
→ Customer transactions (in millions)	720	680	639
→ Average ticket	$67.05	$68.98	$67.67
At end of year			
Number of stores	1,534	1,385	1,234
Sales floor square feet (in millions)	174	157	140
Average store size, selling square feet (in thousands)	113	113	113
Return on average assets (percent)	9.5	11.7	11.9
Return on average shareholders' equity (percent)	17.7	20.8	21.5

Source: Company SEC filings.

offer only a celebration of the past year's performance and a less than comprehensive assessment of shortfalls. Very few discuss the impact of strategic tradeoffs on the numbers—for instance, how a pricing initiative drove growth at the expense of margins. Companies that openly discuss what happened during the year, and disclose where management has identified pockets of underperformance even in good times, will help investors assess the quality of the executive team and thus the potential for future value creation.

More importantly, when strategic decisions go bad, investors want to understand what management has learned. Intrinsic investors in particular understand that business requires taking risks and that not all of them pay off. Intrinsic investors value forthrightness and will probably support a company through a course correction if they were given enough information previously to develop faith in management's judgment.

Says one portfolio manager, "I don't want inside information. But I do want management to look me in the eye when they talk about their performance. If they avoid a discussion or explanation, we will not invest, no matter how attractive the numbers look."

Consider the case of Progressive Insurance. In the third quarter of 2006, the company lowered its policy rates to encourage faster growth, making what CEO Glenn Renwick described as "an explicit trade-off of margin for longer-term customer growth." He acknowledged that "while we will never know the outcome of alternative decisions, we feel very good about the focus on customer growth." When the strategy didn't work out as planned, Renwick addressed the subject directly in the first two sentences of his letter to the shareholders in the 2007 annual report: "Profitability and premium growth are both down and they directly reflect the pricing strategy we enacted," he wrote. That strategy "did not produce the aggregate revenue growth we had hoped for." Long-term investors look for this kind of candid assessment when they decide to bet on a management team.

GUIDANCE

In the view of many executives, the ritual of issuing guidance on their expected earnings per share (EPS) in the next quarter or year is a necessary, if sometimes onerous, part of communicating with financial markets. We surveyed executives about guidance and found that they

EXHIBIT 16.4 **Minimal Impact of Guidance on TRS**

Number of first-year guider firms with returns at given level relative to industry[1]

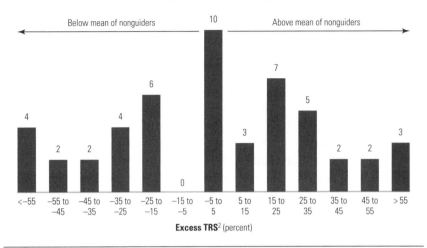

[1] 50 firms in guiding sample, all from the consumer packaged-goods sector.
[2] Excess TRS for a firm is defined as TRS in year of starting guidance minus median TRS in same year for nonguiding firms.

Source: Thomson First Call, McKinsey Corporate Performance Center analysis.

saw three primary benefits of issuing earnings guidance: higher valuations, lower share price volatility, and improved liquidity. Yet our analysis found no evidence that those expected benefits materialize.

Instead of EPS guidance, we believe executives should provide investors with the broader operational measures shaping company performance, such as volume targets, revenue targets, and initiatives to reduce costs.* They can present this information at the beginning of the financial year and issue updates if there are significant changes.

To test whether companies giving EPS guidance were rewarded with higher valuations, we compared the earnings multiples of companies that provided guidance with those that didn't, industry by industry. For most industries, the underlying distributions of the two sets of companies were statistically indistinguishable. Furthermore, in the year companies begin to offer guidance, contrary to what they must have hoped, their total returns to shareholders (TRS) are no different from those of companies that don't offer guidance, as shown in Exhibit 16.4. Returns to shareholders are just as likely to be above the

---

* Peggy Hsieh, Timothy Koller, and S. R. Rajan, "The Misguided Practice of Earnings Guidance," *McKinsey on Finance* (Spring 2006): 1–5.

market as below the market in the year a company starts providing guidance.

On the issue of share-price volatility, we found that when a company begins to issue earnings guidance, the likelihood of volatility in its share price increasing or decreasing is just the same as it is for companies that don't issue guidance. Finally, we found that when companies do begin issuing earnings guidance, they do indeed experience an increase in trading volumes relative to companies that don't provide it, as their management anticipates. However, the effect wears off the next year.

When we asked executives about stopping guidance, many feared that their share price would decline and its volatility would increase. But when we analyzed 126 companies that had discontinued issuing guidance, we found they were just about as likely to see higher or lower shareholder returns as the rest of the market. Of the 126 companies, 58 had higher returns than the overall market in the year they stopped issuing guidance, and 68 had lower returns.

Furthermore, our analysis showed that the lower-than-market returns of companies that discontinued guidance resulted from poor underlying performance and not the act of ending guidance itself. For example, two-thirds of the companies that stopped guidance and experienced lower returns on capital saw lower TRS than the market. For companies that increased ROIC, only about one-third saw lower TRS than the market.

Our conclusion was that issuing guidance offers companies and investors no real benefits. On the contrary, it can trigger real costs and unfortunate unintended consequences. The difficulty of predicting earnings accurately, for example, frequently causes management teams to endure the painful experience of missing quarterly forecasts. That, in turn, can be a powerful incentive for management to focus excessive attention on the short term, at the expense of longer-term investments, and to manage earnings inappropriately from quarter to quarter to create the illusion of stability. Moreover, according to our research with intrinsic investors, they realize that earnings are inherently unpredictable. For that reason, they prefer that companies not issue quarterly EPS guidance.

When Coca-Cola stopped issuing guidance in late 2002, its executives had concluded that providing short-term guidance prevented management from concentrating on strategic initiatives to build its businesses and succeed over the long term. Instead of indicating weak earnings, Gary Fayard (then CFO) believed that the move signaled a renewed focus on long-term goals. The market seemed to agree and didn't react negatively: Coke's share price held steady.*

As an alternative, we believe executives will gain advantages from providing guidance at the start of the financial year on the real short-, medium-, and long-term value drivers of their businesses, giving ranges rather than point estimates. They should update this guidance whenever there is a meaningful change in their targets.

Some companies provide a range of possibilities for revenue growth under a variety of assumptions about inflation, and they discuss the growth of individual business units when that matters. IT research firm Gartner sets out a range of long-term goals, such as growth targets by business unit, margin improvement targets, and capital spending goals. Other companies also provide information on value drivers that can help investors assess the sustainability of growth. Humana, for instance, provides guidance on estimated membership in its health plans—including plans whose membership the company expects will decline.

Ideally, companies would provide the kind of information that would help investors make their own performance projections based on their assessment of external factors. For example, in resource-extraction industries, the prices for the commodities extracted—such as gold, copper, or oil—are volatile. For such companies, a management team's view on future prices is not necessarily better than that of its investors. Production targets would, therefore, be more useful than revenue targets for investors in these industries.

Similarly, exchange rates are unpredictable, yet they can affect the profits of multinationals by five percent or more in a given year. Companies should therefore avoid predicting exchange rates and locking them into EPS targets. Rather, they should discuss their targets at constant currency rates. This would give investors a much clearer picture of their expected performance.

LISTENING TO INVESTORS

The final element of investor communications is listening to investors. Doing this to gain competitive intelligence is, of course, a no-lose proposition. But to what extent should executives be influenced by

* David M. Katz, "Nothing but the Real Thing," CFO (March 2003), http://cfo.com.

investors' opinions about what strategies the companies should pursue (expressed either as opinions or by the nature of the questions the investors ask), particularly when those opinions run counter to what the senior executives believe is the best strategy for creating long-term value?

The answer lies again in the segmentation of the investors, and the interpretation of investor input in light of the investors' own strategies. For example, trading investors (who tend to be the most vocal and frequent voices) base their trading strategies on *events*. So they prefer frequent announcements and short-term actions to create trading opportunities. Intrinsic investors, on the other hand, are more concerned with longer-term strategic initiatives and the broader forces driving the company and industry. Segmenting investor input helps executives sort through the competing views. We typically find that when executives segment the input they receive from investors, the input from intrinsic investors is most helpful.

In the end, though, executives have more information than investors about their company, its capabilities, opportunities, and threats. They need to be confident about their strategic choices and convey that to investors. Executives can't expect to please all investors, and they have to do what's right for long-term value creation.

We liked the recent response by Sam Palmisano, CEO of IBM, to a question about whether IBM should pursue large acquisitions if other high-tech companies did. He confidently described IBM's strategy: "We look for intellectual property that we can scale and leverage. We have a unique base, i.e., distribution in 170 countries. Regardless of what other people say, we don't like big [acquisitions] because you can't scale big, they're already scaled. . . . You tell me how many of these [big acquisitions] ever got their money back much less a premium over their weighted average cost of capital."*

---

* 2010 IBM Investor Briefing, May 12, 2010.

17

Managing for Value

The most difficult part of creating value and applying the four corner-stones is getting the right balance between delivering near-term profits and return on capital, and continuing to invest for long-term value creation.* Configuring the management approaches of the company to reflect this balance is the chief executive's responsibility.

Large companies are complex in their many businesses, markets, stakeholders, and layers of management—and this tends to bias decisions toward short-term profits because they are the most visible measure of performance. One large company we know owes its heritage of success to nurturing small business units with patience, knowing that some of them will become large, successful businesses. But recently we found that the company doesn't have as many small units to nurture anymore, a casualty of its newfound desire to boost current earnings.

We've seen several large companies in industries ranging from consumer products to health care to banking set explicit targets for growing earnings faster than revenues. This can be construed as a clear and bold performance aspiration, and it usually works for a couple of years in an already healthy business. However, it overlooks the fact that the only way to continually grow earnings faster than revenues is to cut necessary costs for growing the business, or to not invest in new markets that will have low or negative margins for several years.

---

* Not just in fixed assets, but in investments that are expensed right away, such as new product development, new geographic markets, and people.

Companies that adopt such a bold but unsustainable performance directive usually regret it.

In Chapter 9, we mentioned a survey by Graham, Harvey, and Rajgopal, who asked 400 chief financial officers what they would do if their companies were at risk of missing their earnings targets. Eighty percent said they would reduce such discretionary expenses as marketing and product development to meet their short-term targets, even though they knew this would damage longer-term performance. Almost 40 percent said they would provide incentives for customers to shift their purchases to an earlier quarter.

Most executives don't set out to shortchange future value creation, yet a variety of forces compel them to focus on near-term performance: investors, equity analysts, the press, their boards of directors, and their own internal management processes. There's no easy way to overcome the short-term bias. It may well require reducing short-term profit growth and ROIC below what they otherwise could be, and sometimes below peers' growth rates and ROICs. To make matters worse, it's virtually impossible for a company to prove to investors or the press that the reason its current profit margin or profit growth is lower than peers' is because of spending for the future, not poor management.

Overcoming the short-term bias while maintaining a strong performance culture often requires changes in several core management processes. Performance measurement should reflect the complexity of the corporation with a better mix of long- and short-term measures, and a greater emphasis on the operating metrics that presage financial results. Executive compensation should move away from simple earnings benchmarks and near-term total returns to shareholders (TRS) measures. Strategic planning and budgeting should embrace the dynamics of portfolio reconfiguration, new-growth platform creation, and growth-related resource reallocation. And the board of directors should understand inevitable trade-offs so it can both challenge and support management on decisions that affect the long-term value of the enterprise.

ORGANIZING FOR VALUE

A common shortfall of most large-company management processes is that they often function at a level that is too high. Value is created by the cash flows from individual products or services in specific customer segments, not at the corporate level (although multibusiness enterprises augment that value with mechanisms we discussed in Chapter 12). Therefore, management processes—like performance measurement, compensation, and planning—need to be conducted in a way that helps the company make decisions at an appropriate level of granularity.

Many larger companies use organizational constructs like divisions (sometimes called groups or sectors), which are collections of related business units. These divisional structures have evolved to groom managers for top jobs and to limit the number of direct reports under the CEO. But this can also reduce business and operational transparency, and it can get in the way of active value-adding actions by the corporation. For example, a head of a small business unit might eye a promising new technology investment—but then dismiss it because his unit doesn't have a sufficient research and development (R&D) budget. If the idea were to make it further up the chain of command, it might be more likely to receive funding. Lack of granular visibility becomes a barrier for future value creation.

Our experience suggests that a typical $10 billion revenue or higher company should probably have 20 to 50 discretely managed performance units. While managing so many units might appear to increase the workload of the CEO and corporate staff, the reverse is often true. Using smaller units actually reduces complexity because managers find it easier to identify and monitor the handful of metrics that truly drive performance.

Instead of aggregating strategies and economics into complex divisions and then spending an inordinate amount of time understanding the overall strategy and performance, the CEO can make a larger number of more rapid, specific, and radical decisions at the more detailed business unit level. With the more granular approach, CEOs and CFOs have better information for taking a more active role in managing a unit's longer-term development.*

These structures also make it easier to actively reallocate money and talent to value creation. One global technology company found that by taking a more granular approach, it shifted its R&D priorities. Under the old approach with only a handful of operating units, one unit regularly reduced R&D spending on a breakthrough renewable energy

* Massimo Giordano and Felix Wenger, "Organizing for Value," *McKinsey on Finance*, Summer 2008, 20–25.

technology to meets its aggregate profit targets. Once the company redefined the reporting units, and this technology and its applications became its own reporting unit, spending was significantly increased based on the technology's long-term revenue potential.

PERFORMANCE MEASUREMENT

Performance measurement typically drives much of the way a large company works. We talked extensively in this book about how accounting profits or profit growth as a sole performance metric doesn't lead to value creation. Supplementing profits with ROIC and revenue growth is a step in the right direction to ensure that the profits a business earns are actually creating value, not simply over-consuming capital that another company could better deploy. However, profits, ROIC, and revenue growth are backward looking. They don't tell you how well the business is positioned for future growth and ROIC improvement.

One company we know had a particular business unit that consistently recorded growing profits and high levels of ROIC for about four years. Since the unit's reported financial results were so good, the executives at the corporate headquarters didn't ask many questions about the drivers of the unit's profits—until it was too late. It turned out that the unit was driving profits by raising prices and cutting marketing and advertising expenditures. Higher prices and reduced advertising created an opening for competitors to take away market share, which they did. So while profits were rising and ROIC was high, market share was declining.

The next thing the company knew, it couldn't raise prices anymore, and market share kept falling. The company had to reset the business with lower prices and more advertising. It took many years for the company to regain its lost position. If the corporate executives and board had probed into the unit's sources of profit expansion, they likely would have taken corrective action earlier. This example also speaks to the obligation of management and boards to challenge high-performing units as much as they challenge those that are troubled.

Good performance measurement can help overcome the short-term bias of financial measures by explicitly monitoring how well a company or business unit is positioned to sustain and improve its financial performance. This is what we call a business's *health*, and related metrics explain how financial results were achieved and provide

EXHIBIT 17.1 **Performance and Health Metrics**

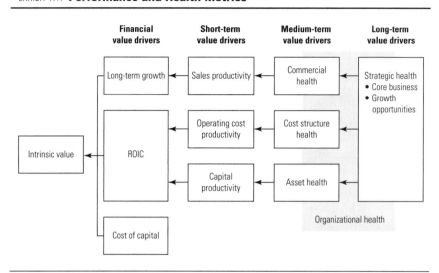

causal insights into future performance potential. An example of systematically measuring both performance and health is illustrated in Exhibit 17.1.

The left-hand side of the exhibit shows the financial drivers of value: revenue growth and ROIC. Companies also need metrics that indicate the short-, medium-, and long-term health of the business, as shown to the right of the financial metrics. While every business needs some metrics tailoring, the eight generic categories presented in Exhibit 17.1 can be used as a starting point to ensure that a company systematically manages all the important areas.

Short-term value drivers are the immediate levers of ROIC and growth. They indicate whether current growth and ROIC can be sustained, will improve, or will decline in the near future. They might include *sales productivity* metrics such as market share, the company's ability to charge premium prices relative to peers, or sales force productivity. *Operating-cost productivity* metrics might include the component costs for building an automobile or delivering a package, the rates of rework, and so forth.

Medium-term value drivers look forward to indicate whether a company can maintain and improve its revenue growth and ROIC over the next one to five years (or longer for companies, such as pharmaceutical manufacturers, that have long product cycles). These metrics may be harder to quantify than short-term measures and are more likely to be measured annually or over even longer periods.

Medium-term *commercial health* metrics indicate whether the company can sustain or improve its current revenue growth, including the company's product pipeline, brand strength measures, and customer satisfaction. *Cost structure* metrics measure a company's ability to manage its costs relative to competitors over three to five years. These metrics might include assessments of continuous improvement programs or other efforts to maintain a cost advantage relative to competitors. *Asset health* measures might show how well a company maintains its assets and consistently improves asset productivity. For example, a hotel or restaurant chain might measure the average time between remodeling projects as an important driver of health.

Metrics for long-term strategic health include a company's progress in identifying and exploiting new growth areas and the company's ability to sustain its competitive advantages against threats. Long-term strategic health metrics might be more qualitative than short- and medium-term metrics, and might be more along the lines of assessments of the company's ability to deal with changes in the environment. Some examples include new technologies, changes in customer preferences, new ways of serving customers, and disruptive threats.

The final category is *organizational health*, which measures whether the company has the people, skills, and culture to sustain and improve its performance. As with the other measures, what is important varies by industry. One dimension of this is the needed flows of talent. Pharmaceutical companies have long needed deep scientific-innovation leadership capabilities but relatively few general managers. This may change with trends like the proliferation of personalized therapeutics into product markets. Retailers historically need trained stored managers, a few great merchandisers, and, in most cases, store staff with a customer service orientation.

This framework shares some elements with the balanced scorecard concept that was introduced in a seminal 1992 *Harvard Business Review* article by Robert Kaplan and David Norton.* Numerous organizations have subsequently advocated and implemented the balanced scorecard

---

* Robert S. Kaplan and David P. Norton, "The Balanced Scorecard: Measures That Drive Performance," *Harvard Business Review* 80, no. 1 (January 1992): 71–79.

idea. Kaplan and Norton point out that customer satisfaction, internal business processes, learning, and revenue growth are important drivers of long-term performance.

Although our concept of health metrics resembles Kaplan and Norton's nonfinancial metrics, we don't advocate their off-the-shelf application. We advocate that companies choose their own set of metrics tailored to their industries and strategies. For example, product innovation may be important to companies in one industry, while in another, tight cost control and customer service may matter more. Similarly, an individual company (or business unit) will have different value drivers at different points in its life cycle.

COMPENSATION

Despite the complexity of running a business and the innumerable decisions that need to be made, most companies still mechanically link compensation to accounting earnings or TRS, and maybe one or two additional metrics such as revenue growth. We believe companies need to fundamentally change how they assess and pay for executive performance. Specifically, they need to complement shorter-term, mechanical formulas with deeper assessments of how effectively the executives have driven the company's long-term value creation.

This more balanced approach requires more judgment and is more time consuming, but it's worth the effort. At our firm, for instance, a committee of senior partners devotes three to four weeks per year evaluating each partner in the firm. Each committee member spends two to three weeks interviewing colleagues about the five to eight partners they're assessing. The committee then meets for a week to discuss the findings and makes development, advancement, and compensation decisions. It's a significant amount of time and effort, but it overcomes the problems with purely mechanical approaches.

An approach like ours isn't subjective; it relies on objective facts as inputs into a nonmechanical process that doesn't compensate people according to a simple formula. Much like a healthy scorecard for a corporation, the scorecard for the individual is also balanced according to holistic metrics. For example, in addition to basing executive compensation on financial results, a company might assess an executive's progress with regard to product development, customer satisfaction, and employee development objectives.

We believe that the current practice of linking compensation to a company's stock price performance, particularly the use of stock options, doesn't create strong incentives to manage for the longer term. First, as we demonstrated in Chapter 7, much of a company's share performance over one- to three-year periods is driven more by broader market movements than anything the company or its executives do. From the early 1980s through the end of the 1990s, stock prices went up largely due to declines in interest rates and a strong economy, not due to the actions of managers. Conversely, share prices fell across the board in 2008, once again without regard to individual company performance.

Second, as we saw in Chapter 4, share price movements in the short term are largely driven by changes in expectations (company and sector), rather than actual company performance. While using share price performance relative to sector peers would be a simple and appropriate step in the right direction, we would still give such a metric small weight in the overall package.

STRATEGIC PLANNING AND BUDGETING

Along with performance measurement and compensation, planning and budgeting shape the corporate culture and drive behaviors throughout the organization. Yet few senior leaders are satisfied with the productivity or effectiveness of these processes. Too often, the processes have structural biases to the short term, hindering the steps required to build long-term value.

As we said earlier in this chapter, the effectiveness of strategic planning and budgeting has little to do with the formal flow of work or the templates a company requires each unit to complete. These processes are effective only when they lead to good decisions based on informed and open dialogue within the company; but at many companies, the annual budgeting process has hijacked strategic planning. Too much of the strategy process has been organized around providing neat, multiyear financial forecasts; too little of the process entails the often messy questions of, say, what should and shouldn't be in the business portfolio, or what combination of organic and acquired growth can create value.

We see numerous ways to improve how strategic planning contributes to value creation. First, break the links between strategic planning and budgeting. The strategic planning process should operate under a different time line than budgeting to ensure that it doesn't reemerge as a glorified three- to five-year budget.

Second, business unit strategic planning should migrate away from detailed financial forecasts toward a focus on the long-term drivers of value creation and, most importantly, a discussion of the issues and opportunities facing the unit. Instead of a 50-line-item, bottom-up financial forecast, maybe a company should have each unit prepare three 10-line-item financial scenarios that can help frame the issues and opportunities, along with their required investments.

Companies should also create a stand-alone *corporate* strategy process distinct from their business unit strategic planning. The corporate strategy process should be designed to understand opportunities for better ownership, growth platforms, and resource reallocation.

Both business unit and corporate strategic discussions need to address radical changes to the status quo, such as exiting businesses, dramatically boosting expenditures on promising growth opportunities, or taking bold steps to reduce asset intensity or the way the company develops or markets its products.

The budgeting process at many companies has become too top-down and delinked from strategy. Executives often tell us that certain investments in growth were approved during the strategy discussion (meaning product or market development investments that flow through the income statement rather than the balance sheet). But when budgeting time comes around, there's no money to spend.

Furthermore, too many budgeting processes are designed for one size to fit all: every unit is expected to cut costs by a certain amount or grow by a certain amount regardless of its unique circumstances. We find merit in the budgeting processes of companies that don't start with a top-down target like 10 percent earnings per share (EPS) growth for the entire company. Top-down targets work only when they've been developed through a thoughtful analysis of each unit's potential and needed investments.

A better approach is for the corporate center to work with each unit to figure out the right target and budget for that unit first, then see how they add up. When all the units are summed, the company may find that it doesn't like the aggregated results. That's okay. If a company has done its homework, it will know which units need to cut costs according to their relative value creation potential, not according to the application of a rote formula to cut the same percentage across the board. Even better, this process could lead the corporation to realizing that it isn't in a position to fully fund the opportunities of all units—sparking a thoughtful discussion about whether the corporation is the best owner of certain units.

BOARD OF DIRECTORS

Another management process that may not appear to be a *process* is the way the board of directors works with and influences a company's top management. Instead of helping executives make courageous long-term decisions, many boards of directors, usually inadvertently, do the opposite: encourage a focus on short-term earnings. This comes from direct decisions they make (such as executive compensation design) and from the kinds of questions they ask (such as focusing on EPS to the exclusion of other performance metrics).

This is not to say that boards shouldn't pressure managers for short-term results, since a strong performance ethic starts with what the business is doing today. But as the investors' permanent representatives, the board's job is to make sure that the company's management team gets the balance right between delivering current profits/ROIC and building future profitable growth. Making complex judgments about value creation choices requires what the board brings: distance, freedom to ask tough questions, and diverse perspectives.

Many board discussions focus on aggregate financial results: the earnings of the entire company or a handful of divisions at best. As we discussed earlier, that's not good enough. High-level financial results don't help the board understand the decisions that senior management is making to prepare the company for the future. If the board focuses on aggregate results, so will the management team. Both the board and the management team should focus on disaggregated results, as well as on health metrics, not just performance metrics. If the business needs to be managed at the level of 20, 30, or even 50 units, the board should see the results at that level as well.

It's a formidable task to understand the strategies and performance of 20 or more units, in terms of both financial performance and the potential for future growth and value creation. Yet the amount of time boards spend on these tasks is alarmingly low, especially given the complexity of many large companies.

Several of our colleagues interviewed 20 directors who had served on the boards of both listed companies and private equity owned companies.* They found that, on average, these directors spent nearly three times as many days on their roles as directors at private equity owned companies versus listed companies (54 vs. 19). Most of the difference wasn't time spent in formal board meetings but, rather, on field visits, ad hoc meetings with executives, phone calls, and e-mails. Furthermore, our colleagues also found that the boards of listed companies spent more of their limited time on risk avoidance rather than on strategy and performance management. One interviewee said of the listed company boards that "the focus is on box-ticking and covering the right inputs, not delivering the right outputs."

According to our colleagues, "the nature and intensity of the performance-management culture is perhaps the most striking difference between the two environments. Private equity boards have what one respondent described as a 'relentless focus on value creation levers.' . . . In contrast, public boards were described as much less engaged in detail. . . . Public boards focus much less on fundamental value creation levers and much more on meeting quarterly profit targets. . . . [Public boards] are focused more on budgetary control, the delivery of short-term accounting profits, and avoiding surprises for investors."

Boards also need a full understanding of the company's share price performance if they are to avoid reinforcing short-term biases or diverting management time. For example, the board members of one company were concerned that its price-earnings (P/E) ratio as reported on financial web sites was about 20 percent lower than the P/Es of many of its peers. However, a deeper analysis showed that, when adjusted for differences in the capital structures of peers and some nonoperating items, its valuation multiple (measured by enterprise value/EBITA) was right in line with peers. Clarifying this allowed the CEO and board to shift the conversation to more important issues, such as how to maintain longer-term growth in light of external pressure on the industry.

When public company boards and their chairs work with the top management team on important value creation questions, the results

---

* Viral Acharya, Conor Kehoe, and Michael Reynor, "The Voice of Experience: Public versus Private Equity," *McKinsey on Finance*, Spring 2009, 16–21.

can be remarkable. In one case, despite solid growth and ROIC, the CEO and CFO of a large company had a sense that the corporation wasn't adding value to its businesses. In close cooperation, the board and management asked the ultimate question: should the company continue to exist? They decided it should not and subsequently broke it into several stand-alone, focused companies. Freed from having to make compromises as a single company, the stand-alone companies changed their strategies and performance trajectories and created substantially more value for their shareholders.

It's difficult to offer a recipe for how boards can help drive value creation. Company and industry demands are different, as are the habits and preferences of existing boards, chairs, and CEOs. That said, we offer some suggestions.

First, find ways for the board to develop a deeper understanding of the performance, strategies, and opportunities of individual business units. Value creation occurs at the business unit level, not the corporate level, so boards need to have insights and discussions at this level.

One approach might be to create a performance management and strategy committee, recognizing that fewer than 10 percent of public company boards in the United States and Europe have such a committee. This committee could be tasked with delving deeper into the performance of key business units to ensure that the board fully understands the drivers of current results, as well as each unit's positioning for future value creation. A company might even ask members of this committee to devote more time than other board members to do this well.

An alternative might be to create a mechanism that provides deeper board member expertise for each major business. Individual board members or small committees might each get involved with a specific business unit. The assigned board member or committee could meet regularly with the business unit leader and its CFO to assess its strategy and performance in more detail than the full board ever could. While the entire board can't abdicate strategy and performance management to a committee or subset of members, it might benefit from the insights that more dedicated members could provide.

Another way to bring more insight into the performance of the company and its units would be to provide direct staff support to the board; the staff could provide unbiased, in-depth analyses about performance and health, opportunities for value creation, and risks. For example, the board or its subsets could spend time informally with the CFO or designated staff members to critically review the performance and outlook for key businesses and the company as a whole. The CFO or staff would be tasked with identifying major competitive risks and opportunities and independently assessing the longer-term outlook for the business. This might be analogous to the way internal auditors meet in private with the board to discuss internal controls. While many executives, particularly business unit heads, will be uncomfortable with the board learning information that hasn't been filtered through their offices, we believe that responsible boards can use the information to improve dialogue and trust.

It's not easy to get the board properly set and to get the other management processes right when it comes to balancing near-term financial performance with longer-term value creation in large, complex companies. The risk is oversimplification, which leads to a lopsided management focus on more immediate earnings. If companies can't find a way to make more granular decisions that maintain short-term performance while also generating long-term value, they should ask themselves if they've become too big and complex.

The Math of Value

For the mathematically inclined, this appendix shows the core-of-value cornerstone as a simple formula along with its derivation. We call this the key value driver formula as it relates the value of a company to growth and ROIC:

$$\text{Value} = \frac{\text{NOPLAT}_{t=1}\left(1 - \dfrac{g}{\text{ROIC}}\right)}{\text{WACC} - g}$$

Where:

Net operating profit less adjusted taxes (NOPLAT) represents the profits generated from the company's core operations after subtracting corresponding income taxes.

Return on invested capital (ROIC) is the return the company earns on each dollar invested in the business:

$$\text{ROIC} = \frac{\text{NOPLAT}}{\text{Invested Capital}}$$

Invested capital represents the cumulative amount the business has invested in its core operations—primarily property, plant and equipment, and working capital.

Weighted average cost of capital (WACC) is the rate of return that investors expect to earn from investing in the company and, therefore, the appropriate discount rate for the free cash flow.

Growth (g) is the rate at which the company's NOPLAT and cash flow grow each year.

To derive the core value driver formula, we also need to define the following variables:

Net investment is the increase in invested capital from one year to the next:

$$\text{Net Investment} = \text{Invested Capital}_{t+1} - \text{Invested Capital}_{t}$$

Free cash flow (FCF) is the cash flow generated by the core operations of the business after deducting investments in new capital:

$$\text{FCF} = \text{NOPLAT} - \text{Net Investment}$$

Investment rate (IR) is the portion of NOPLAT invested back into the business:

$$\text{IR} = \frac{\text{Net Investment}}{\text{NOPLAT}}$$

Assume that the company's revenues and NOPLAT grow at a constant rate, and the company invests the same proportion of its NOPLAT in its business each year. Investing the same proportion of NOPLAT each year also means that the company's free cash flow will grow at the same rate as NOPLAT.

Because the company's cash flows are growing at a constant rate, we can begin by valuing a company using the well-known cash flow perpetuity formula:

$$\text{Value} = \frac{\text{FCF}_{t=1}}{\text{WACC} - g}$$

This formula is well established in the finance and mathematics literature.*

---

*For the derivation, see T. E. Copeland and J. Fred Weston, *Financial Theory and Corporate Policy*, 3rd ed. (Reading, MA: Addison Wesley, 1988), Appendix A.

Next, define free cash flow in terms of NOPLAT and the investment rate:

$$FCF = NOPLAT - Net\ Investment$$
$$= NOPLAT - (NOPLAT \times IR)$$
$$= NOPLAT(1 - IR)$$

In Chapter 2, we developed the relationship between the investment rate (IR), the company's projected growth in NOPLAT (g), and the return on investment (ROIC):*

$$g = ROIC \times IR$$

Solving for IR, rather than g, leads to

$$IR = \frac{g}{ROIC}$$

Now build this into the definition of free cash flow:

$$FCF = NOPLAT \left(1 - \frac{g}{ROIC}\right)$$

Substituting for free cash flow gives the key value driver formula:

$$Value = \frac{NOPLAT_{t=1} \left(1 - \frac{g}{ROIC}\right)}{WACC - g}$$

Migrating the forecast assumptions for Value Inc. and Volume Inc. (from Exhibit 2.3) into the key value driver formula results in the same values we came up with when we discounted their cash flows:

Company	$NOPLAT_{t=1}$	Growth (percent)	ROIC (percent)	WACC (percent)	Value
Volume Inc.	100	5	10	10	1,000
Value Inc.	100	5	20	10	1,500

We call the key value driver formula the *Tao of corporate finance* because it relates a company's value to the fundamental drivers of

---

* Technically, we should use the return on new or incremental capital, but for simplicity here, we assume that the ROIC and incremental ROIC are equal.

economic value: growth, ROIC, and the cost of capital. You might go so far as to say that this formula represents all there is to valuation. Everything else is mere detail.

However, we usually don't use this formula in practice. In most situations, the model is overly restrictive, as it assumes a constant ROIC and growth rate going forward. For companies whose key value drivers are expected to change, we need a model that is more flexible. Nevertheless, the formula is very useful in helping keep the mind focused on what drives value.

We can also use the key value driver formula to show that ROIC and growth determine earnings multiples, such as price-to-earnings and market-to-book ratios. To see this, divide both sides of the key value driver formula by NOPLAT:

$$\frac{\text{Value}}{\text{NOPLAT}_{t=1}} = \frac{\left(1 - \dfrac{g}{\text{ROIC}}\right)}{\text{WACC} - g}$$

As the formula shows, a company's earnings multiple is driven by both its expected growth and its return on invested capital.

You can also turn the formula into a value-to-invested-capital formula. Start with the identity:

$$\text{NOPLAT} = \text{Invested Capital} \times \text{ROIC}$$

Substitute this definition of NOPLAT into the key value driver formula:

$$\text{Value} = \frac{\text{Invested Capital} \times \text{ROIC} \times \left(1 - \dfrac{g}{\text{ROIC}}\right)}{\text{WACC} - g}$$

Divide both sides by invested capital:

$$\frac{\text{Value}}{\text{Invested Capital}} = \text{ROIC} \left(\frac{1 - \dfrac{g}{\text{ROIC}}}{\text{WACC} - g}\right)$$

The Use of Earnings Multiples

Earnings multiples, particularly the P/E ratio, are a common shorthand for summarizing a company's value. We showed in Chapter 2 that value and earnings multiples can be explained by ROIC and growth. In practice, though, analyzing and interpreting earnings multiples can be messy. Even worse, a superficial analysis of earnings multiples can be misleading. This appendix explains some of the techniques behind a thorough analysis of multiples, to help you avoid misleading results.

A company recently asked us what could be done to increase its earnings multiple. The company was trading at a P/E multiple of 11 times, while most of its peers were trading at a P/E of 14, a discount of 25 percent. The management team believed the market just didn't understand its strategy or performance, but it turned out that this company had much more debt than its peers. We estimated that if the company had the same relative debt as its peers, its P/E would also have been about 14.

The difference was pure mathematics, not judgment by investors. Everything else equal, a company with higher debt will have a lower P/E ratio. The economic explanation is that companies with higher debt levels are riskier and, therefore, have higher costs of capital—which translates into lower P/Es.

This example points out the pitfalls in the superficial use and interpretation of earnings multiples. You have to dig into the accounting statements to make sure you're comparing companies on a comparable basis. Done properly, multiples analysis can provide useful insights into a company and its valuation; but doing a sloppy multiples analysis can lead you to wrong conclusions, which can be worse than not doing any analysis at all.

Many successful investors use earnings multiples to analyze potential investments, but they emphasize the need to use multiples with caution. For example, the disciples of Ben Graham don't use reported earnings to estimate multiples; instead they use what they call *earnings power*.* They adjust accounting earnings for a number of items, including nonrecurring profits or charges, the current position in the business cycle, capital structure, and so on. Using this data and information, they then estimate a sustainable level of earnings.

These days, sophisticated investors and bankers use forward-looking, enterprise value-to-EBITA multiples. These multiples provide a more apples-to-apples comparison of company values.

The forward-looking, enterprise value-to-EBITA multiple improves the simple P/E multiple that's reported in the newspaper or on a web site in three ways: it strips out nonoperating items, it eliminates the effect of different capital structures and, by using estimates of forward earnings, it more closely reflects the level of earnings over a company's business cycle.

When constructing multiples carefully, making the proper adjustments, you'll notice that the differences in multiples across companies in the same industry tend to narrow considerably. Exhibit B.1 shows the P/E and enterprise-value multiples for some of the large pharmaceutical companies. The raw backward-looking P/E multiples range from 12 to 38 times. Looking forward one year, and adjusting to enterprise multiples, note that the range declines to 12 to 17 times. Use earnings four years out and the variation across companies disappears.†

The convergence of multiples four years out in the pharmaceuticals industry is extreme and most likely due to the market's penchant for projecting near-term earnings well, because drug introductions and patent expirations are well known, while the long-term success of the companies is hard to differentiate because it depends on the company's ability to invent new drugs.

---

* Bruce C. N. Greenwald, Judd Kahn, Paul D. Sonkin, and Michael van Biema, *Value Investing: From Graham to Buffett and Beyond* (New York: John Wiley & Sons, 2001).
† P/E multiples are higher than enterprise multiples in most cases because the P/E multiple uses earnings after tax, while most enterprise value multiples use higher pretax earnings.

EXHIBIT B.1 **Forward Enterprise Multiples Have Less Dispersion Than Traditional P/E Multiples**

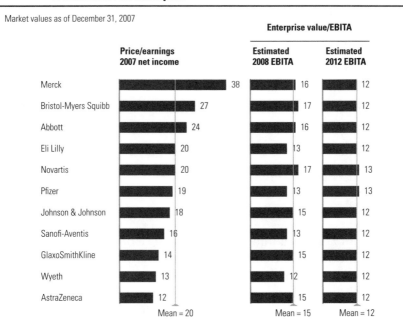

Market values as of December 31, 2007

Enterprise value/EBITA

	Price/earnings 2007 net income	Estimated 2008 EBITA	Estimated 2012 EBITA
Merck	38	16	12
Bristol-Myers Squibb	27	17	12
Abbott	24	16	12
Eli Lilly	20	13	12
Novartis	20	17	13
Pfizer	19	13	13
Johnson & Johnson	18	15	12
Sanofi-Aventis	16	13	12
GlaxoSmithKline	14	15	12
Wyeth	13	12	12
AstraZeneca	12	15	12
	Mean = 20	Mean = 15	Mean = 12

Source: Compustat, McKinsey Corporate Performance Center analysis.

Because earnings multiples are driven by the combination of growth and return on capital, it's essential to compare the multiples of companies with similar growth and ROIC expectations. A typical flaw in using multiples is to compare a company with an average of other companies in the same industry, regardless of differences in performance. Another flaw is that companies tend to compare themselves with peers which are not in their performance class, rather than peers with similar performance. Once you find the right peer group, multiples that otherwise seem far off base often become perfectly sensible.

Exhibit B.2 shows the multiples of six technology companies and their expected performance. Our client, Company C, had simply looked at the left side and expressed discontent that its multiple was lower than some of its peers. When you factor in performance, however, the multiples make sense.

EXHIBIT B.2 **Multiple Comparisons Require Right Peer Group**

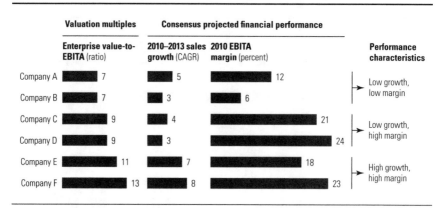

Source: McKinsey Corporate Performance Center analysis, Datastream.

The companies fall into three performance buckets that align with different multiples. The companies with the lowest margins and low growth expectations had multiples of seven times. The companies with low growth but high margins had multiples of nine times. And the companies with high growth and high margins had multiples of 11 to 13 times.

Index